D0939365

How to Grow More Vegetables

8TH EDITION

How to Grow
MORE VEGETABLES*

(and fruits, nuts, berries, grains, and other crops)

than you ever thought possible on less land than you can imagine

JOHN JEAVONS

Ecology Action of the Midpeninsula

A primer on the life-giving GROW BIOINTENSIVE® method of sustainable horticulture

TEN SPEED PRESS
Berkeley

Copyright © 1974, 1979, 1982, 1991, 1995, 2002, 2006, 2012 by Ecology Action of the Midpeninsula

All rights reserved. Published in the United States by Ten Speed Press, an imprint of the Crown Publishing Group, a division of Random House LLC, a Penguin Random House Company, New York.
www.crownpublishing.com
www.tenspeed.com

Ten Speed Press and the Ten Speed Press colophon are registered trademarks of Random House LLC.

www.growbiointensive.org
www.bountifulgardens.org
www.commongroundinpaloalto.org
See also: www.johnjeavons.info

Library of Congress Cataloging-in-Publication Data

Jeavons, John.
  How to grow more vegetables : (and fruits, nuts, berries, grains, and other crops) than you ever thought possible on less land than you can imagine / John Jeavons.
— 8th ed.
      p. cm.
  Includes bibliographical references and index.
  1. Vegetable gardening. 2. Organic gardening. I. Title.
  SB324.3.J43 2012
  635—dc23

                              2011040066

ISBN 978-1-60774-189-3
eISBN 978-1-60774-190-9

Printed in the United States
Design by Betsy Stromberg
Illustrations by Pedro J. Gonzalez, Ann Miya, Susan Stanley, Sue Ellen Parkinson, Betsy Jeavons Bruneau, and Dan Miller
Photos on pages 14 and 235 by Cynthia Raiser Jeavons
Cover photograph (pumpkin) and spine photograph courtesy of Bountiful Gardens
Cover photograph (red chard) © iStockphoto.com/swalls
Cover photograph (soil) © iStockphoto.com/AdShooter
Cover photograph (red boots) © iStockphoto.com/cjp

10 9 8 7 6 5 4

Eighth Edition

DEDICATED TO CYNTHIA RAISER JEAVONS

CONTENTS

ACKNOWLEDGMENTS

Betsy Bruneau, Rachael Leler, Tom Walker, Craig Cook, Rip King, Bill Spencer, George Young, Claudette Paige, Kevin Raftery, Marion Cartwright, Paka, Phyllis Anderson, Wayne Miller, Paul Hwoschinsky, Dave Smith, Steve and Judi Rioch, Louisa Lenz, Bill Bruneau, Dean Nims, Tommy Derrick, Carol Cox, Cynthia Raiser Jeavons, Rose Raiser Jeavons, Dan Whittaker, Shirley Coe, David Basile, Jed Diamond, Sensei, John Raiser, Helen Raiser, Jennifer Raiser, Phill Raiser, Victoria Raiser, Sheila Hilton, Mia Walker, Bill Somerville, John Beeby, Salvador Diaz, Bill Liebhardt, Jack and Virginia Jeavons, John Doran, Emmanuel Omondi, Joshua Machinga, Sandra Mardigian, Fernando Pia, Juan Manuel Martinez Valdez, Mercedes Torres Barrones, and, especially, Jennifer Ungemach, Carol Vesecky, Vicci Warhol, Mary Zellachild, William Wardlaw and Patricia Arnold, Maryanne Mott and Herman Warsh, Richard Rathbun, Mike and Diane Griggs, Steve and Carol Moore, Clancy Drake, Jasmine Star, Langtry Williams, Mark Larratt-Smith, Gayle Fillman, Jed Diamond, Karina McAbee, Julian Gorodsky, Ellen Bartholomew, Brian Bartholomew, Randy Fish, Dawn Griffin, Marie Laure Roperch, Jake Blehm, Mark House, Robert de Gross, Patricia Becker, Don Larson, Veronica Randall, Betsy Stromberg, members of Ecology Action, and friends have all made important contributions to the book's content and spirit.

We assume responsibility for any inaccuracies that may have been included; they are ours and not Alan Chadwick's or Stephen Kafka's. This book is not intended to be an exhaustive work on the subject, but rather one of simple completeness. Most of us at Ecology Action are only beginning- to intermediate-level GROW BIOINTENSIVE gardeners. The purpose of this book is to turn on as many people as possible to a beautiful, dynamically alive method of horticulture and life.

FOREWORD BY ALICE WATERS

In the early days at Chez Panisse, forty years ago, we had to scrounge for decent beans, pick lemons from neighbors' trees, and hunt far and wide for a variety of produce of any quality whatsoever. But farming has evolved in California. We now work with, at last count, nearly fifty local, small-scale, family-run farms that grow—organically and sustainably—the seasonal fruits and vegetables that are the foundation of our cooking. In large part, we have John Jeavons to thank for this.

I met John on the twentieth birthday of Chez Panisse just as he was preparing for the twentieth anniversary of Ecology Action. We both had a lot to celebrate. The work that John had begun in a small garden at Stanford had inspired small farms on nearly every continent; he had already worked with the Peace Corps in Togo, helped found an agricultural center in Kenya, taught in Mexico, and supported programs in Russia and the Philippines. His work has gone right on inspiring, and at a pace that is fast enough to give us real hope that we will be able to grow sustainable communities around the world.

John's methods are nothing short of miraculous. He has shown that almost any soil can be prepared for the planting of food, and that astonishing quantities of high-quality produce can be grown on even the most devastated land. He has worked tirelessly to bring self-sufficiency to the poorest people in the poorest parts of the world. As I write, he's preparing to share his methods with the five thousand small-scale farmers from one hundred and thirty-one countries who are expected at Terra Madre, the biannual gathering of farmers in Turin, Italy, organized by the eco-gastronomes of Slow Food International. I can think of no more appropriate place for the dissemination of his ideas.

Vandana Shiva, the outspoken Indian food activist, has said that farms are zones of peace on this planet. A peaceful revolution in agriculture—what I like to call the delicious revolution—has begun, and John is one of its most brilliant leaders. *How to Grow More Vegetables* may be one of the most important how-to guides ever written.

Ecology Action and the Common Ground Project

by the Ecology Action Staff

ECOLOGY ACTION GOAL: Act as a catalyst, instruct teachers, and train students

The work has always been worthwhile despite the continuing challenge of attracting strong, ongoing support. The biggest single asset to this undertaking is John Jeavons's unfailing stamina and dedication. Over and over, when we all ask, "Can it work?" he answers, "How are we going to make it work?" It is becoming increasingly clear that GROW BIOINTENSIVE Sustainable Mini-Farming will be an important part of the solution to starvation and malnutrition, dwindling energy supplies, unemployment, and exhaustion and loss of arable land, if the social and political challenges can be met.

After forty years of testing, GROW BIOINTENSIVE food-raising has produced amazing benefits. Yields can average 2 to 6 times those of U.S. agriculture, and a few range up to 31 times higher—a plus at a time of *peak food*. But there's still more to learn; for example, we are still working to develop an optimally healthy soil system. Compost and calorie crops present the most challenges because they are crucial in meeting the nutritional needs of people and the soil. Experiments include alfalfa, fava beans, wheat, oats, cardoon, and comfrey. So far our yields are from one to five times the U.S. average for these crops. Water use is well below that of commercial agriculture per pound of food produced, and is about 33% to 12% that of conventional techniques per unit of land area. This is especially important in a world that has reached a point of *peak water*.

Energy expenditure, expressed in kilocalories of input, is 6% to 1% of that used by commercial agriculture, and this helps meet the challenge of *peak oil*. The human body is still more efficient than any machine we have been able to invent. Several factors contradict the popular conception that this is a labor-intensive method. Using hand tools may seem to be more work, but the yields more than compensate. Even at 50¢ a pound wholesale, zucchini can bring as much as $18 to $32 per hour depending on the harvest timing because it is easy to grow, maintain, and harvest. Time spent in soil preparation is more than offset later in less need for weeding, thinning, cultivation, and other chores per unit of area and per unit of yield. Hand watering and harvesting appear to take the most time. Initial soil preparation, including fertilization and planting, may take 5 to 9½ hours per 100-square-foot raised bed. Thereafter, the time spent decreases dramatically. A new digging tool, the U-bar, has reduced subsequent bed preparation time to as little as 20 minutes. A new hand watering tool that waters more quickly and more gently is also being developed.

Nature has answered our original queries with an abundance even greater than expected, and we have narrowed our research to the most important question that can be asked of any agricultural system: Is it sustainable? The GROW BIOINTENSIVE[1] method currently uses 50% or less of the purchased fertilizer that commercial farmers use. Can we maintain all nutrient levels on site, once they have been built up and balanced? Or is some outside additive always necessary? We need to look more closely at all nutrients: nitrogen, phosphorus, potash, calcium, and trace minerals. Anyone can grow good crops on good soil, cashing in on nature's accumulated riches. The GROW BIOINTENSIVE method appears to allow anyone to take "the worst possible soil" (Alan Chadwick's appraisal of our original Palo Alto research site) and turn it into a bountiful garden or mini-farm. Preliminary monitoring of our soil-building process by a University of California soil scientist was probably the most important information garnered about our initial site. Continued monitoring will unlock new secrets and provide hope for people with marginal, worn-out, or desertified soils. However, a complete answer to the long-term question of sustainable soil fertility will require at least fifty years of observation as the living soil system

Note: The GROW BIOINTENSIVE method is very energy efficient, in large part because it relies on the work of the capable and efficient human body rather than on the work of machines. One person annually consumes in food the energy equivalent of 32.6 gallons of gasoline. In contrast, the most efficient economy car will use that much gas in a month or two of ordinary driving. Imagine the fuel consumed by a tractor in a year!

changes and grows! We continue to work on that opportunity. Why not create *ecosystems of hope*?

Nine years of growing and testing in Ecology Action's urban garden mini-farm came to an end in 1980 due to the termination of our lease and new construction on that land. Like so much other agricultural land in the United States, our lovingly tended beds succumbed to the press of urbanization. The city growing area prepared us for a rural site. The facilities of grocery store and electric lines were exchanged for open skies and room to grow more herbs, flowers, vegetables, beans, grains, and compost crops than we ever imagined. At the Common Ground Mini-Farm in Willits, California, we are enjoying a permanent site where we can grow trees of all kinds—for food, fuel, and beauty. Other projects include a self-fertilizing lawn composed of fragrant herbs and clovers, and a working mini-farm. In 1973, we initially estimated that a one-person small holding (1/8 to 1/2 acre) could grow crops bringing in a net income of $5,000 to $20,000 a year (about $100 to $400 a week) after four to five years. However, one woman on Vancouver Island, British Columbia, was earning about $400 a week growing gourmet vegetables for restaurants on 1/16 of an acre twenty years after we began. At first she thought it could not be done, but when she tried growing crops for income it worked. She then passed her skills on to twelve other women. Crops grown may include collards, chard, beets, mangels, spinach, green onions, garlic, radishes, romaine and Bibb lettuce, zucchini, pattypan squash, cucumbers, and lavender. Rather than solely looking to Ecology Action for answers, we hope you will dig in and try GROW BIOINTENSIVE for yourself! The techniques are simple to use, as this book shows. No large capital expenses are necessary to get started. The techniques work in varied climates and soils. American farmers are feeding the world, but mini-farming can give people the knowledge and empowerment to feed themselves.

Posted on the wall of our local environmental center, there once was a tongue-in-cheek guide called *50 Really Difficult Things You Can Do to Save the Earth*. The second item was "Grow all your own vegetables." We had to laugh. We moved up to our new mini-farm in Willits with a plan for short-term food self-sufficiency. That was forty years ago. We still take a neighborly ribbing for racing down to the farmers' markets to buy sweet corn, carrots, and other vegetables and fruits to feed an extended family of staff, apprentices, interns, and friends at our research site. Research priorities often interfere with growing all our vegetables and fruits. It is difficult to research, write, publish, teach, do outreach around the world—and farm—all at the same time!

Rachael Leler said, "My first garden was a total failure. I planned, dug, and planted, but I had not really learned how to garden yet. Now my favorite class to teach is compost. I bring a glass jar of waste— a slimy brew of potato peels, coffee grounds, and last week's rotting roses. The other jar has compost—sweet smelling, earthy, and alive, and, by the way, nothing like the sifted and homogenized product sold at garden centers. These two jars remind me of the magical transformation of a garden: health from garbage, riches out of waste. I can 'see' that magic immediately, though it may take me years to fully comprehend it!"

Betsy Bruneau, a senior staff person, has an affinity for tiny life-forms. She taught us to appreciate the infinitely variable lichens that cling to bare rock and fallen trees, creating soil for larger life-forms to follow. People used to bring insects into our store for identification. Betsy's first response was usually a hushed "How beautiful!" She marvels at the intensely colorful tomato hornworms, the intricate markings on the shells of wise old snails, and the fact that earwigs are wonderful mothers.

We live in an age of consumption, when we are constantly exhorted to measure ourselves by our possessions. Yet no matter how rich we manage to become, something human in us says our true worth is reflected by what we ourselves create. Why not make it full of life and beauty rather than pollution? Our neighbor Ellen spent all day putting up jars of string beans and piccalilli, then worked until midnight to finish up a batch of raspberries. One of her notes reads, "There is no rest for the gardener . . . but there is always dessert!"

Gardening is not always easy, but the rewards are personal and fun. For most of us, the environment is what is around us, separate from human activity. Gardening offers the chance to become partners with nature. The reward is not just a salad from the backyard or a gleaming jar of peaches. Gardening is the process of digging the soil, starting small seeds, watching an apple tree grow. Gardening is an education in observation, harmony, honesty, and humility—in knowing and understanding our place in the world.

But the impact is also global. Alan Chadwick felt that gardening was the only way to prevent another world war—to bring a living, active peace on Earth by working with healthy, creative, positive life forces. In doing this, we become one with those life forces. He felt that, *as we breathe life back into the soil, we breathe life back into ourselves.* The homegrown tomato requires no fuel for transportation, no packaging to be sent to the landfill, no political decisions about who will be allowed to work the fields or what level of pollutants is acceptable in our groundwater. Nature is not always a Garden of Eden. Some partnership is required to bring out the best in both nature and people. *"Give to Nature, and she will repay you in glorious abundance"* was one of Chadwick's favorite sayings. Gardening and mini-farming give us the opportunity to participate in the subtle the transformation of desert into dessert. *All we need to do is to start with one growing bed and tend it well, and we have begun the exciting, expansive, giving process of enlivening and healing the Earth and ourselves.*

ENDNOTES

1 In this book you will see the terms grow biointensive and Biointensive. Both refer to individuals, projects, and programs using some and more, respectively, of biologically intensive techniques before Ecology Action's 1999 trademark registration of GROW BIOINTENSIVE and/or not using all of the GROW BIOINTENSIVE features, which have a goal of maximizing closed-system sustainable food-raising.

Ecology Action and the Common Ground Project

Building Soil, Building the Future

There is an exciting challenge ahead of us. How can we revitalize our extraordinary planet, ensuring life and health for the environment, the life-forms of a myriad of ecosystems, humankind, and future generations? The answer is as close to us as the food we consume each day. We can begin to create a better world from right where we are—in home gardens and mini-farms. Millions of people in over 140 countries are already using GROW BIOINENSIVE Sustainable Mini-Farming techniques to work toward this better world.

We "farm" as we eat. If we consume food that has been grown using methods that inadvertently deplete the soil in the growing process, we are responsible for depleting the soil. It is how we are "farming." If, instead, we raise or request food grown in ways that heal the Earth, then we are healing the Earth and its soils. Our daily food choices make the difference. We can choose to sustain ourselves while increasing the planet's vitality. In the process, we preserve resources, breathe cleaner air, enjoy good exercise, and eat pure food.

What are the dimensions of the challenge of raising food that sustains the soil? Current agricultural practices reportedly destroy approximately 6 pounds of soil for each pound of food produced.[1] United States croplands are losing topsoil about 18 times faster than the soil formation rate. This loss is not sustainable.

They're making more people every day, but they ain't makin' any more dirt.
—WILL ROGERS

1

In fact, worldwide only about 33 to 49 years' worth of farmable soil remains.[2]

Why is this happening? Conventional agricultural practices often deplete the soil 18 to 80 times more rapidly than nature builds soil. This phenomenon happens when the humus (cured organic matter) in the soil is used up and not replaced, when cropping patterns are used that tend to deplete the soil's structure, and when minerals are removed from the soil more rapidly than they are replaced. Even organic farming probably depletes the soil 9 to 67 times faster than nature builds it, by importing organic matter and minerals from other soils, which thereby becomes increasingly depleted. The planetary result is a net reduction in overall soil quality.

In contrast, the techniques used in GROW BIOINTENSIVE Sustainable Mini-Farming can build the soil up to 60 times faster than in nature.[3] *The overall goal of GROW BIOINTENSIVE techniques, which distinguishes these techniques from Biointensive practices, is the miniaturization of food production in a closed system.* GROW BIOINTENSIVE features the use of the following eight techniques in a closed system that does not use any chemical substances. Ten years ago, Ecology Action coined the term "GROW BIOINTENSIVE" to refer to this style of production.

Biointensive techniques include:

Deep soil preparation, which develops good soil structure. Once this structure is established, it may be maintained for several years with 2-inch-deep surface cultivation (until compaction once again necessitates deep soil preparation).

The use of compost (humus) for soil fertility and nutrients.

Close plant spacing, as in nature.

Synergistic planting of crop combinations so plants that are grown together enhance each other.

Carbon-efficient crops by which approximately 60% of the growing area is planted in dual-purpose seed and grain crops for the production of large amounts of carbonaceous material for compost and significant amounts of dietary calories.

Calorie-efficient crops by which approximately 30% of the growing area is planted in special root crops, such as potatoes, leeks, garlic, parsnips, and Jerusalem artichokes, which produce a large amount of calories for the diet per unit of area.

The use of open-pollinated seeds to preserve genetic diversity.

A whole, interrelated farming system. When GROW BIOIN-TENSIVE is used properly—with all of its components and so all wastes are recycled and enough organic matter is grown to ensure that each farm can produce enough compost to create and maintain sustainable soil fertility—*GROW BIOINTENSIVE Sustainable Mini-Farming can create soil rapidly and maintain sustainable soil fertility*. It is *how* each of us uses GROW BIOINTENSIVE, or other food-raising practices, that makes a living difference!

Note: Up to 6 billion microbial life-forms can live in 5 grams of cured compost, about the size of a quarter.

The combination of these techniques makes it possible to greatly reduce resources compared to conventional agricultural practices while greatly increasing soil fertility and productivity.

- A **67% to 88% reduction** in water consumption per unit of production

- A **50+% reduction** in the amount of purchased fertilizer in organic fertilizer form required per unit of production

- A **94% to 99% reduction** in the amount of energy used per unit of production

- A **100+% increase** in soil fertility, while productivity increases and resource use decreases

- A **200% to 400% increase** in caloric production per unit of area

- A **100+% increase** in income per unit of area

However, GROW BIOINTENSIVE Sustainable Mini-Farming (or any other sustainable farming practice) is not a panacea. If *not* used properly GROW BIOINTENSIVE practices can deplete the soil more rapidly than other farming practices because of the high yields. But above all, using only a single agricultural approach to grow food would not be vital. It would be another form of "monocropping" in a living world ecosystem that thrives on diversity. Sustainable approaches in the future will probably be a synthesis, a sustainable collage, of:

- GROW BIOINTENSIVE

- Agroforestry

- No-till Fukuoka food raising

- Traditional Asian blue-green algal wet rice farming

- Natural rainfall "arid" farming

- Indigenous farming

These food-growing techniques are only part of a sustainable future. *To preserve the plant and animal genetic diversity upon which we all depend, we will need to keep one-half of the world's farmable land in a wild, natural state.* As we begin to use sustainable, land- and resource-conserving food-raising approaches, more wilderness areas can remain untouched so more of the endangered plant and animal diversity on this Earth can be preserved. This wealth of genetic diversity is necessary if the planet on which we live is to support abundance.

Generally, the challenges of world hunger, soil depletion, and diminishing resources seem so overwhelming that we tend to look for big solutions, such as shipping massive amounts of grain, breeding high-yield miracle crops, or establishing infrastructures—bank loans, machinery and fertilizer purchases, markets, and roads. These solutions create long-term dependency. What is so exciting about a personal approach is that it seeks to answer the question, "How do we enable ourselves to take care of our own needs?" Personal solutions will have as many varied applications as there are people, soils, climates, and cultures. Our research of one of these sustainable proposals, GROW BIOINTENSIVE, is a way for people to begin to develop these solutions.

Our work grew out of personal concern about worldwide starvation and malnutrition, augmented by a sober assessment of the unsustainability of the most dominant current methods of producing our food. We came to believe that if we could determine the smallest amount of land and resources needed for one person to supply all of his or her own needs in a sustainable way, we might arrive at a personal solution. What if a person could, in a tiny area, easily raise all the crops that would supply all food, clothes, building materials, compost materials, seeds, and income for an entire year? We asked whether others knew the smallest

Population will increase rapidly, more rapidly than in former times, and 'ere long the most valuable of all arts will be the art of deriving a comfortable subsistence from the smallest area of soil.
—ABRAHAM LINCOLN

area required. No one did. So we began our 40-year (and counting) quest.

The way humankind is currently living and increasing in population, *we will not be able to provide for our own food needs soon if we do not grow living soil at a time of peak farmable soil.* The charts in Appendix 2 illustrate how that in as little as two years, there may only be an average off 9,000 square feet of farmable land per person for a large number of people. We also need to leave half of that land in its natural, wild state to preserve plant and animal genetic diversity in thriving mini-ecosystems. This in turn will enable Nature's natural cycles to provide a wonderful life for us all.

Therefore, much of that theoretically accessible land becomes limited to about 4,500 square feet, and this availability may be limited further as water becomes less available to water crops. The UN-FAO has reported that, in as little as 13 years, in 2025, increasingly limited water availability means that as many as two-thirds of the world population, about 5 billion people, may not have enough water to grow sufficient food. With GROW BIOINTENSIVE Sustainable Mini-Farming, it may be possible to grow all the food for one's nutrition, as well as "food" for the soil, on as little as 4,000 square feet, without a great amount of difficulty—and with 67% to 88% less water per pound of food produced. This is important, as 70% to 80% of the water used by people is used for farming. If we all have the will, we can transform a water scarcity into water abundance.

The energy crisis is not in a barrel of oil, it is primarily in ourselves!

We also believe that GROW BIOINTENSIVE can produce more net income per acre than conventional farming practices. In striving for quality gardening, a person may thus be able to provide a diet and income with a living soil more than sufficient for his or her needs. **The effort will produce a human renaissance and a cornucopia of food for all.**

The whole world is becoming urbanized. Currently, 91% of the people in India live in cities. Soon, 90% of the people in China will be urban. Japan, Mexico, and Kenya are importing approximately 60% of their calories. People are moving to cities for a better life and more "food security," yet increasingly the world surplus food supply is dwindling. What if we were unable to import food at a reasonable price, or not at all? Most of the world's people have lost the skill of farming literacy. The Chinese used to call their farmers Living Libraries, because they knew that the farmers knew more than they learned in school, from their parents or from millennia of experience and tradition. *They felt it in their hands, hearts and hands.*

Our future security now depends . . . on developing new, more productive farming technologies.
—LESTER BROWN

We need to relearn this! The Hananoo culture in the Philippines grew into place in the Stone Age. They still thrive. Its members are illiterate. Eighty percent of their meal conversations are about food-raising, and their children play farmer. This culture has a 200-crop, 5-year rotation growing system with 40 varieties of rice grown each year—so that whether the climate is hot, cold, wet or dry, they will have a good harvest of calories! The Mayan culture in Guatemala survived when other civilizations around them faded. They did this, in part, through neighborhood biologically intensive food-raising. No one knows why this very skilled and intelligent culture eventually disappeared. There are many possibilities, including disease, but one is that the food-raising practices may not have been used with full sustainability. Many cultures have faded due to insustainable soil practices. North Africa used to be the granary for Rome—until it was overfarmed. Now it is in great part a desert. The Sahara desert used to be a forest, until it was clear cut too frequently. At the rate the world has been becoming desertified since 1977, the planet may be completely desertified in just 70 years. There may even be as little as 33 to 49 years of farmable soil remaining in the world.

We all have an opportunity now to become farming literate! The world has spent the last 30 years becoming computer literate. Why not spend the next 30 years becoming farming literate? If we can get to the moon and back with all of our intelligence, skill and wisdom, we can grow soil—and this living spongecake can grow healthy food for us plus good compost materials to enrich our soils. *Newsweek* magazine once called the soil produced by biologically intensive food-raising the sacher torte, or rich high quality pastry, of gardening.

We may think this is impossible, yet an Early Stone Age culture in northern Iran 10,000 years ago grew its calorie needs in just 20 hours a year—20 minutes a day for 60 days—according to anthropologists. Let's give ourselves a fivefold handicap and work on rediscovering how to grow all our food in just 100 hours a year per person!

How can we live better on fewer resources? It is possible!
Why not begin now and avoid the rush?

Building Soil, Building the Future

The History and Philosophy of the GROW BIOINTENSIVE Method

The GROW BIOINTENSIVE method of horticulture is a quiet, vitally alive art of organic gardening that links people with the whole universe—a universe in which each of us is an interwoven part of the whole. People find their place by relating and cooperating in harmony with the sun, air, rain, soil, moon, insects, plants, and animals rather than by attempting to dominate them. All of these elements will teach us their lessons and do the gardening for us if we only watch and listen. We become gentle shepherds providing the conditions for plant growth.

Biologically intensive farming dates back to four thousand years ago in China, two thousand years in Greece, and one thousand years ago in Latin America. In fact, the Mayan culture grew food this way at their homes on a neighborhood basis. This is one of the reasons their culture survived when others around them were collapsing.

The GROW BIOINTENSIVE method is a combination of two forms of horticulture practiced in Europe during the 1800s and early 1900s. French intensive techniques were developed in the 1700s and 1800s outside Paris. Crops were grown on 18 inches of horse manure, a fertilizer that was readily available. The crops were grown so close to each other that when the plants were mature, their leaves would barely touch. The close spacing provided a mini-climate and a living mulch that reduced weed growth and helped hold moisture in the soil. During the winter, glass jars were placed over seedlings to give them an early start. The gardeners grew up to nine crops each year and could even grow melon plants during the winter.

Biodynamic techniques were developed in the early 1920s by Rudolf Steiner, a brilliant Austrian philosopher and educator. His work began after the introduction of chemical fertilizers and pesticides. Initially, only nitrogen fertilizers were used to stimulate growth. Later, phosphorus and potassium were added to strengthen the plants and to minimize disease and insect problems. Eventually, trace minerals were added to the chemical larder to round out the plants' diet. The single, physical nutrients in soluble salt forms in chemical fertilizers were not complete and vital meals for the plants, causing imbalances that attracted disease and insects. These fertilizers caused chemical changes in the soil that damaged its structure, killed beneficial microbioitic life, and greatly reduced its ability to make nutrients already in the air and soil available to the plants. Steiner noticed that the number of crops affected by disease and insect problems increased while nutritive value and yields dropped.

Steiner traced the cause of these problems to the use of the newly introduced synthetic chemical fertilizers and pesticides. He returned to the gentler, diverse, and balanced diets of organic fertilizers as a cure for the ills brought on by synthetic chemical fertilization. He stressed the holistic growing environment for plants: their rate of growth, the synergistic balance of their environments and nutrients, their proximity to other plants, and their various companion relationships. And he initiated a movement to scientifically explore the relationships that plants have with each other.

The biodynamic method also brought back raised planting beds. Two thousand years ago, the Greeks had noticed that plant life thrives in landslides. The loose soil allows air, moisture, warmth, nutrients, and roots to properly penetrate the soil. The curved surface area between the two edges of the landslide bed provides more surface area for penetration and interaction of the natural elements than a flat surface. The simulated landslides or raised beds used by biodynamic gardeners were usually three to six feet wide and of varying lengths.

Between the 1920s and the 1930s, Alan Chadwick, an Englishman, combined the biodynamic and French intensive techniques into the biodynamic/French intensive method. The United States was first exposed to the combination when Mr. Chadwick brought the method to the four-acre organic Student Garden at the University of California's Santa Cruz campus in the 1960s. Chadwick, a horticultural genius as well as an avid dramatist and artist, had been gardening for half a century. He had studied under Rudolf Steiner, the French gardeners, and as a gardener for the Union of South Africa. The site he developed at Santa Cruz was on the side of a hill with poor soil with high clay content. Only poison oak grew well in this area. Chadwick and his apprentices removed the poison oak with pickaxes and created a rich soil in two to three years by hand. A true Garden of Eden grew from Chadwick's vision and hard work. Barren soil was made fertile through extensive use of compost, with its life-giving humus. The humus produced a healthy soil that grew healthy plants less susceptible to disease and insect attacks. The many nuances of the biodynamic/French intensive method—such as transplanting seedlings into a better soil each time a plant is moved and sowing by the phases of the moon—were also used. The results were beautiful flowers with exquisite fragrances and tasty vegetables of high quality.

In 1971, Larry White, Director of the Nature and Science Department for the City of Palo Alto, invited Stephen Kafka, Senior Apprentice at the university's garden, to give a four-hour class on the biodynamic/French intensive method gardening. Members from a local, young nonprofit environmental research and education organization, Ecology Action, attended the class and recognized that the time was ripe: the city had made land available to the public for gardening two years before, citizens were interested in learning how to grow food and garden, and they were inspired by the local Eden that had been created at the university. Aside from a two-year apprentice program at Santa Cruz and periodic classes given by Alan Chadwick or Stephen Kafka, training in Biointensive was not available to the public. Neither detailed public classes nor yield research were being conducted regularly anywhere. In January 1972, the board of directors approved a project that would include a research garden (the Common Ground Garden) to teach regular classes; collect data on the reportedly high yields by the environmentally sound Biointensive method; make land available for gardening to additional Midpeninsula residents; and publish information on the method's techniques.

Instructed by Alan Chadwick and Stephen Kafka, Ecology Action members began teaching their own classes in the spring of 1972 on a 3¾-acre plot belonging to the Syntex Corporation in the Standard Industrial Park offered to Ecology Action. *How to Grow More Vegetables,* originally only 96 pages, sprouted from clamors for information. Ecology Action began to investigate what agricultural techniques would make food-raising by small farmers and gardeners more efficient. The concept of "mini-farming" began to be developed.

In 1980, Ecology Action lost the lease to the site in Palo Alto. A new Common Ground Mini-Farm was inaugurated in Willits, California. The facilities of grocery store and electric lines were exchanged for open skies and room to grow more herbs, flowers, vegetables, beans, grains, and compost crops than we ever imagined. The site offered a permanent site to grow trees of all kinds—for food, fuel, and beauty. It also offers a place to grow. A world-class library, housing and office space grace the current site. The infrastructure has grown over time to lend itself to short-term and long-term training programs. Every year, hundreds of people visit the site on scheduled tours and through workshops. Interns from around the world study in the 6-month training program. They play a key role in documenting data from the 100-bed-plus research garden within a myriad of experiments.

Research continues on quantitative aspects as listed above, but has also deepened in areas related to diet and compost design. For example, what crops can produce calories and compost? What is the smallest size of land that one needs to produce an entire diet sustainably? What income-generating strategies are possible in the small scale? What are the best strategies for establishing a Biointensive garden while inputting the minimum of external nutrients?

In 1999, Ecology Action coined the term GROW BIOINTENSIVE to differentiate its work from other Biointensive initiatives. Over the course of time, Biointensive had come to refer to many practices, some involving chemical approaches. Ecology Action looked to distinguish its work from these initiatives and highlight its work in designs that involved the miniaturization of agriculture in a closed system.

How to Use This Book

Alan Chadwick advised, "Just grow one small area, and do it well. Then, once you have it right, grow more!" The genius of these guiding words should form the backbone of your learning. One of the advantages of *How to Grow More Vegetables* is that it describes a complete general approach to gardening. Another is that it lets you start small and build your skill as a gardener over the years.

Bed preparation, fertilization, composting, seed propagation, transplanting, watering, and weeding are performed essentially the same way for all crops. The principal difference among crops is seedling flat and growing-bed space recommendations. (Spacing recommendations are found in columns M, E and I in the Master Charts which begin on page 134). As you become familiar with different crops and their "personalities," you will see other nuances. However, the principal work will have been done: to build a framework for your sustainable food-growing. So, once you know how to grow lettuce, you know most of the basics for growing onions, tomatoes, wheat, apple trees, and even cotton!

If you are a **beginning gardener** or mini-farmer reading *How to Grow More Vegetables,* you will likely concentrate on learning basic techniques of bed preparation, compost-making, and close-space planting. You may want to concentrate on planting seedlings that have already been started at a local nursery. Starting your own seedlings requires a higher skill level, and you may want to wait to try it until your second or third year. Your use of the Master Charts in chapter 8 will likely concentrate in Column M which gives in-bed spacing of plants.

If you are an **intermediate gardener,** we recommend that you use more of the tables and charts to grow seedlings, compost crops, grains, and fruit trees. We hope that you will become fascinated with producing soil fertility crops (carbon-and-calorie crops) in your own garden as way to feed your soil and yourself.

A **fully experienced food grower** takes about ten years in the garden. You will be able to draw on all of the information provided in this book as you work on growing most or all of your family's food at home, or teach others the skills you have already mastered.

Throughout the learning process, we recommend that carbon-and-calorie crops (see pages 39–41) should occupy an increasing part of your garden throughout your learning process. Carbon-and-calorie crops feed the soil as well as ourselves. Examples include corn, millet, wheat, oats, barley, cereal rye, and amaranth. These crops grow a lot of carbonaceous material for the compost pile, which in turn feeds the soil with humus, as well as providing a great deal of *nutritious food*. For more information, see chapter 8 in particular. (Information about these **dual-purpose crops**, which provide both dietary calories and compost materials, is included in the Master Charts section beginning on page 129, as well in the Compost Crop sections of Ecology Action's Self-Teaching Mini-Series, Booklets 14, 15, 25, 26, 28, 34, 35, and 36.)

How to Grow More Vegetables provides you with everything that you need to *create a garden symphony*—from the basic techniques to advanced planning skills for a beautifully planted backyard home-stead. Each of us can revitalize ourselves, the soil, and the Earth—one small growing area at a time. Before we know it, we will all live on a thriving, vibrant Earth consisting of personal and community mini-preserves, reestablished with health as a vital, dynamic whole!

The real excitement is that each of us will never know every-thing. After fifty years of gardening, Alan Chadwick exclaimed, "I am still learning!" And so we are all. In fact, while the universal scientific principles operate within GROW BIOINTENSIVE Sustainable Mini-Farming's biological systems, our gardening results change each year. As we explore, we will come to understand the underlying principles, and a whole new world will unfold. We will be able to make changes to improve the health, fertility, effec-tiveness, and sustainability of the way we farm for an even better life on this planet.

This latest revision includes new material to make your job easier: key clarifications in the compost and seed propagation chapters;

crop rotation information; improved techniques, understandings, and approaches; corrected and updated Master Charts and planning data; a whole new organization of the eight key concepts; a reorganization of the most accessible bibliography. The edition represents forty years of working with plants, soils, and people—in virtually all climates and soils around the world.

We each have a lifetime of growing before us, and the opportunity to continually improve our understanding of the living canvas we are painting. Many more people are becoming involved in home food-raising and mini-farming as a result of peak-oil challenges, as well as for a love of nature and working with a soil teeming with life. Start now with just one raised growing bed. Self-reliance in your own "foodshed" will make all the difference in the world. Each one of us has tremendous potential to heal the Earth. Let us begin. As Gandhi observed, "to forget how to dig the earth and tend the soil is to forget ourselves." In *Candide,* Voltaire points the way: **The whole world is a garden, and what a wonderful place this would be, if only each one of us took care of our part of the Earth—our garden!** Each of us is needed. Building a truly sustainable agriculture is an essential part of building sustainable communities. As we build soils, we also build a culture made of healthy living and effective farming, as well as enduring communities. In order to accomplish these goals, we need to shift our agricultural perspective. *We need to stop growing crops and start growing soil.* Granted, in order to grow soil, we need to grow crops. But rather than growing crops for the sole purpose of consumption, the goal changes to one of giving and creating life-producing soil, and in the process, an abundance of food. We must begin by educating ourselves, then sharing what we have learned by teaching people to *understand the importance of growing soil.* Life makes more life, and we have the opportunity to work together with this powerful force to expand our own vitality and that of this planet.

Join us in this exploration! Despite its worldwide impact, Ecology Action has remained a small organization, believing that small is effective and human. We consider ourselves to be a catalyst: Our function is to empower people with the skills and knowledge necessary to enable them to improve their lives and thus transform the world into a garden of health and abundance. The message is to live richly in a simple manner—in a way we can all enjoy.

You can assist Ecology Action in this work by finding five friends and getting them involved in GROW BIOINTENSIVE Sustainable Mini-Farming and/or other sustainable food-raising practices.[4] Together we can make a significant difference in the world, one small area at a time. This is our opportunity. It is fun to be part of the whole picture and part of the long-term world environmental solution!

ENDNOTES

1 Developed from U.S. Department of Agriculture statistics.

2 Developed from P. Buringh, "Availability of Agricultural Land for Crop and Livestock Production," in D. Pimental and C.W. Hall (eds.), *Food and Natural Resources* (San Diego: Academic Press, 1989), pp. 69–83, as noted in "Natural Resources and an Optimum Human Population," David Pimental et al., *Population and Environment: A Journal of Interdisciplinary Studies,* Vol. 15, No. 5, May 1994; and with statistics from the United Nations.

3 Ibid.

4 To help accelerate this process, in the last 20 years Ecology Action has taught 1,855 participants at Introductory 3-Day Workshops from 47 states and the District of Colombia, plus 29 countries and initiated a Self-Teaching Section on its website www.growbiointensive.org.

Nothing happens in living nature
that is not in relation to the whole.
—GOETHE

1

DEEP SOIL CREATION AND MAINTENANCE

Preparing the raised bed is an important step in GROW BIO-INTENSIVE gardening. A correctly prepared bed facilitates proper soil structure. Proper **soil structure** and nutrients allow uninterrupted and healthy plant growth. Loose soil with good nutrients enables roots to penetrate the soil easily, and a steady stream of nutrients can flow into the stem and leaves. How different from a situation in which a plant is transferred from a flat with loose soil and proper nutrients into a hastily prepared backyard plot or a chemically stimulated field. The plant suffers not only from the shock of being uprooted, but also from an environment where it is difficult to grow. The growth is interrupted and the roots have difficulty getting through the soil and obtaining food. As a result, the plant produces more carbohydrates and less protein than usual. This imbalance attracts insects. A debilitating cycle can begin that ends in the use of pesticides which kill soil life and make the plants even less healthy. Fertilizers are then used in an attempt to boost the plants' health. Instead, the fertilizers destroy more soil life, damage the soil structure further, and lead to even less healthy plants that attract more insects and "need" more toxic "medicines" in the form of additional pesticides and fertilizers.

Beds vs. Rows: The planting rows usually made by gardeners and farms today are only a few inches wide with wide spaces in between. The plants have difficulty growing in these rows due to the extreme penetration of air and the greater fluctuations in temperature and moisture content. During irrigation, water floods the rows; immerses the roots in water; and washes soil away from the rows and upper roots. Consequently, much of the beneficial microbiotic life around the roots and soil, which is so essential to disease prevention and to the transformation of nutrients into forms that plants can use, is destroyed and may even be replaced by harmful organisms. (About three quarters of the beneficial microbiotic life inhabits the upper 6 inches of the soil.) After the water penetrates the soil, the upper layers dry out and microbial activity is severely curtailed. The rows are then more subject to wide temperature fluctuations. Finally, to cultivate and harvest, people and machine trundle down the trough between the rows, compacting the soil and the roots, which eat, drink, and breathe—a difficult task with someone or something standing on the equivalent of your mouth and nose!

Well-documented reports tell us that a wide variety of commercial pesticides kill beneficial invertebrate predators while "controlling" pest populations. These pesticides exterminate earthworms and other invertebrates that are needed to maintain soil fertility. The pesticides also destroy microorganisms that provide symbiotic relationships between the soil and plant root systems. We propose striving for good soil health in the first place, starting with the preparation of the soil—and easier soil preparation next time.

The initial preparation and planting a raised bed, a time investment of as much as $6\frac{1}{2}$ to 11 hours to dig and transplant a 100-square-foot bed. If you are lucky enough to have loose soil, the time commitment will be much less. The time invested pays off with increased yields and healthier soil and plants.

As you become more skilled at double-digging, the time invested is greatly reduced. Often a 100-square-foot bed can be done in two hours or less. We estimate that only 4 to $6\frac{1}{2}$ hours should be required on an ongoing basis for the entire bed preparation and planting process as the soil develops better structure over time with correct care and compost.

Getting Started—Correct Tools

We recommend investing in quality tools from the beginning. Poor tools will wear out or tire you out while you are preparing your garden area. For all-around ease, D-handled flat spades and D-handled spading forks of good temper should be used for bed preparation. D-handles allow you to stand straight with the tool directly in front of you. A long-handled tool means that you must hold it at your side. This position does not allow for a simple, direct posture. Most people find that D-handled tools are less tiring. However, people with back problems may need long-handled tools. In fact, anyone with chronic pain or other health problems should check with their physician before proceeding with the physically active process of doubling-digging.

The flat spade has a particular advantage in that it digs equally deep all along its edge rather than in a pointed V pattern. The flat edge is preferable as all points in the bed should be dug to an equal depth. The blade on the flat spade also goes into the soil at less of an angle and without the usual shovel's curve. Therefore, the sides of the bed can be dug perpendicular or even diagonally outward into the path, a plus for root penetration and water flow.

For Seed Propagation

The proper tools will make the work easier and more productive.

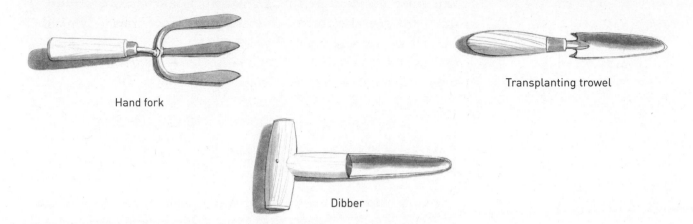

Hand fork

Transplanting trowel

Dibber

For Soil Preparation

The 39-inch-long spades and forks are generally for people 5'5" or shorter; 43-inch-long tools are for people 5'6" or taller.

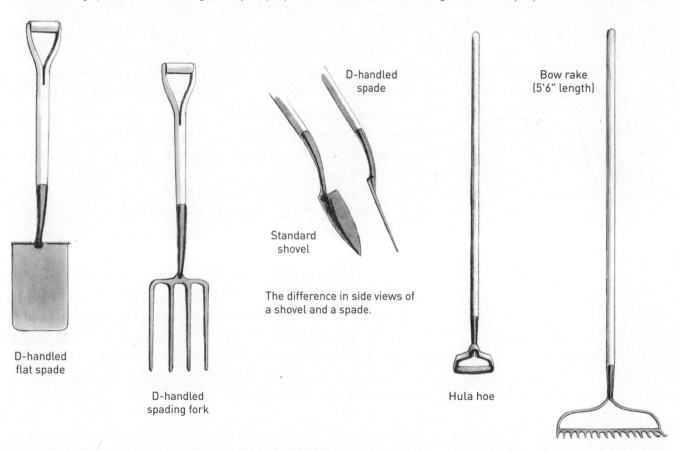

D-handled
spade

Bow rake
(5'6" length)

Standard
shovel

The difference in side views of
a shovel and a spade.

D-handled
flat spade

D-handled
spading fork

Hula hoe

A ⅝-inch-thick plywood board, 2 to 3 feet long by 3 to 5 feet wide, serves as a "digging board" to stand on. The size of the board will depend on your height and the width of the bed. Treat the board with linseed oil to protect it against soil moisture. This board will distribute your weight over the bed as you dig or work on the bed.

A bow rake (preferably 5 feet 6 inches in length) makes leveling and forming the bed easy. A hula hoe is the perfect tool for cultivating the upper 2 to 4 inches of soil.

Laying Out Your Beds

Carefully choose a place for your raised beds that has access to water and sunlight—preferably 7 to 11 hours of direct sunlight each day.

To begin, mark out a bed 3 to 5 feet wide and at least 3 feet long. A 3 foot by 3 foot space assures a minimum mini-climate. Most people prefer beds to be 5, 10 or 20 feet long, as it makes calculating easier.

The maximum length should be determined by ease of work.

Consider your source of compost. Ideally, you will have compost that you have prepared available as you begin to prepare your beds. However, many decide to purchase compost or aged manure to begin. For this initial application of organic matter, one may consider aged manure. While compost is preferable, if one chooses aged manure, assure that it is two-year-old steer or cow manure, or two-year-old horse manure that originally contained a lot of sawdust, or two-month-old horse or chicken manure not containing much sawdust.

The best time to double-dig the soil is in early morning or evening in spring or autumn. The air temperature is cooler at these times so less soil organic matter is lost in the process. Dig only when the soil is evenly moist. It is easier and also better for the soil. Digging a hard, dry soil breaks down the structure, and it is difficult to penetrate. Wet soil is heavy and easily compacted. Compaction destroys friable structure and minimizes aeration. These conditions kill microbiotic life. Correct soil moisture can be determined by a simple hand test. Soil is too dry for digging when it is loose and will not hold its shape after being squeezed in the palm of your hand (in cases of sands or loams) or when it cannot be penetrated by a spade (in the case of clays). Soil is too wet when it sticks to the spade as you dig.

The goal of double-digging is to loosen the soil to a depth of 24 inches below the surface. The first year, you may only be able to reach 15 to 18 inches with reasonable effort. Be satisfied with this result. Do not injure yourself or your tools. More important than reaching 24 inches in the first years is improvement over the course of time. Nature, the loosened soil, worms, and plant roots will further loosen the soil with each crop, so digging will be easier each year and the depth will increase over time. Be patient in this soil-building process. It takes 5 to 10 years to build up a good soil (and one's skills). Actually, this is very rapid. Nature usually requires a period of 3,000 years or more to build the 6-inch layer of farmable soil needed to grow a good crop of food.

After the soil has been initially prepared, you will find that the GROW BIOINTENSIVE method requires less work per unit of food produced than the gardening technique you presently use. The Irish call this the "lazy bed" method of raising food.

Types of Deep Soil Preparation

The double-dig is the principal way one prepares a GROW BIOIN-TENSIVE bed until good structure is established. Afterwards, one will depend on surface cultivating the top 2 to 4 inches. Another way to keep soil loose between double-digging is to single-dig (loosening the top 12 inches with the spading fork). We recommend doing so between crops in the same growing year.

Proper soil structure and nutrients allow uninterrupted and healthy plant growth.

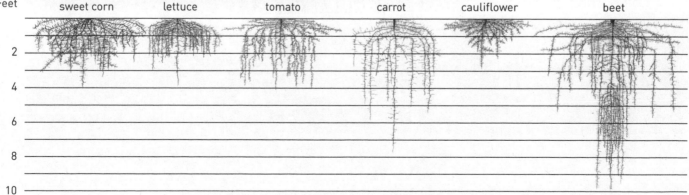

Selected Vegetable Root Systems Shown in Scale

Feet

sweet corn · lettuce · tomato · carrot · cauliflower · beet

2

4

6

8

10

General Double-Digging Procedure— Each year before the main crop until good soil structure is established

After marking the bed, place the digging board on the bed, leaving approximately 12 inches from the end of the bed for the first trench. Remove 7 five-gallon buckets of soil from the upper level of the first trench (assuming a 5-foot-wide growing bed; see illustration on page 25). Be sure to dig trenches across the width of the bed. This will give you 3 buckets of soil to make compost (these will eventually be returned to the growing beds in the form of cured compost), 1 bucket of soil to make flat soil to grow seedlings, and the remaining 3 buckets are returned to the bed after it is dug.

Now, standing in the trench or on the digging board above

Note: The soil at the upper and lower trench levels should be prepared when the soil is evenly moist—at approximately the 50% humidity level.

The Initial Double-Dig Process: Step-by-Step

1. Spread a 1/2-inch layer of compost over the entire area to be dug. (Compost is added *after* the double dig and bed shaping for Basic Ongoing Double Digs [see page 26].)
2. Using a spade, remove the soil from a trench 1 foot deep and 1 foot wide across the width of the bed and put the soil into buckets or a wheelbarrow for use in making compost and flat soil. If the bed is 5 feet wide, the soil will fill 7 five-

gallon buckets. (The trench is being dug across the width of the bed.)

3a. Loosen the soil an additional 12 inches with a spading fork by digging the tool in to its full depth and then pushing the tool handle downward so the fork tines will lever through the soil, loosening and aerating it. (See illustrations opposite for loosening compacted soil.)

Deep Soil Creation and Maintenance

the trench, insert the spading fork 12 inches from the end of the bed and dig down another 12 inches (or as deep as possible) with a spading fork, a few inches at a time if the soil is heavy or tight. Leave the fork as deep as it has penetrated, and loosen the subsoil by pushing the fork handle down and levering the tines through the soil. If the soil is not loose enough for this process, lift the chunk of soil out of the trench on the fork tines. Then throw it slightly and gently upward, and allow it to fall back on the tines so it will break apart some. If this does not work, use the points of the fork tines to break the soil apart. Work from one end of the trench to the other in this manner.

Next, move back the digging board (approximately the 12-inch width of the next trench). Dig another trench behind the first one, moving each spadeful of the top 12 inches of soil forward into the first trench. When digging, make as few motions and use as little

Note: If the spading fork will not easily penetrate the soil fully, with your complete weight on the shoulder of the tool, arc the tool slowly back and forth. Your weight and the arcing will draw the tool all the way into the soil.

The Initial Double-Dig Process: Step-by-Step

3b(i). FOR COMPACTED SOIL: While standing in the trench, loosen the soil an additional 12 inches with a spading fork by digging in the tool to its full depth and lifting out a tight soil section on the fork pan.

3b(ii). Then, by moving your arms upward in a small jerk, the soil will break apart as it falls downward, hits the fork tines, and falls into the hole below.

4. Dig out the upper part of a second trench 1 foot deep and 1 foot wide. Move each spadeful of soil forward (into the first trench), mixing the soil layers as little as possible.

muscle as possible in this process. This will conserve your energy and involve less work. In fact, as you dig the soil, you will discover you can use an Aikido-like economy of motion and energy in which you are virtually just shifting your balance and weight rather than digging. Sometimes you will have to work over a trench a second or third time to remove all the soil and obtain the proper trench size. Repeat the subsoil loosening process in the second trench.

Dig a third trench, and so on, until the entire bed has been double-dug. It helps to level the soil with a rake every 3 to 4 trenches during the digging process. If you do not, you may end up with a very deep trench at the end of the bed. Then you will have to move a large amount of soil from one end of the bed to the other to even it out when you are ready to be finished. This action also causes a disproportionate misplacing of topsoil into the subsoil area.

When you are sliding the soil forward from one trench into another, notice a couple of things. If you spread compost on the bed before beginning, note that some of the layer slides 3 to 6 inches down into the trench, creating a small mound of soil or landslide. This approximates the way nature adds leaves, flower bodies, and other decaying vegetation to the top of the soil, where they break down and their essences percolate in the soil.

Always make sure that the upper layer of soil (the top 12 inches) is not turned over during the double-dig. Most of the microbiotic life lives in the upper 6 inches of the soil. Also, the natural layering of the soil that is caused by rainfall and leaching, leaf litter, temperature, gravity, and other natural forces is less disturbed when the soil is not generally mixed, even though the soil is loosened up and distributed somewhat. Aim for a balance between nature's natural stratification and the loosened landsliding soil. (As a goal, strive not to mix the soil layers. Even though some mixing will occur, it is important to avoid excessive disruption of the soil layers.)

When you are through double-digging, the aerated surplus soil in the bed will be enough to fill the final trench at the end of the bed. You may also add some of the buckets from the first trench. If you add compost that you have made with soil, that will also contribute soil to the bed.

Take buckets of surplus soil to the soil bin pile.

Level and shape the bed. Sprinkle on compost and any soil amendments as recommended by your soil test over the surface of the bed. These may include organic nitrogen, phosphorus, potash, calcium and trace mineral fertilizers. (For more detail, see page 68.) Include any pH modifiers (such as special leaf or pine needle compost to make the soil less alkaline, or lime to make the soil less acid) as indicated by your soil test. Sift in compost and fertilizers and pH modifiers only 2 to 4 inches deep with a spading fork. After sifting them in, do no further raking to avoid disturbing the even distribution of fertilizers and compost.

Considerations for Initial Dig with Very Poor Soils

You may choose to add compost at different points for the initial double-dig and when working with a soil with very low amounts of organic matter. Instead of applying compost only *after* the double-dig, consider spreading a 1/2-inch layer over the bed *before* double-digging and/or a 1/2-inch layer *during* the dig by incorporating it thoroughly into the 12-inch-deep trench.

BED PREPARATION PER 100 SQUARE FEET

1. Check the soil moisture. The soil should be evenly moist to facilitate digging, but not saturated. If needed, water the area to be dug. For hard, dry clays that have not ever been cultivated, this may mean up to 2 hours with a sprinkler. Begin next steps when soil is evenly moistened.

2. Loosen 12 inches of soil with a spading fork, and remove any plant cover.

3. Check soil moisture and water again if necessary. If your soil has particularly large clods, consider waiting several days and let nature help do the work. The warm sun, cool nights, wind, and water will help break down the clods. Water the bed lightly every day to aid the process.

   OPTIONAL (ONE TIME): At this time, sand may be added to a bed with a clayey soil, or clay to a bed with sandy soil, to improve texture. Normally you should add no more than 1/2 inch (4 cubic feet) of sand or clay. (More sand may allow water-soluble fertilizers to percolate down too rapidly.) Mix the sand or clay thoroughly into the loosened 12 inches of soil with a spading fork.

OPTIONAL (ONE TIME): If the soil is poor (very sandy or very clayey), add on a one-time-only basis up to a 1/2-inch layer (8 cubic feet) of compost or aged manure.

Remove the soil from the upper part of the first trench and place it in a soil storage area for use in making compost and flat soil or to return to the last trench.

4. Loosen the soil an additional 12 inches.

OPTIONAL (ONE TIME): Spread a 1/2-inch layer of compost on the loosened soil of the first trench.

5. Dig out the upper part of the second trench and move it forward into the first upper trench.

6. Loosen the lower part of the second trench.

7. Continue the double-digging process (repeating steps 7 and 8) for the remaining trenches. Rake every 3 to 4 trenches to ensure even bed height.

8. Fill in the final trench. Shape the bed by raking it. Evenly spread compost and any needed fertilizers over the entire area. Sift in compost and any fertilizers 2 to 4 inches deep with a spading fork. Your bed is ready to be transplanted!

TYPES OF DEEP SOIL PREPARATION—SIMPLIFIED SIDE VIEWS

Ecology Action uses 4 basic types of deep soil preparation processes:

- the initial double-dig, shown opposite

- the basic ongoing double-dig, shown on page 26

- the complete texturizing double-dig, shown on page 27

- the U-bar dig, shown on page 28

The **complete texturizing double-dig** was developed to improve soil quality more rapidly and is used one time only. It is used usually in place of the initial double-dig, but it can be used at a later point in time. We have found this soil preparation process greatly improves plant health and yields immediately in poor, compacted,

Initial Double Dig

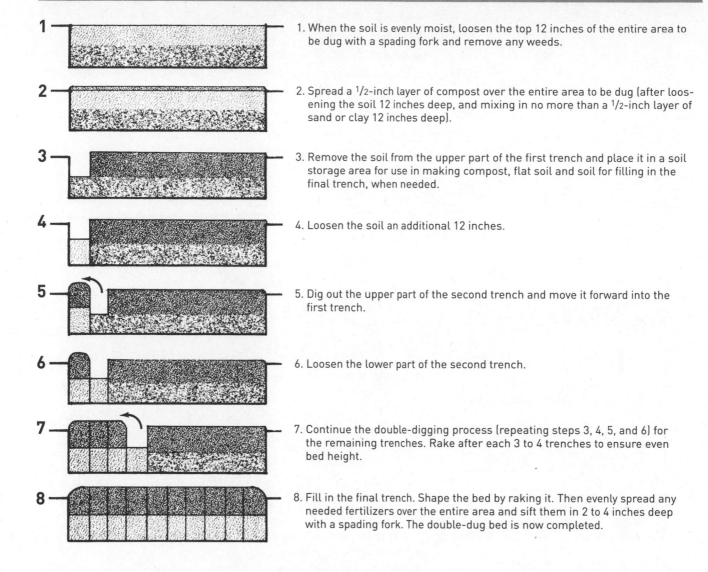

1. When the soil is evenly moist, loosen the top 12 inches of the entire area to be dug with a spading fork and remove any weeds.

2. Spread a 1/2-inch layer of compost over the entire area to be dug (after loosening the soil 12 inches deep, and mixing in no more than a 1/2-inch layer of sand or clay 12 inches deep).

3. Remove the soil from the upper part of the first trench and place it in a soil storage area for use in making compost, flat soil and soil for filling in the final trench, when needed.

4. Loosen the soil an additional 12 inches.

5. Dig out the upper part of the second trench and move it forward into the first trench.

6. Loosen the lower part of the second trench.

7. Continue the double-digging process (repeating steps 3, 4, 5, and 6) for the remaining trenches. Rake after each 3 to 4 trenches to ensure even bed height.

8. Fill in the final trench. Shape the bed by raking it. Then evenly spread any needed fertilizers over the entire area and sift them in 2 to 4 inches deep with a spading fork. The double-dug bed is now completed.

and heavy soil. It is often worth the extra digging time involved. However, it does use an insustainable amount of organic matter.

The **U-bar dig** can be used as a substitute for the ongoing double-dig in soil that is in reasonably good shape. This usually means after one normal double-dig or more. The 18-inch-long U-bar tines (see page 28) do not prepare the soil as deeply as a spade and a spading fork used to double-dig 24 inches deep, but the lower 12 inches of the growing bed compact more slowly over time than the upper 12 inches. Also, the U-bar appears to have the advantage of mixing up the soil strata much less than double-digging with a spade and a spading fork. It aerates the soil less, however. This is an advantage in looser, sandier soil and can be a problem in tighter clays. If you use a U-bar regularly, do a normal double-dig as often as increased compaction indicates. U-barring is quicker and easier than using a spade and a spading fork, though some knowledge of how your soil is improving, or not improving, is lost with the decreased personal contact with the soil. (For detailed plans on how to build a U-bar, see pages 193–195 or Ecology Action's *The Backyard Homestead, Mini-Farm and Garden Log Book*.) At Ecology Action, we prefer to double-dig, as we learn more from it and stay more in touch with the soil.

Basic Ongoing Double Dig

A primary difference between the ongoing and the initial double-dig is that the compost is put on *after* the digging and shaping process in the ongoing double-dig.

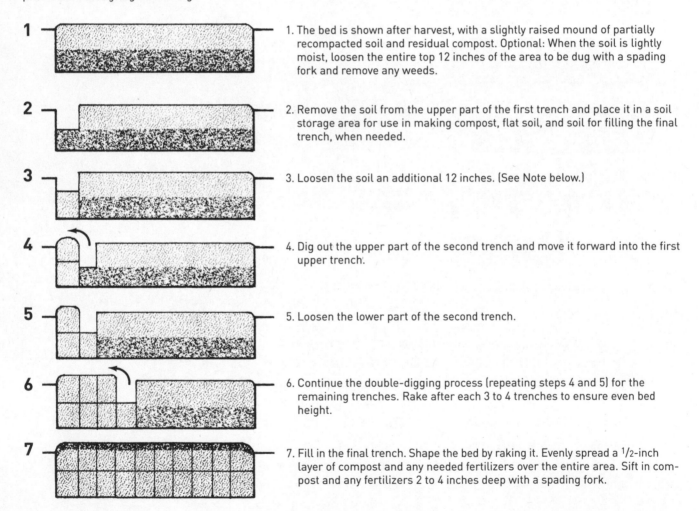

1. The bed is shown after harvest, with a slightly raised mound of partially recompacted soil and residual compost. Optional: When the soil is lightly moist, loosen the entire top 12 inches of the area to be dug with a spading fork and remove any weeds.

2. Remove the soil from the upper part of the first trench and place it in a soil storage area for use in making compost, flat soil, and soil for filling the final trench, when needed.

3. Loosen the soil an additional 12 inches. (See Note below.)

4. Dig out the upper part of the second trench and move it forward into the first upper trench.

5. Loosen the lower part of the second trench.

6. Continue the double-digging process (repeating steps 4 and 5) for the remaining trenches. Rake after each 3 to 4 trenches to ensure even bed height.

7. Fill in the final trench. Shape the bed by raking it. Evenly spread a 1/2-inch layer of compost and any needed fertilizers over the entire area. Sift in compost and any fertilizers 2 to 4 inches deep with a spading fork.

*Note: After the lower trench has been loosened, **potatoes** may be placed on its surface on 9-inch centers using offset spacing (see pages 76–78). The soil from the next trench's upper level may then be moved forward onto them. This is the easiest way we have found to plant potatoes. (Mark the location of the potatoes with stones or sticks in the outside paths before covering them with soil. This will indicate where potatoes should be placed on the surface of each succeeding lower trench.)*

Complete Texturizing Double-Dig

One time only for compacted heavy soils.

1

1. When the soil is lightly moist, loosen the top 12 inches of the entire area to be dug with a spading fork and remove any weeds.

2

2. Spread a 1/2-inch layer of compost including 50% soil over the entire area to be dug (after mixing in a 1/2-inch layer of sand or clay 12 inches deep; optional, see page 24).

3

3. Thoroughly mix in compost 12 inches deep.

4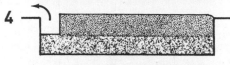

4. Remove the soil from the upper part of the first trench and place it in a soil storage area for use in making compost, flat soil, and soil for filling the final trench, when needed.

5

5. Loosen the soil an additional 12 inches.

6

6. Spread a 1/2-inch layer of compost including 50% soil on the loosened soil in the first trench.

7

7. Thoroughly mix the compost placed on top of the lower first trench into the soil 12 inches deep.

8

8. Dig out the upper part of the second trench and move it forward into the first trench.

9

9. Loosen the lower part of the second trench.

10

10. Spread a 1/2-inch layer of compost including 50% soil on the loosened soil in the second trench.

11

11. Thoroughly mix in the compost on the lower second trench 12 inches deep.

12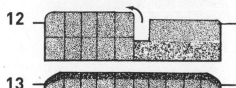

12. Continue the complete texturizing double-digging process (repeat steps 8 through 11) for the remaining trenches. Rake after each 3 to 4 trenches to ensure even bed height.

13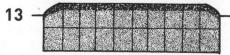

13. Fill in the final trench. Shape the bed by raking it. Then evenly spread any needed fertilizers over the entire area and sift them in 2 to 4 inches deep with a spading fork. The complete texturizing double-dug bed is completed.

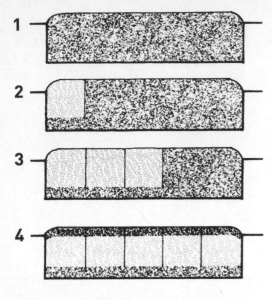

1 1. After harvest, weed the entire slightly raised bed if necessary.

2 2. When the soil is lightly moist, begin U-barring the soil along the length of the bed. No digging board is used. The soil will be loosened three-quarters as deep as in the double-dig.

3 3. Continue U-barring until the bed is done; 2 or 3 U-bar passes along the length of the bed may be necessary depending on the bed's width. The U-bar is about 2 feet wide and loosens the soil 2 to $2^1/2$ feet wide.

4 4. Break up any remaining large clumps with a spading fork. Shape the bed by raking it. Then evenly spread $1/2$-inch layer of compost and any needed fertilizers over the entire area and sift them in 2 to 4 inches deep with a spading fork.

Note: See pages 193–195 on the proper techniques for building and using a U-bar.

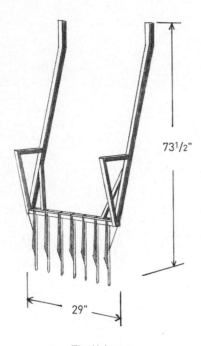

73$^1/2$"

29"

The U-bar.

unsustainable. The amounts needed for applying multiple layers of compost are not typically able to be produced in a garden. Therefore, Ecology Action recommends applying compost before and/or during the double-dig only as the initial double-dig or a one-time application. As you get higher yields, you may even be able to "payback" the borrowed compost to its original source.

Compost applications will help very sandy or clayey soils to have better structure. However, sometimes food-growers decide to add sand or clay to improve the texture. Ecology Action recommends experimenting with a bed a season or two before making such a decision. If you choose to add sand or clay, spread a $1/2$-inch layer on the bed area before the double-dig and mix in thoroughly in the top 12 inches with a spading fork.

Prepared Beds

Whenever you reprepare a bed (after each crop or season) until good structure is created, the 24-inch depth of the bed should be measured from the bed, not from the path surface. Ecology Action repreapares the soil between crops with a double- or single-dig (loosening the first 12 inches of soil with the fork). As your soil improves and the large clods disappear, your bed may not raise as high as initially. Do not worry about this. It is a sign that you and your soil are successful. The goal of double-digging is not the height of the bed, but a reasonable looseness and good structure of the soil.

Once good structure has been established by double-digging, it is preferable to use surface cultivation (the loosening of the upper two inches of soil with a cultivating tool such as a hula hoe) for several years, or more. In this way, the developed structure and soil organic matter are better preserved.

One simple way to determine whether our soil has good structure follows. Squeeze a sample of reasonably moist soil firmly in your hand. Then open your hand. If the soil falls apart easily, it does not have good structure. If it holds the shape of your hand even when you press it gently with the fingers of your other hand, it does not have good structure. If the soil breaks apart into small clumps when you press it with your fingers, it probably has good structure.

When surface cultivation is used, *compost made without soil* **will be used** because soil will not be removed from the bed during the soil preparation process. Whenever the lower soil becomes compacted, the bed may be double-dug again to encourage reestablishment of a well-aerated structure.

Remember that *structure is different from texture*. The **texture** is determined by its basic ingredients: silt, clay, and sand particles. The soil **structure** is the way these ingredients hold together. With your assistance, sticky "threads" exuded by microbial life and the roots produced by the plants help to loosen a clay soil and improve a sandy soil.[1] The goal is to create a sumptuous "living sponge cake." Bon appétit!

Once the bed is prepared, you will truly appreciate its width. The distance between the tips of your fingers and your nose is about 3 feet when your arm is extended out to the side. Thus a 3- to 5-foot-wide bed can be fertilized, planted, weeded, and harvested from each side with relative ease, and insects can be controlled without walking on the bed. A 3- to 5-foot width also allows a good

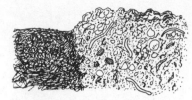

path   bed

Soil in the path is subject to compaction; soil in the bed remains loose.

The loosened soil of the planting bed makes weeding easier.

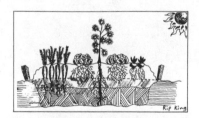

The GROW BIOINTENSIVE raised bed. A balance between nature's natural stratification and our loosened land-sliding soil.

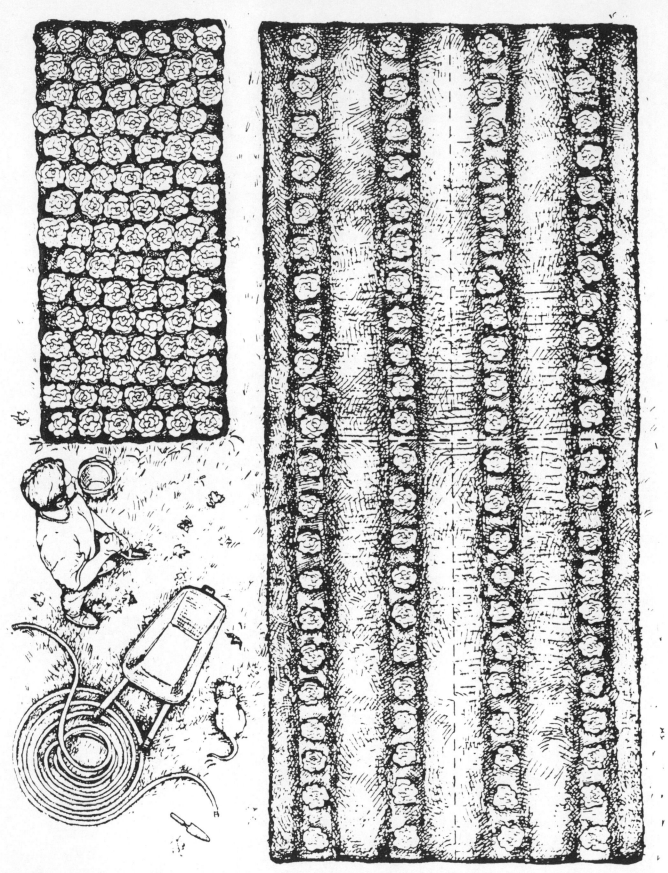

Good soil preparation makes GROW BIOINTENSIVE fertility possible—up to 4 times the productivity per unit of area!

mini-climate to develop under closely spaced plants. You may wish to use a narrower bed, 1½ to 2½ feet wide, for plants supported by stakes, such as tomatoes, pole beans, and pole peas, for easier harvesting.

Try not to step on the growing beds once they have been prepared. To do so compacts the soil and makes it more difficult for the plants to grow. If the bed must be walked on, use the double-digging board. This will displace your weight over a large area and minimize the damage. Plants obtain much of their water and nutrients through the contact of their root hairs with the soil. If they do not develop an abundant supply of root hairs, less water and fewer nutrients are taken in. The root hairs are more numerous and vigorous in looser soil, so keep your soil loose.

When weeding, note that the entire weed root usually comes up out of loosened raised-bed soil. This is welcome weeding, and if you get all the root, you will not have to weed as often. Also, you do not need to cultivate the soil of raised beds as much as other gardens. The **living mulch** shade cover provided by mature plants helps to keep the soil surface loose. If the soil compacts between young plants before the mini-climate takes effect, you should cultivate.

Once this beautifully alive bed is prepared, it should be kept evenly moist until and after planting so the microbiotic life and plants will stay alive. The bed should be planted as soon as possible so the plants can take advantage of the new surge of life made possible by bringing together the soil, compost, air, water, sun, and fertilizers.

A good growing bed will often be 2 to 10 inches higher than the soil's original surface. A good soil contains 50% air space. (In fact, adequate air is one of the missing ingredients in most soil preparation processes.) Increased air space allows for increased diffusion of oxygen (which the roots and microbes depend on) into the soil, and of carbon dioxide (which the leaves depend on) out of the soil. The increased "breathing" ability of a double-dug bed is a key to improved plant health. Thus, the prepared depth will be as much as 34 inches in clayey soil. A sandy soil will probably not raise as high as clayey soil at first. To prevent erosion and promote more even water saturation in a clay bed with a high rise, create a lip around the top of the bed (see page 73).

If the bed raises higher than 10 inches as you are double-digging, be sure to level it out with a rake as you go along. Otherwise you will end up with a very wide and deep trench at the end of the bed. Then you will have to move a large amount of soil from

Note: For different types of ongoing soil cultivation practices to use after soil preparation, refer to the "Cultivation" information sheet in the Information Packets—Complete Set (item BEA-0770), available from Bountiful Gardens at www.bountifulgardens.org.

one end of the bed to the other to even it out when you are tired. This would also cause a disproportionate misplacing of topsoil into the subsoil area.

SOIL STRUCTURE

We currently re-prepare the soil after each crop, except for autumn compost crops. Some people prefer to do this only once each year. As your soil improves and the large clods disappear, your bed may not raise as high as initially. Do not worry about this. It is just a sign that you and your soil are successful. *The goal of double-digging is not the height of the bed, but the looseness and good structure of the soil.*

ENDNOTES

1 For More information on growing soil quality and soil structure, see "Table 20.1—Qualitative Soil Health Indicators" in U.S. Department of Agriculture/ Agriculture Research Service, Soil Quality Test Kit (Washington, DC: U.S. Department of Agriculture/Agriculture Research service, 1999); and Fred Magdoff and Harold van Es, *Building Soils for Better Crops, 2nd ed.* (Burlington, VT: Sustainable Agriculture Network, 2000).

GOAL: Grow and maintain sustainable soil fertility with sufficient humus in the soil while creating thriving mini-ecosystems

SUSTAINABILITY

Sustainable Soil Fertility

Sustainability means living in such a way that there are enough resources to live well in an alive, diverse, thriving environment—indefinitely.

Sustainability *is* possible—individual people, families, and communities accomplish this frequently all around the world. Yet most people find this challenging. Many of us are living on six times—or more—the resources that would be available to each person in the world if the resources were divided up equally!

The food we purchase is how we farm, or grow, our food. When we purchase food that has been grown with less sustainable practices, these are the types of practice we are encouraging.

We often think of sustainability in terms of using *nonrenewable resources* carefully. More important, however, is learning to use *renewable resources* well. If all the Earth's agriculture became organic tomorrow, it would be wonderful and challenging. A healthier resource-conserving, food-raising, and planetary ecosystem would be possible. However, there would be new challenges to how to manage the renewable resources within the system. The

The grandfather keeps sheep, the son keeps goats, the grandson keeps nothing.

—RICHARD ST. BARBE BAKER,
My Life, My Trees

cost of purchasing the cured compost needed to grow food organically would skyrocket because the demand would exceed current supply. It is a reason for which we need to learn how to properly preserve, manage, and develop our renewable resources. Soil, for example, needs a given level of humus, or cured compost, in order to thrive. Therefore, we each need to make sure we grow enough organic matter to properly preserve the renewable resource of soil.

For a garden or mini-farm to be sustainable, it must be able to produce sufficient crops to provide the grower with what she or he needs over an indefinite period of time. This is possible *only* if the mini-farm's soil is kept fertile in a way that relies neither on non-renewable resources, such as petroleum, nor on the nutrients or health of another soil. Most chemical fertilizers and pesticides are created in part from petroleum, which also fuels tractors, processing machinery, and transport vehicles. While organic fertilizers may seem to be a good alternative, their production often relies on another farm's soil being able to produce the raw materials, such as alfalfa, cottonseed, and feed for animals that provide hoof and horn and blood meals. With these materials constantly taken away from the soil that produces them, these soils lose nutrients and eventually become depleted and infertile.

When our focus is on harvesting as much as we can from the soil, we forget to give the soil what it needs to remain fertile. We must grow soil in a way that is sustainable. Only then can it continue to provide us with abundant food. If we farm in a way that does not sustain soil fertility, the soil that is currently used functionally to grow crops will soon be depleted. Like a non-renewable resource, it will be used up.

The Loss of Soil Nutrients and Humus

When soil grows crops, the crops extract nutrients as well as humus from the soil. To maintain the soil's fertility, the nutrients and humus must be replenished. Both of these needs can be met simultaneously when the crop and all other residues from those who consumed the edible portion of the crop are composted and returned to the soil. The cured compost will have almost all of the nutrients that the crop contained and, depending on the crops that are grown, enough humus to replenish the soil's supply.[1] The carbon that left the soil in the form of carbon dioxide will be returned if plants that store large amounts of carbon in their mature bodies (such as corn, amaranth, wheat, and rice) are grown and added to the soil as cured compost.

Initially Adding Nutrients and Humus to the Soil

Not all soils naturally have all of the nutrients that they need for their optimum health and crop productivity. Deep-rooted crops such as alfalfa and comfrey can be grown to bring up nutrients from below the range of most roots, then composted and added to the topsoil. Additionally, when cured compost is added to the soil, nutrients that were previously unavailable in the soil may be made available by the biogeologic cycle. (In this cycle, humic acid—which is produced from the decomposition process and is contained in the cured compost—along with the carbonic acid developed around the plant's roots, can increase soil microbial activity, decompose larger minerals, and possibly alter soil pH so that previously unavailable nutrients are made available.) However, if the needed nutrients are not in the deeper regions of the soil, they will not be present in the cured compost. In other words, if the nutrients are not present, **the cured compost made from plants grown on the nutrients-deficient soil will not contain the deficient nutrients, and the soil will still be unbalanced even after the cured compost is added.** Therefore, in some cases, you may need to bring nutrients in the form of organic fertilizers into the mini-farm from the outside. Your goal should be to bring in a minimum of outside organic fertilizers and maintain them cycling in the system through compost.

You may also decide to bring carbonaceous materials into the garden or mini-farm in the beginning so sufficient humus can be added to the soil. Humus is the food of soil microorganisms that are responsible for creating good soil structure and soil fertility. It also helps hold the nutrients in the soil. If there is not enough humus (about 4% to 6% organic matter in temperate regions; about 3% organic matter in tropical ones), nutrients that are returned to the soil in the form of cured compost may leach out.

100% Sustainability Impossible

Some nutrients will escape from the garden or mini-farm, whether from leaching, from rainfall runoff, or from wind picking them up and carrying them away (although water and wind erosion are usually not a problem when the soil's humus supply is maintained and all of the GROW BIOINTENSIVE techniques are used). At the same time, however, nutrients are added naturally to the mini-farm through rainfall, wind, the breakdown of the soil's parental rock material, and the upsoaking of groundwater. With GROW BIOIN-TENSIVE sustainable gardening and mini-farming, **the gain in nutrients may eventually near the loss of nutrients and the soil's nutrient balance may be maintained if all nutrients are recycled.**

According to the second law of thermodynamics, all systems proceed toward a state of entropy or disorder. Therefore, no system, including agriculture, can be sustained indefinitely. At the extreme, all life will cease as we know it when the sun burns out millions of years from now. However, until this happens, we can maintain our soils at a level close to complete sustainability (instead of close to complete insustainability as is now the situation with most agricultural systems). Within a garden or mini-farm, some soil nutrients may not be replenished by natural forces, or the same natural forces may add soil nutrients in excess. In both situations, if proper soil nutrient maintenance is not pursued, the soil may cease to be able to grow significant amounts of crops in a very short period of time.

The Need for Up to 99% Sustainability

At Ecology Action, we are investigating the components of GROW BIOINTENSIVE as possibly one of the quickest, most effective, most resource-conserving, and most ecologically sound ways to replenish and balance soil nutrients. Once the soil's nutrient base has been properly built and balanced, we need to learn how best to maintain those nutrients in our gardens and mini-farms. One promising approach is to grow all of our own compost materials. If we grow sufficient quantities of crops that produce material for compost, our goal is that the resulting cured compost will contain as many of the nutrients that the crops removed from the soil as possible, as well as enough humus to feed the soil microbes and prevent nutrient leaching. In this way, our food-raising area becomes a

A [farmer] took up land [in Saskatchewan], dug a cellar and built a frame house on top of it; ploughed up the prairie and grew wheat and oats. After twenty years he decided the country was no good for farming, for eight feet of his soil had gone and he had to climb up into his house.

—RICHARD ST. BARBE BAKER,
My Life, My Trees

source rather than a *sink*—of carbon, nutrients, and fertility. (The net loss of carbon dioxide, or "leakage," from the system is a key concern. Worldwide, the loss of carbon from our soils—and plants in the form of harvested trees and their use for fuel—is a situation causing increasing problems.)

Keeping the nutrients within the mini-farm, as well as learning how to minimize the amount of nutrients we need to bring in from the outside, are important tasks if we are to grow all of our food, clothing, and building materials on the 9,000 square feet (or about one-fifth of an acre) that may soon be all that is available to each man, woman, and child living in developing nations (see Appendix 2). Soon we simply will not have the luxury of taking nutrients from one soil to feed another.

With about 33 to 49 years' worth of topsoil remaining in the world, learning how to enrich, improve, and maintain soil—in a way that is sustainable—is of vital importance if we as a species are to survive. If current agricultural systems can only provide food for about a century before the soil is depleted, they clearly are not sustainable. Ancient civilizations sustained their soils to feed large populations for lengthy periods of time. China's soils, for example, remained productive for 4,000 years or more until the adoption of mechanized chemical agricultural techniques that have been responsible, in part, for the destruction of 15% to 33% of China's agricultural soil in the period from 1950 to 1990. Many of the world's great civilizations have disappeared when their soil's fertility was not maintained. Northern Africa, for example, used to be the granary for Rome until overfarming converted it into a desert, and much of the Sahara Desert was forested until it was overcut.

Learning from the past and present: The Chinese biologically miniaturized agriculture and grew food organically by closely spacing plants and maintaining soil fertility (using nutrient- and carbon-containing compost) for thousands of years without depleting their resources. By 1890, this process enabled the Chinese to grow all the food for 1 person on about 5,800 to 7,200 square feet, including animal products used at the time.

Ecology Action's Pursuit of Sustainability

When Ecology Action began the Common Ground Mini-Farm in Willits, California, the soil was so infertile that many carbonaceous compost crops did not grow well. In an effort to improve the soil, so it could grow all of the carbonaceous compost material needed to provide sufficient cured compost, high-carbon content compost material (sawdust mixed with nutrient-containing horse manure was imported to the mini-farm). This approach eventually was deemed inappropriate because of the significant importation. Consequently, we limited our compost building to include materials produced by the mini-farm whenever possible. However, because

In order to preserve diversity on Earth: It is important to keep at least half of the Earth's viable land as a natural pre-serve. GROW BIOINTENSIVE Sustainable Mini-Farming—with its high yields and low local resource needs—can help make this possible.

many crops we were testing did not contain much carbon, the mini-farm produced significantly less carbonaceous compost material than was needed to increase and maintain the soil's fertility. Without sufficient cured compost, the soil began losing the humus it had, and its ability to grow sufficient organic matter declined. By 1985, we began to grow more of our own compost material than before and supplemented our supply of carbonaceous compost material with purchased straw and alfalfa for special compost tests, and goat litter (from outside fodder inputs).

Today, we are much closer to achieving closed-system soil humus sustainability *within the limits of the mini-farm*. We rarely import any compost materials from outside the beds (besides weeds from path spaces and kitchen scraps that contain scraps from outside sources). In addition, we are exploring different levels of maintaining sustainable soil fertility. These methods involve using different amounts of cured compost with different corresponding crop yield levels resulting (see chapter 3).

Because we are not currently returning the nutrients in our human urine and manure to the mini-farm's soil, we need to import some organic fertilizers to maintain the nutrient levels and bal-ance in the soil. (Over time, the amounts and number of fertilizers has decreased significantly as the nutrients are retained and cycled in the compost.) For the future, we are exploring ways to safely, effectively, and legally return the nutrients in our waste to the soil from which they came. Our original goal was to produce relevant yield averages with the same amount, or less, of equivalent inputs as conventional agriculture. Today our goal is to eventually produce at least relevant averages with no additional inputs after the soil is built up on a one-time basis.

CURRENT GOALS OF UNDERSTANDING AND ACHIEVING 99% SUSTAINABILITY

Our goals are to understand how a garden or mini-farm can:

- Produce all of its own compost material initially without having to import any straw, manure, or other carbonaceous material for the soil's humus sustainability

- Maintain nutrient sustainability

How to Design for Your Soil's Fertility

In order to more easily sustain the fertility of your soil and decrease the space necessary to produce a large percentage or your entire diet in the smallest area, Ecology Action recommends that you:

- Maintain approximately 60% of your growing area in carbon-and-calorie crops that produce large amounts of carbon for compost and that also produce food in the form of significant amounts of calories. Legumes can also be interplanted to produce immature biomass and fix nitrogen in the soil if they are harvested at 50% flower.[2]

- Grow approximately 30% in special root diet crops that produce large amounts of calories in limited space per unit of time.

- Have a maximum of 10% in vegetable crops for additional vitamins and minerals. (Up to three-quarters of this area may be planted in income crops if the missing needed vitamins and minerals are provided by one-quarter of the area.)

See the information on the following pages for details. We hope that these guidelines will make your path to sustainability easier. Remember that the goal is to grow sufficient compost material in your growing space in order to maintain levels of organic matter as well as cycle nutrients. Annual soil tests provide you with the information to monitor your success and direction.

The GROW BIOINTENSIVE Sustainable Mini-Farm

APPROXIMATE CROP AREA PERCENTAGES FOR SUSTAINABILITY: 60/30/10

APPROXIMATELY 40 BEDS (4,000 SQ FT) FOR 1 PERSON (5,000 SQ FT INCLUDING PATHS)

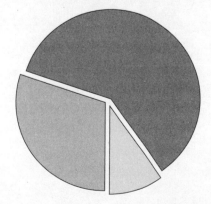

60% carbon-and-calorie crops (e.g., grains) for maximum carbon and satisfactory calorie production
- 24 beds

30% high-calorie root crops (e.g., potatoes) for maximum calories
- 12 beds

10% vegetable crops (e.g., salad crops) for vitamins and minerals
- 4 beds

If desired, 50% to 75% of the vegetable crops area may be used for income crops

In order to mini-farm sustainably, take these goals into account as you grow compost crops and apply compost.

Compost Application Goals (including 50% soil)					
Per 100 sq ft, at least annually before main crop, and, if possible, per 4- to 6-month growing season					
				Dry Weight Mature Material to Grow (lb/100 sq ft)	Wet Weight Immature Material to Grow (lb/100 sq ft)
Beginning	1 cu ft	1.5 five-gallon buckets	$1/8$ inch	15 lb and up	90 lb and up
Intermediate	2 cu ft	3 five-gallon buckets	$1/4$ inch	30 lb and up	180 lb and up
High	4 cu ft	6 five-gallon buckets	$1/2$ inch	60 lb and up	360 lb and up

Notes: Application of 1 cu ft/100 sq ft is not sufficient to prevent minerals from leaching out because the soil will likely lack sufficient organic matter (unless the organic matters were originally high).

Compost production will likely increase as a system operates over time and the gardener becomes more adept and experienced and soil conditions improve.

Ecology Action's research shows that very few systems on the average will be able to produce more than 4 cu ft/100 sq ft sustainably. A sustainable mini-farm will apply the compost created from the system that is available.

High-Calorie Root Crops	
Most Area-Efficient	Most Weight-Efficient
Leeks (6.6 beds)	Garlic (3.6 lb)
Garlic (10.8 beds)	Sweet potatoes (5.0 lb)
Parsnips (10.8 beds)	Salsify (6.5 lb)
Salsify (11.8 beds)	Potatoes (6.7 lb)
Potatoes (12.2 beds)	Jerusalem Artichokes (7.0 lb)
Jerusalem Artichokes (12.3 beds)	Parsnips (7.1 lb)
Sweet Potatoes (12.4 beds)	Leeks (8.7 lb)

To be considered in Vegetable Category	
Area-Efficient but Not Weight-Efficient	Weight-Efficient but Not Area-Efficient
Turnips, including tops (8.8 beds); requires 19.4 lb/day*	Peanuts (0.9 lb); requires 34.1 beds
Onions, regular (12.7 beds); requires 14.0 lb/day*	Cassava (3.3 lb); requires 20.1 beds
Rutabagas (13.4 beds); requires 14.7 lb/day	Soybeans (3.8 lb); requires 58.0 beds
	Burdock (7.3 lb); requires 17.8 beds
	Beans (excluding Fava Beans) (4.7 lb); requires 56.8 beds

*Assumes 2 crops per year OR yields that are 2 times the intermediate level

Note: Other root crops such as carrots, beets, mangels, and radishes are neither weight nor area efficient and should likewise be considered as vegetable crops.

The 60/30/10 design ratio was developed after observing the results of theoretical GROW BIOINTENSIVE mini-farm designs over ten years of workshops. We noted that many of the designs were in this range for planning a 40-bed growing area (using 4,000 square feet as a target area to grow a complete diet). A 40-bed growing area is fairly manageable for one person to do part time, once one's soil and skill are built. We also chose to use 40 beds as a target as many of the world's people only have access to such a limited area. A growing world population will only reduce the available farmable land. The skill of growing all your nutrition sustainably in a reduced area will be invaluable. We offer the ratio as a guiding tool to assist you in creating the initial designs for your growing area.

Over the years, we have seen numerous design ratios that work well within the 40-bed design constraint. Below, we offer a series of considerations.

- If you chose to eat more carbon-and-calorie crops, the weight of the food you eat will generally be less per day, but the area needed to grow your diet will generally increase.

- If you chose to eat more high-calorie root crops, the weight of the food you eat will generally be more, but the area needed to grow your diet will generally decrease.

- If you choose to eat a diet with a large variety of crops, planning your garden/mini-farm will be more complex as there will be more considerations in terms of phasing crops, harvesting, and preservation.[7]

- If you grow a lot of non-interplanted legumes (besides fava beans) as part of your diet, they will reduce the weight of the diet you eat, but will significantly increase the area needed for the growing of your diet, as legumes are not very area-efficient for the production of calories. In addition, your design may produce more protein than is optimal for a person to consume.

- The 40-bed unit is a guideline. In many climates and soils with sufficient water availability, a complete balanced diet may be grown on as few as 25 growing beds and sometimes fewer, assuming intermediate-level yields. In challenging climates with soils lacking water, it may take more to much more than 40 growing beds.

Clarifications and Examples of the 60/30/10 Design Ratio

GENERAL AIDS FOR PLANNING YOUR DIET:

60%: Carbon-and-calorie crops produce high amounts of carbon and significant calories.[3]
- Grains: wheat, cereal rye, oats, barley, triticale, corn, sorghum, amaranth, quinoa, pearl millet, etc.
- Fava beans (grown to maturity for dry bean and biomass production)
- Sunflowers[4]
- Filberts
- Grapes (eaten in form of raisins)

30%: High-calorie root crops produce a large amount of calories in a limited space. They are area and weight efficient.[5] (See middle table on page 40.)

10%: Vegetable crops: Low-calorie-producing, low-carbon-producing vegetables for vitamins and minerals. (See lower table on page 40.)

NB: Vegetable and income crops do not produce a large amount of calories or carbon in a limited space.

Note: Even if, when you become especially skilled at diet design, you choose other ratios of these crops[6]—you will find that the 60/30/10 approach best teaches you the nature and strength of crops.

Sustainability Lessons:
Biosphere2, a closed-system living project in Arizona during the 1990s, used techniques based on those rediscovered/ systematized by Ecology Action. The result: They raised 80% of their food for two years within a closed system. Their experience demonstrates that a complete year's diet for one person can be raised on the equivalent of just 3,403 square feet! In contrast, it currently takes commercial agriculture 15,000 to 30,000 square feet to do the same. Moreover, commercial agriculture has to bring in large inputs from other areas and soils just to make this production possible, depleting other soils in the process. To raise all the food for one person in a developing nation takes about 16,000 square feet, given the diets eaten and the food-raising practices used.

The Environmental Research Laboratory at the University of Arizona performed the first tests for Biosphere2, documenting the status of the soil and crop yields over time. In the Human Diet Experiment, all crop tests involved sustainable Biointensive crop rotations including grains, legumes, and green manures. All crop residues were returned to the soil after harvest and composting. Dr. Ed Glenn, who conducted *continued on page 43*

We are excited whenever people and programs adopt GROW BIOINTENSIVE practices, but there is still a challenge to be met. Many people are successfully using Biointensive farming techniques to grow food for nutrition intervention, but few are trying to grow all their calorie food needs on a basis that also feeds the soil adequately. When people say that they are growing their own food, they tend to refer to 5% to 10% of their diet (the vegetables that they can produce during the growing season). Calorie and sustainable soil fertility mini-farming and gardening are the next step, which needs to be catalyzed by each of us. Ecology Action publications *One Circle, the Sustainable Vegetable Garden* and the Self-Teaching Mini-Series Booklets 14, 15, 25, 26, 28, 34, 35, and 36 deal with growing a complete diet. Once this additional 90% of calorie-growing area has been established in the garden and your soil and skill are improved, it may take an average of about 15 minutes or less each day per bed to maintain.

There has been a great shift in human consciousness since Ecology Action set up its first research garden mini-farm over 40 years ago. This shift occurred because individuals around the world began to realize that although they might not be able to change the world, they could change the way they do things in their own lives. Raising food sustainably in a gentle and conscious manner makes a difference. Once you become skilled, have built up the fertility of your soil, use simple efficient tools such as U-bars and scythes with grain cradles, and, if you choose the most effective crops—you may be able to grow your food in as little as 2 hours a day.

In fact, anthropologists tell us that 10,000 years ago, a culture in northern Iran raised one person's calories with just 20 hours of work a year—20 minutes a day for 60 days. Their staple crop was *Einkorn hornemanni,* Early Stone Age wheat—the second most simple wheat and an early spelt wheat.

Calories are the most challenging nutritional element to grow in the smallest area with the least labor, and this culture found one solution. Any missing vitamins and minerals can be grown to complement the calories in a relatively small area and amount of time in the form of vegetables and soft fruits.

We as humans are part of the Earth's nutrient cycle, just as the plants and animals are. The Earth welcomes us by creating what we need. Trees are a wonderful example. They absorb our carbon dioxide and give us back oxygen to breathe. As we become more aware of and attuned to our place in the circle of life, it will seem natural to plant carbon-producing crops that also produce calories. *In this way our crops give life back to the Earth that has fed us.* As we become more responsible for our place in this exciting nutrient flow, we will want to grow *all* of our diet.

Consider getting together with five friends and becoming involved in GROW BIOINTENSIVE Sustainable Mini-Farming and/or other sustainable food-raising practices. The Mayan culture practiced biologically-intensive food-raising as neighborhoods. In such a way we can make a significant difference in the world, one small area at a time!

continued from page 42
the tests, stated: Although funding was not available to continue these experiments for the number of years necessary to draw final conclusions, the results support the hypothesis that sustainable food production with few or no outside inputs will not only continue to produce high yields but will improve rather than deplete the organic constituents in the soil.

ENDNOTES

1 Of course, the nutrients that we eat then pass through our bodies as "waste." Recycling humanure and urine is often considered a taboo subject, but it is an area greatly in need of study to be able to recycle those nutrients, in particular, phosphorus, in a safe, legal, and effective way. See Human Waste section in the online Bibliography at www.growbiointensive .org for resources on recycling human waste.

2 To grow the nitrogen needed to make a good compost, legumes also need to be planted. One way to achieve additional nitrogen production without increasing space is to interplant. For example, fava beans can be planted among wheat in winter and bush beans with corn in summer.

3 Carbon-and-calorie crops produce at least 15 lbs of mature material per 100 sq ft at intermediate yields as well as are weight-efficient.

4 Sunflower seeds are very high in fat; to avoid copper toxicity no more than 0.62 lbs should be eaten per day.

5 As defined by Ecology Action, a crop is considered to be area efficient if the annual area needed for total calories is 16 beds (1,600 sq ft) or less, assuming GROW BIOINTENSIVE intermediate yields. A crop is considered to be weight efficient if 2,400 calories are contained in 9 pounds or less.

6 High-calorie crops that are ~30% of the area need to be both area- and weight- efficient. As defined for this worksheet, a crop is considered to be area-efficient if the annual area needed for total calories is 16 beds (1,600 sq ft) or less, assuming GROW BIOINTENSIVE intermediate yields; it is considered to be weight-efficient if the daily weight of food to be eaten for total calories is 9 pounds or less. In *One Circle*, by David Duhon, an area-efficient crop can provide total daily calories for a year with 700 sq ft or less (550 sq ft for a woman, 850 sq ft for a man); a weight-efficient crop can provide total daily calories for a year in 6 pounds or less for a man or 5.5 pounds or less for a woman.

7 For diet diversity, you may choose crops that are less weight-efficient (e.g., regular onions, 14.0 pounds per day); in which case, you need to have a significant amount of food from crops that are *more* weight-efficient (e.g., filberts, 0.8 pounds per day) and/or increase your design area.

Root Crops That Are Not Good Choices for This Category:
- Carrots (30.0/12.3)
- Beets or mangels, roots only (40.8/12.3)
- Radishes (48.1/26.4)

Give to Nature, and she will repay you in glorious abundance.
—ALAN CHADWICK

3

THE USE OF COMPOST AND SOIL FERTILITY

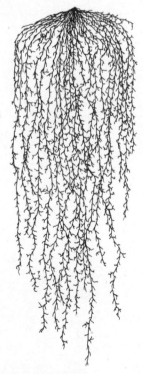

Cereal rye roots grow to 6 feet deep.

A "Natural" System

In nature, living things die, and their death allows life to be reborn. Both animals and plants die on forest floors and in meadows to be composted by time, water, microorganisms, sun, and air to produce a soil improved in structure and nutrients. Organic plant growing follows nature's example. Leaves, grass, weeds, prunings, spiders, birds, trees, and plants should be returned to the soil and reused—not thrown away. Composting is an important way to recycle such elements as carbon, nitrogen, magnesium, sulfur, calcium, phosphorus, potash, and trace minerals. These elements are all necessary to maintain the biological cycles of life that exist naturally. All too often we participate instead in agricultural strip-mining.

Composting in nature occurs in at least 3 ways:

1. It occurs in the form of manures, which are plant and animal foods composted inside an animal's body (including earthworms) and then further aged outside the animal by the heat of fermentation. Earthworms are especially good composters. Their castings

are 5 times richer in nitrogen, 2 times richer in exchangeable calcium, 7 times richer in available phosphorus, and 11 times richer in available potassium than the soil they inhabit.[1]

2. It occurs in the form of animal and plant bodies that decay on top of and within the soil in nature and in compost piles.

3. And it occurs in the form of roots, root hairs, and microbial life-forms that remain and decay beneath the surface of the soil after harvesting. It is estimated that one cereal rye plant in good soil grows 3 miles of hairs a day, 387 miles of roots in a season, and 6,603 miles of root hairs each season![2]

Qualitatively, some people feel that compost made from plants is 4 times better than that made from manure and that compost in the form of plant roots is twice as good as plant compost! It is interesting that the roots (which have a special relationship with the soil microbes and the soil itself) can weigh 45% to 120% of the aboveground weight of the plants.

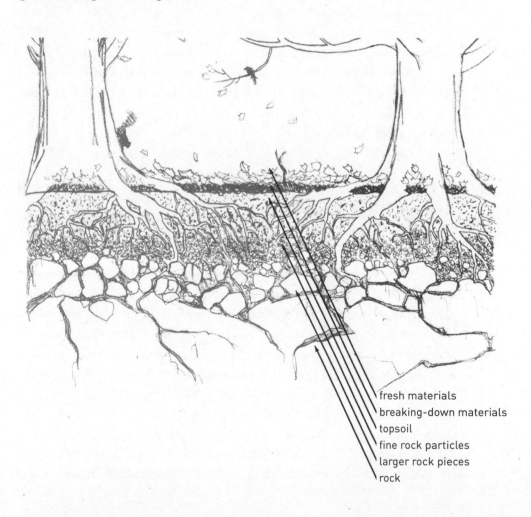

fresh materials
breaking-down materials
topsoil
fine rock particles
larger rock pieces
rock

Compost Functions

Compost has a dual function. It improves the **structure** of the soil. This means the soil will be easier to work, will have good aeration and water-retention characteristics, and will be resistant to erosion. Compost also provides **nutrients** for plant growth, and its organic acids make nutrients in the soil more available to plants. Fewer nutrients leach out in a soil with adequate organic matter.

Improved structure and nourishment produce a healthy soil. A **healthy soil produces healthy plants** better able to resist insect and disease attacks. Most insects look for sick plants to eat. The best way to control insects and diseases in plants is with a living, healthy soil rather than with poisons that kill beneficial soil life.

Compost keeps soil at maximum health with a minimum expense. Generally, it is unnecessary to buy fertilizers to be able to grow healthy plants. At first, organic fertilizers may have to be purchased so the soil can be brought to a satisfactory level of fertility in a short period of time. Once this has been done, the soil's health can be maintained with compost, good crop rotation, and the recycling of plant residues into the compost pile.

It is important to note the difference between *fertilization* and *fertility*. There can be plenty of fertilizer in the soil, and plants still may not grow well. Add compost to the soil, and the organic acids it contains will release the hidden nutrients in a form available to the plants. This was the source of the amazing fertility of Alan Chadwick's garden at Santa Cruz.

The Process

Compost is created from the decomposition and recombination of various forms of plant and animal life, such as leaves, grass, wood, garbage, natural-fiber clothes, hair, and bones. These materials are **organic matter.** Organic matter is only a small fraction of the total material that makes up the soil—generally between 1% and 8% by weight. Yet organic matter is absolutely essential to the sustenance of soil life and fertility. Organic matter refers to dead plant and animal residues of *all* kinds and in *all* stages of breakdown or decay. Inseparable from these decaying dead residues are the living microorganisms that decompose, or digest, them.

Microscopic life-forms (bacteria and fungi) in the soil produce the recombining process, which creates the warmth in the compost pile. Most of the decomposition involves the formation of carbon dioxide and water as the organic material is broken down. You can monitor the temperature of your compost pile with a compost thermometer. You can also do this by inserting a 1 by 1-inch piece of wood into the pile, removing it periodically and feeling the warmth with your hand. You can judge whether the latest measurement is hotter or cooler than before.

As the available energy is consumed, microbial activity slows down, their numbers diminish—and the pile cools. Most of the remaining organic matter is in the form of **humus compounds.** Humus includes the living and dead bodies of microbial life. As humus is formed, nitrogen becomes part of its structure. This stabilizes nitrogen in the soil because the humus compounds are resistant to decomposition. They are worked on slowly by soil organisms, but the nitrogen and other essential nutrients are protected from too-rapid solubility and dissipation. Organic matter includes humus and some undecomposed organic matter.

Humus also acts as a site of nutrient adsorption (accumulation of nutrients on its surface) and exchange for plants in the soil. The surfaces of humus particles carry a negative electric charge. Many of the plant nutrients—such as calcium, sodium, magnesium, potassium, and most trace minerals—carry a positive electrical charge in the soil solution and are thereby attracted to and adhere to the surface of humus. Some of the plant nutrients—such as phosphorus, sulfur, and the form of nitrogen that is available to plants—are not positively charged. Fortunately, a good supply of these nutrients becomes available to the plants through biological transformation in the compost pile and soil.

As plant roots grow through the soil in search of nutrients, they feed on the humus. Each plant root is surrounded by a halo of hydrogen ions that are a by-product of the roots' respiration. These ions also carry a positive electric charge. The root actually "bargains" with the humus, exchanging some of its positively charged hydrogen ions for positively charged nutrient ions stuck onto the surface of the humus. An active exchange is set up between humus and roots, the plants "choosing" which nutrients they need to balance their own inner chemistry.

Therefore, humus is the most reliable plant food, and plants pull off whatever combinations of nutrients they choose from its surface. GROW BIOINTENSIVE practices rely on this natural, continual, slow-releasing biological process for nutrient release to the plants, rather than making available all the season's nutrients chemically at one time.

The beauty of humus is that it feeds plants with nutrients that the plants pick up on its surface and it also safely stores nutrients in forms that are not readily leached. The humus contains much of the remainder of the original nitrogen that was put in the compost pile in the form of grass, kitchen wastes, and so on. The humus was formed by the resynthesizing activity of numerous species of microorganisms feeding off that original "garbage."

The microorganisms in the soil then continue to feed on the humus after the finished compost is spread on the soil. As the microorganisms feed, the core nutrients in the humus are released in forms available to plant roots. Thus, the microorganisms are an integral part of the humus, and one cannot be found without the other. The only other component of the soil that holds onto and exchanges nutrients with plant roots is clay, but humus can hold onto and exchange a far greater amount of these nutrients.

Soil and Other Materials in the Compost Pile

It is important to add soil to your compost pile. The soil contains a good starter supply of microorganisms. It also contains some bacteria of a type that helps stabilize nitrogen in a pile. The organisms help in several ways. Some break down complex compounds into simpler ones the plants can utilize. There are many species of free-living bacteria that fix nitrogen from the air in a form available to plants. Many microorganisms tie up nitrogen surpluses. The surpluses are released gradually as the plants need nitrogen. An excessive concentration of available nitrogen in the soil (which makes plants susceptible to disease) is therefore avoided. There are predaceous fungi that attack and devour nematodes (see page 114), but these fungi are only found in large amounts in a soil with adequate humus.

The microbial life provides a living pulsation in the soil that preserves its vitality for the plants. The microbes tie up essential nutrients in their own body tissues as they grow, and then release them slowly as they die and decompose. In this way, they help stabilize food release to the plants. These organisms are also continuously excreting a whole range of organic compounds into the soil. Sometimes described as "soil glue," these excretions contribute to the building of the soil structure. The organic compounds also contain disease-curing antibiotics and health-producing vitamins

---

Give back to the soil as much as you have taken—and a little bit more—and Nature will provide for you abundantly!

—ALAN CHADWICK

Note: The soil for your compost piles comes from the first trench of your double-dug beds. As your bed soil improves, your compost will also improve. Also, the soil in the compost pile becomes "like compost." It holds compost juices, microbes, and minerals that would otherwise leach out of the pile. It is one way to get "more" compost.

The Use of Compost and Soil Fertility

and enzymes that are integral parts of biochemical reactions in a healthy soil.

The use of soil in compost is important, because it:

- Enables the pile to hold moisture better—facilitating the decomposition of the pile

- Contains microbes that enable the pile to decompose more easily

- Holds many of the nutrient-laden compost "juices"—keeping them from leaching out.

Note that at least three different materials of three different textures are used in the GROW BIOINTENSIVE method compost recipe and in many other recipes. The varied textures will allow good drainage and aeration in the pile. The compost will also have a more diverse nutrient content and greater microbial diversity. A pile made primarily of leaves or grass cuttings makes the passage of water and air through the pile difficult without frequent turning because both tend to mat. Good air and water penetration are required for proper decomposition. The layering of the materials further promotes a mixture of textures and nutrients and helps ensure even decomposition.

Microbe diversity is very important in the growing soil. Many microbes produce antibiotics that help plants resist diseases, and healthy plants have fewer insect challenges. Each microbe tends to have a food preference—some prefer beet refuse, others wheat straw, and so on. Therefore, a way to maximize microbe diversity in the compost pile is to build your compost pile with a large variety of materials.

Locating the Pile

Compost piles can be built in a pit in the ground or in a pile above the ground. The latter is preferable, since during rainy periods a pit can fill up with water. A pile can be made with or without a container. We build our compost piles without using containers. They are unnecessary and use wood and metal resources.

The pile should optimally be built under a deciduous oak tree. This tree's nature provides the conditions for the development of excellent soil underneath it. And compost is a kind of soil. The

Tip: Always be sure to add at least 3 different kinds of crops to your compost piles. Different microbes flourish in specific kinds of crops. The result of this crop diversity is microbe diversity in the soil, which ensures better soil and plant health.

Tip: You will probably want to build some compost *without* soil for your perennial growing areas. This is because you cannot easily take soil from these areas to build compost piles. Also, the perennial roots will necessitate **surface cultivation** to an approximately 2-inch depth in most cases.

Compost

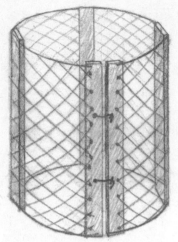

The least expensive type of compost container is homemade.

second-best place for a compost pile is under any other kind of deciduous tree (with the exceptions of walnut and eucalyptus). As a last resort, you can build your pile under evergreen trees or any shady place in your backyard. The shade and windbreak provided by the trees help keep the pile at an even moisture level. (The pile should be placed 6 feet away from the tree's trunk so it will not provide a haven for potentially harmful insects.)

For those who wish to use them, containers can help shape a pile and keep the materials looking neat. The least-expensive container is made of 12-foot-long, 3-foot-wide pieces of 1-inch mesh chicken wire with five 3-foot-long, 1 by 2-inch boards and 2 sets of small hooks and eyes. The boards are nailed along the two 3-foot ends of the wire and at 3-foot intervals along the length of the wire. The hooks and eyes are attached to the 2 end boards as shown. The

Some Other Kinds of Compost Piles

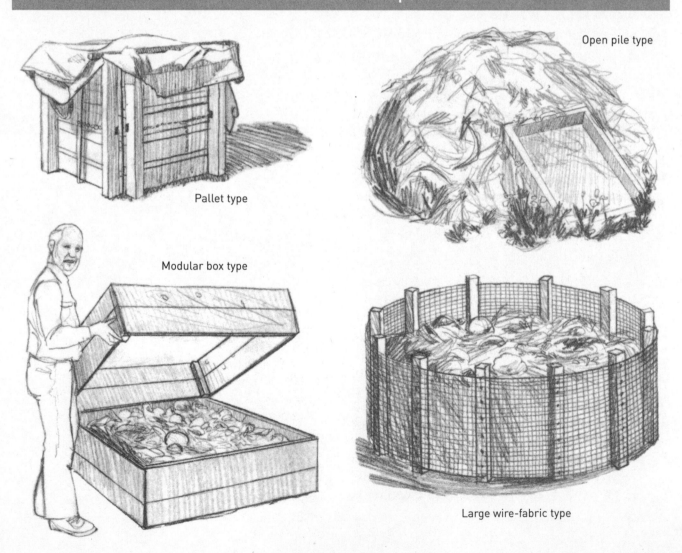

Open pile type

Pallet type

Modular box type

Large wire-fabric type

The Use of Compost and Soil Fertility

unit is then placed as a circle on the ground, the hooks attached to the eyes, and the compost materials placed inside. The materials hold up the circle. After the pile is built, the wire enclosure may be removed and the materials will stay in place. You may now use the enclosure to build another pile, or you may use it later to turn the first pile into if you want to speed up the decomposition process. We rarely try to accelerate this natural process.

Note: There are more than 6 billion microbial life-forms in only 1 level teaspoon of cured compost—almost the number of people on Earth!

Size and Timing

A minimum compost pile size of 3 feet by 3 feet by 3 feet (1 cubic yard of lightly moist, built compost, weighing about 1,000 pounds) is recommended. (In colder climates, a minimum compost pile size of 4 feet by 4 feet by 4 feet will be needed to properly insulate the heat of the composting process.) Smaller piles fail to provide the insulation necessary for appropriate heating (up to 140°F) and allow too much air to penetrate. It is all right to build up piles slowly to this size as materials become available, though it is best to build an entire pile at one time. A large compost pile might be

Cross Section of a GROW BIOINTENSIVE Compost Pile

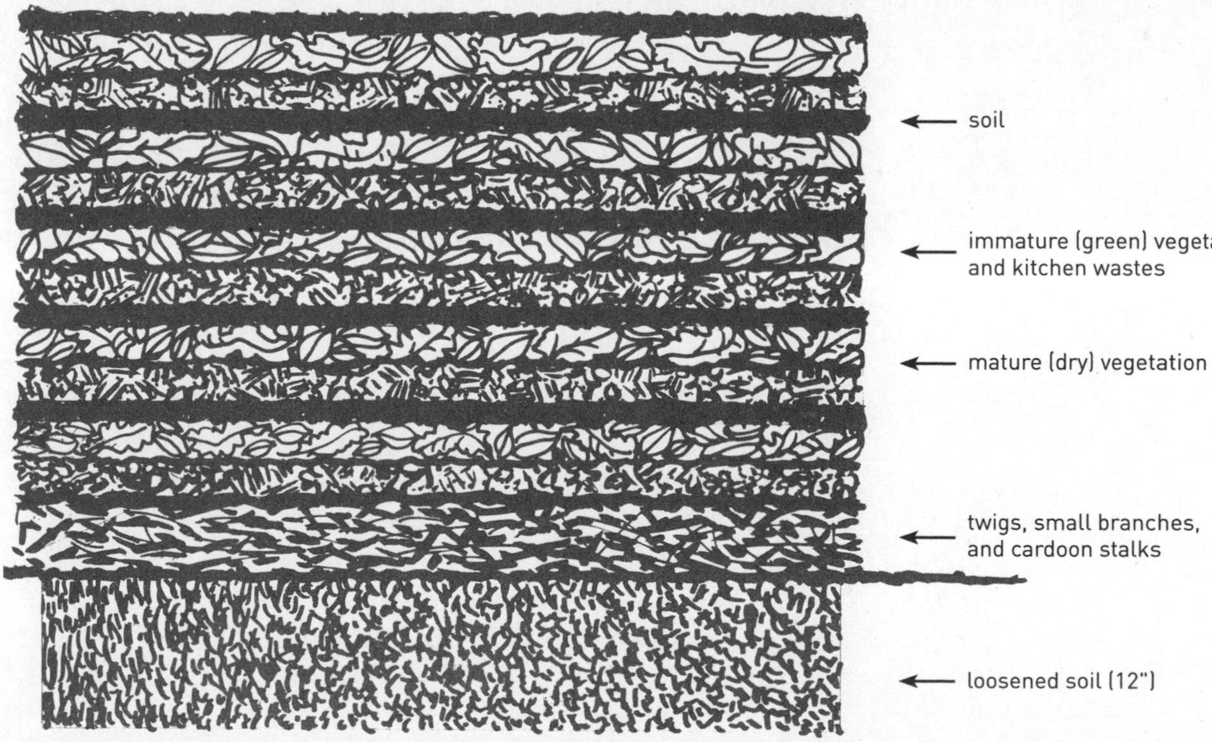

← soil

← immature (green) vegetation and kitchen wastes

← mature (dry) vegetation

← twigs, small branches, and cardoon stalks

← loosened soil (12")

4 feet high, 5 feet wide, and 10 feet long. A pile will cure to one-third to one-quarter of its original size, depending on the materials used.

The best time to prepare compost is in the spring or autumn, when biological activity is highest. (Too much heat or cold slows down and even kills the microbial life in the pile.) The two high-activity periods conveniently coincide with the maximum availability of materials in the spring, as grass and other plants begin to grow rapidly, and in the autumn, as leaves fall and other plant life begins to die. Compost built at other times will simply cure more slowly.

KEY ORGANIC MATTER FUNCTIONS

1. Organic matter feeds plants through nutrient exchange and through nutrient release upon its decomposition.

2. It is a continual slow-release source of nutrients for plants.

3. Organic acids in humus help dissolve minerals in the soil, making the mineral nutrients available to plants. Organic acids also increase the permeability of plant root membranes and therefore promote the plant roots' uptake of water and nutrients.

4. Organic matter is the energy source for the soil's microbial life-forms, which are an integral part of soil health. In 1 gram of humus-rich soil there are several *billion* bacteria, 1 million fungi, 10 to 20 million actinomycetes, and 800,000 algae.

5. The microbes that feed on organic matter in the soil temporarily bind the soil particles together. The fungi, with their *threadlike* mycelia, are especially important. They literally sew the soil together. The microbes secrete compounds into the soil as they live, metabolize, and ultimately decompose. Their secretions are a bacterial glue (polysaccharides) that holds soil particles, thus improving the soil's structure. Structure is vital to soil productivity because it ensures good aeration, good drainage, good water retention, and erosion resistance.

6. Organic matter is the key to soil structure, keeping it safe from severe erosion and keeping it in an open, porous condition for good water and air penetration.

Building the Pile

The ground underneath the pile should be loosened to a depth of 12 inches to provide good drainage. Next, lay down roughage (brush, tree prunings, cardoon stalks, or other woody materials) 3 inches thick, if available, for air circulation.

One recipe for GROW BIOINTENSIVE compost is, **by volume,** *45% mature (dry) material, 45% immature (green) vegetation* (including kitchen wastes), and *10% soil*. Each layer should be watered well as it is created. This 45/45/10 recipe will give you a carbon-to-nitrogen ratio in your built compost pile of about 30 to 1, and will produce compost with a significant amount of high-quality, short-term humified carbon. The result will be a hotter (*thermophilic* 113° to 149°F) pile with faster-releasing cured compost that generally releases nutrients over a 3-month to 2-year period. A lot of the carbon in this type of compost pile is lost, however, and the resulting cured compost only contains about one-third to one-half the cured organic matter that a cooler (*mesophilic* 50° to 113°F) 60-to-1 compost pile will produce.

A 60-to-1 pile is built with approximately 8 parts mature material to 2 parts green vegetation (including kitchen wastes) and 1 part soil. The result of this pile will be a slower-releasing cured compost that generally releases nutrients over a 3-month period (and up to 5,000 years!) especially if the mature materials contain a large amount of lignin, such as corn and sorghum stalks. This can be a way to build up your soil fertility on a long-term basis, but the more readily available nutrients in the cured compost from a 30-to-1 pile will be important for the good growth of most vegetables. We make separate compost piles of small tree branches, since they can take 2 years or more to decompose.

The materials should optimally be added to the pile in 1- to 2-inch layers with the mature vegetation on the bottom, the immature vegetation and kitchen wastes second, and the soil third (in a 1/4- to 1/2-inch layer). You can, however, build a pile spontaneously, adding materials daily or so, as they become available. This kind of pile will usually take a little longer to cure, but can be built more easily. Mature vegetation is high in carbon content. It is difficult for the microbes in the compost pile to digest carbon without sufficient amounts of nitrogen.

Unless you have a large household, it may be necessary to save your kitchen scraps in a tight-lidded unbreakable container for several days to get enough material for the kitchen waste layer. You may want to hold your breath when you dump them because the

Soil is added to a compost pile after a layer of immature vegetation and kitchen waste.

stronger-smelling *anaerobic* form of the decomposition process has been taking place in the closed container. The smell will disappear within a few hours after reintroducing air. All kitchen scraps may be added except meats and sizable amounts of oily salad scraps. Be sure to include bones, tea leaves, coffee grounds, eggshells, and citrus rinds. Always be sure to cover kitchen waste with soil to avoid flies and odors!

Add the soil layer immediately after the immature material and kitchen waste. It contains microorganisms that speed decomposition, keeps the smell down to a minor level, and prevents flies from laying eggs in the garbage. The smell will be difficult to eliminate entirely when waste from members of the cabbage family is added. In a few days, however, even this soil-minimized odor will disappear.

Watering the Pile

As each layer is added, water it thoroughly so the pile is *evenly* moist—like a wrung-out damp sponge that does not give out excess water when squeezed. Sufficient water is necessary for the materials to heat and decompose properly. Too little water results in decreased biological activity, and too much simply drowns the aerobic microbial life. Water the pile, when necessary, as you water your garden. The particles in the pile should glisten. During the rainy season, some shelter or covering may be needed to prevent waterlogging and the less optimal anaerobic decomposition that occurs in a waterlogged pile. (The conditions needed for proper functioning of a compost pile and those required for good plant growth in raised beds are similar. In both cases, the proper mixture of air, soil nutrients, structure, microorganisms, and water is essential.)

Compost Curing and Application Rates

Usually, a compost pile needs one turning to adjust the moisture level and make the mixture more homogeneous for complete breakdown. This should be done at about the 3-week point, after the temperature of the compost pile has peaked and fallen. A decrease in moisture usually occurs at the same time, the color begins to change to brownish from the original green and yellow, and the compost's odor begins to change from musty to an earthy, freshly plowed soil aroma. The compost will normally be ready about 2 months later.

Compost does not necessarily need to be turned. If you do not, the pile takes longer to cure, but you will probably produce more cured compost per unit of built material. This is because less oxidation may occur compared to when you turn the pile. If you turn the compost frequently, you will have cured compost faster, but may produce less cured compost per unit of built material.

Compost is ready to use when it is dark and rich looking and it crumbles in your hands. The texture should be even, and you should not be able to discern the original source of materials. Mature compost even smells good—like water in a forest spring! A GROW BIOINTENSIVE pile should be ready in about 3 months for a pile built and cured during the hot main growing season to about 6 months for a pile built and cured in the cooler season.[3]

Parts of a regular compost pile that have not broken down completely by the end of the composting period should be placed at the bottom of a new pile. This is especially true for twigs and small branches that can use the extra protection of the pile's height to speed up their decomposition in a situation of increased warmth and moisture.

In the garden a *maximum* maintenance dressing of 1/2 inch of compost should be added to the soil annually before the main crop, and, if possible, before each additional 4- to 6-month crop. Guidelines for general maintenance dressings are a 1/8- to 1/2-inch layer of compost (1 to 4 cubic feet) per 100 square feet, if available.

Composting Methods Compared

The GROW BIOINTENSIVE method of making compost differs in particular from the **biodynamic method** in that the GROW BIOINTENSIVE method is simpler, normally uses no manure, and usually uses no herbal solutions to stimulate microorganism growth.[4] Manure, used continually and in large amounts in biodynamic compost piles, is an imbalanced fertilizer, although it is a good texturizing agent because of its usual decomposed sawdust content. Rather than using herbal solutions, GROW BIOINTENSIVE practices sometimes use weeds, such as stinging nettle, and other plants, such as fava beans, as part of the ingredients in compost piles. Special compost recipes may be created in GROW BIOINTENSIVE to meet particular pH, structure, and nutrient requirements.

Notes:
- When you turn a compost pile, make the base of the new pile smaller than the original base to give the turned pile more internal volume and less surface area.
- If you are not ready to use your compost when it is fully cured, stop watering it and spread it out to dry. (See Ecology Action's booklet 32, *GROW BIOINTENSIVE® Composting and Growing Compost Materials*.)
- Compost sifted through 1/2-inch wire fabric is less likely to attract root hair-eating symphylans. For an easy-to-use sifter, see pages 204-206.

Compost

no rock powder fertilizers or nitrogen supplements.[5] Fertilizers do not need to be added to the pile since successful compost can be made from a mixture of ingredients. The nitrogen supplements do, however, speed up the decomposition process. Both the biodynamic and Rodale methods are good ones, proven by use over a long period of time. Chadwick's Biointensive recipe seems simpler to use and equally effective.

Some people use the **sheet composting,** a process of spreading uncomposted organic materials over the soil and then digging them into the soil, where they decompose. The disadvantage of this method is that the soil should not be planted for 3 months or so, until decomposition has occurred. Soil bacteria tie up the nitrogen during the decomposition process, thereby making it unavailable to the plants. Sheet composting may be beneficial if it is used during the winter in cold areas because the tie-up prevents the nitrogen from leaching out during winter rains.

Other people use **green manures**—cover crops such as vetch, clover, alfalfa, beans, peas, or other legumes, grown until the plants are at 10% to 50% flower. The nitrogen-rich plants are then dug into the soil. By using these legumes in this manner, a maximum of nitrogen is fixed in their root nodules. (The nitrogen is taken from the nodules in the seed-formation process. You can tell whether the nodules have fixed nitrogen by cutting one in half with a fingernail. If the inside is pink, they have fixed nitrogen.) This is a way to bring unworked soil into a better condition. These plants provide nitrogen without your having to purchase fertilizer, and they also help you dig. Their roots loosen the soil and eventually turn into humus beneath the earth. Fava beans are exceptionally good for green manuring if you plan to plant tomatoes; their decomposed bodies help eradicate tomato wilt organisms from the soil.

However, we find that green-manure crops are much more effective when used as compost materials, and their roots still have their good effect in the soil. There are several reasons for this. Due to their high nitrogen content, green manures decompose rapidly and even deplete some of the soil's humus. Another disadvantage of the green manuring process is that the land is not producing food crops during the period of cover crop growth and the 1-month period of decomposition. Additionally, green manures generally produce only about one-quarter the carbon in a given area that carbonaceous compost crops do, and carbon in the form of **humus** is the most limiting and essential element in maintaining sustainable soil fertility (by serving as the energy source for microbial life and holding minerals in the soil so they cannot easily leach out of it).

The advantage of the small-scale GROW BIOINTENSIVE method is that backyard composting is easily feasible. When you use compost crops without digging in the crop residues, the growing process will put nitrogen into the soil and make it possible to grow plants, such as corn and tomatoes which are heavy nitrogen feeders. And the plant residues are valuable in the compost pile.

Materials to Use Minimally or Not at All

If you need to use manures and/or less desirable materials in your compost pile, they should make up only one-sixth of your pile by volume so their less optimum effects will be minimized. Some materials should not be used in the preparation of compost, including:

- Plants infected with a disease or a severe insect attack where eggs could be preserved or where the insects themselves could survive in spite of the compost pile's heat.

- Poisonous plants, such as oleander, hemlock, and castor beans, which harm soil life.

- Plants that take too long to break down, such as magnolia leaves.

- Plants that have acids toxic to other plants and microbial life, such as eucalyptus, California bay laurel, walnut, juniper, and cypress.

- Plants that may be too acidic or contain substances that interfere with the decomposition process, such as pine needles, which are extremely acidic and contain a form of kerosene. (However, special compost piles are often made of acidic materials, such as pine needles and leaves. This compost will lower the soil's pH and stimulate acid-loving plants, like strawberries.)

- Ivy and succulents, which may not be killed in the heat of the decomposition process and can regrow when the compost is placed in a planting bed.

- Pernicious weeds, such as wild morning glory and Bermuda grass, which will probably not be killed in the decomposition process and will choke out other plants when they resprout after the compost is placed in a planting.

Note: In order to maintain good soil fertility, approximately 4% to 6% (by weight) organic matter is needed in temperate soils. About 3% is desirable in tropical soils. It is noteworthy that the soil organic matter level used to be measured 11 inches deep many years ago. Later, the measurement level was reduced to $6^2/3$ inches. Today, it has been further reduced to less than 6 inches deep.

- Cat and dog manures, which can contain pathogens harmful to infants. These pathogens are not always killed in the heat of the compost pile.

Plants infected with disease or insects and pernicious weeds should be burned to be destroyed properly. Their ashes then become good fertilizer. The ashes will also help control harmful soil insects, such as carrot worms, which shy away from the alkalinity of ashes. (Use ashes in moderate amounts.)

Benefits of Compost in the Soil

Improved structure—Compost breaks up clay and clods and binds together sandy soil. It helps make proper aeration in clayey and sandy soil possible.

Moisture retention—Compost holds 6 times its own weight in water. A soil with good organic matter content soaks up rain like a sponge and regulates the supply to plants. A soil stripped of organic matter resists water penetration, thus leading to crusting, erosion, and flooding.

Aeration—Plants can obtain 96% of the nutrients they need from the air, sun, and water. A loose, healthy soil assists in diffusing air and moisture into the soil and in exchanging nutrients. Carbon dioxide released by organic matter decomposition diffuses out of the soil and is absorbed by the canopy of leaves above in a raised bed mini-climate created by closely spaced plants.

Fertilization—Compost contains some nitrogen, phosphorus, potassium, magnesium, and sulfur, but is especially important for trace elements. The important principle is to return to the soil, by the use of plant residues and manures, all that has been taken out of it.

Nitrogen storage—The compost pile is a storehouse for nitrogen. Because it is tied up in the compost-breakdown process, water-soluble nitrogen does not leach out or oxidize into the air for a period of 3 to 6 months or more—depending on how the pile is built and maintained.

pH buffer—A good percentage of compost in the soil allows plants to grow better in less-than-optimal pH situations.

pH buffer—A good percentage of compost in the soil allows plants to grow better in less-than-optimal pH situations.

Soil toxin neutralizer—Important recent studies show that plants grown in organically composted soils take up less lead, heavy metals, and other urban pollutants.

Nutrient release—Organic acids dissolve soil minerals and make them available to plants. As organic matter decomposes, it releases nutrients for plant uptake and for the soil microbial population.

Food for microbial life—Good compost creates healthy conditions for organisms that live in the soil. Compost harbors earthworms and beneficial fungi that fight nematodes and other soil pests.

Ultimate in recycling—The Earth provides us with food, clothing, and shelter, and we close the cycle in offering fertility, health, and life through the shepherding of materials.

Building a Compost Pile Step-by-Step

1. Under the pile area (9 or 16 square feet), **loosen the soil,** to 12 inches deep with a spading fork.

2. **Lay down roughage,** such as brush or other woody material, 3 inches thick, if it is available, for air circulation.

3. Put down a 2-inch layer of **mature material,** such as dry weeds, leaves, straw, hay, and old garden wastes. Water it thoroughly.

4. Put down a 2-inch layer of **immature material,** such as fresh weeds, grass clippings, hedge trimmings, green cover crops, and kitchen wastes you have saved. Water well.

5. **Cover lightly with** a 1/4- to 1/2-inch layer of **soil** to prevent flies and odors.

6. **Moisten the soil.**

7. **Add new layers** of mature vegetation, immature vegetation,

Note: We sometimes build a compost pile on an unused growing bed so the next crop grown in that bed will pick up and utilize any nutrients leached out from the pile into the soil. The next season we build compost on another unused growing bed.

8. **Cover the top** of the pile with a 1/2- to 1-inch layer of **soil.**

9. **Water** the completed pile **regularly** until it is ready for use.

10. **Let the completed pile cure** 3 to 6 months while you are building a new pile. Turn the pile once for faster decomposition. For planning purposes, remember that a 4-foot-high compost pile will be 1 to 1 1/3 feet high when it is ready to use.

All Compost Is *Not* Equal

FIVE IMPORTANT FACTORS TO MORE COMPOST EFFICIENCY

We have discovered five factors that may enable GROW BIO-INTENSIVE compost to have much more power *quantitatively* and *qualitatively*:

1. More total compost due to **higher yields.** The result can be up to 2 to 6 times the cured compost.

2. More possible compost when using a **cold composting** process. You can try this by using:

   - slightly more carbonaceous material and/or less nitrogenous material,

   - more coarse materials and less fine ones,

   - slightly more soil when building the pile,

   - slightly more water when building the pile, and

   - a "no turn" approach.

   The first time we did this, we got 38% more cured compost. One publication implies that up to 100% more may be possible.

3. Building a pile with a **carbon/nitrogen ratio of 44/1,** instead of 30/1 or 60/1. Over time the 44/1 cured compost consistently produces higher yields of grain and biomass. (In one test com-

Note: Do you know that some of the compost—you build and put into the soil for nutrients for the plants to eat, to act as a sponge to hold water, and to prevent disease, because it contains antibiotics—can last in the soil up to 5,000 years? What a wonderful commitment to sustainable soil fertility!

paring these three types of compost, the 44/1 derived cured compost produced double the grain and dry biomass.)

4. Building a pile which uses **more structural forms of carbon,** such as cellulose and lignin (mature straw and stalks) and **less metabolic forms of carbon,** such as sugars and starches (immature leaves and stalks). The result may be more durable, lasting cured compost.

5. **Maintaining the curing compost piles,** carefully. A cured compost pile that has been properly maintained can contain 20% or more organic matter rather than the more typical 8% to 10%. All cured compost is not equal. One cubic foot of cured compost may have double or more the compost power!

   In a world with increasingly depleted and desertified soils, sufficient amounts of compost will be key.

Many people advocate **hot compost piles,** because they are said to kill weed seeds, disease organisms, and insect larvae. Hot compost piles cure around 139°F. At this temperature, probably only 25% of these are destroyed. It takes a temperature of about 178°F to kill 100% of them—and this temperature "burns off" a lot of the organic matter that could become cured compost, *so we are considering adopting a cooler pile approach.* Such piles make greater use of coarse materials, more structural carbon or the mature material input (rather than metabolic carbon), and a little more soil and water. All this means some less nitrogen in the pile and a lower temperature.

In fact, in multi-year tests, we have found that using cured compost built with closer to a 45/1 carbon to nitrogen ratio than using compost built closer to a 30/1 or 60/1 ratio, have yielded noticeably higher amounts of dry matter and calories. We are looking forward to better understanding why the difference has occurred.

Note: We are finding that **cold compost piles,** which are built with more carbon and can take up 4 months or more to fully cure, may produce much more cured carbon (humus) and compost per unit of "built" carbon—possibly even double. This type of composting process is predominantly one of moldering rather than significant heat. If the test results prove consistent over time, the process could be essential to maintaining global sustainable soil fertility, since sufficient humus is the essential to making the fertility possible. You may wish to experiment with this!

ENDNOTES

1 Care must be taken to avoid overdependence on worm castings as a fertilizer; the nutrients in them are very available and can therefore be more easily lost from the soil system.

2 Helen Philbrick and Richard B. Gregg, *Companion Plants and How to Use Them* (Old Greenwich, CT: Devin-Adair Company, 1966), pp. 75–76.

3 If for some reason you need compost cured quickly, there are three ways to speed up the decomposition rate in a compost pile—though they will probably

leave you with much less cured compost per unit of material added to your pile originally, rather than the greatest quantity of life-enhancing compost you must seek.

One way is to increase the amount of nitrogen. The ratio of carbon to nitrogen is critical for the breakdown rate. Materials with a high carbon-to-nitrogen ratio—such as dry leaves, grain straw, corn stalks, and small tree branches—take a long time to decompose alone since they lack sufficient nitrogen, which the bacteria depend upon for food. To boost the rate of decay in carbonaceous materials, add nitrogen-rich materials such as newly cut grass, fresh manure, vegetable wastes, green vegetation, or a fertilizer such as alfalfa meal. About 12 to 20 pounds of alfalfa meal per cubic yard of compost will fortify a compost pile with a high carbon content. Lightly sprinkle these fertilizers on each layer as you build your compost pile.

A second method is to increase the amount of air (aeration). Beneficial aerobic bacteria thrive in a well-aerated pile. Proper layering and periodic turning of the pile will accomplish this.

Third, you may increase the surface area of the materials. The smaller the size of the materials the greater the amount of their exposed surface area. Broken-up twigs will decompose more rapidly than twigs that are left whole. We discourage the use of power shredders because nature will do the job in a relatively short time, and everyone has sufficient access to materials that will compost rapidly without resorting to a shredder. The noise from these machines is quite disturbing and spoils the peace and quiet of a garden. They also consume increasingly scarce fuel.

4 For the biodynamic method of compost preparation, see Alice Heckel (ed.), *The Pfeiffer Garden Book* (Stroudsburg, PA: Biodynamic Farming and Gardening Association, 1967), pp. 37–51.

5 For the Rodale method of compost preparation, see Robert Rodale (ed.), *The Basic Book of Organic Gardening* (New York: Ballantine, 1971), pp. 59–86.

4

GOAL: Build and maintain proper levels of and balances among soil nutrients while maintaining an adequate level of humic and carbonic acids for good nutrient cycling

FERTILIZATION

The goal of a GROW BIOINTENSIVE Sustainable Mini-Farm is *to produce essentially all of the soil's fertility sustainably and to eventually need no outside inputs.* A GROW BIOIN-TENSIVE system endeavours to build nutrients up to their proper levels and in balance for your particular soil type, rainfall, climate, sun exposure, altitude, and cation-exchange capacity (a measurement of the availability of nutrients in a given soil), while keeping these nutrients in your food-raising area by composting properly and recycling all wastes. This is possible once the soil nutrients are balanced through competent soil analysis followed by the application of the appropriate quantities of organic fertilizers. Sustainability can be achieved by accomplishing two goals:

- growing "compost crops" to generate sufficient cured compost, and

- returning all of the soil nutrients contained in the crop to the soil through sufficient compost and the proper, safe, and legal recycling of human waste.

Lessons Learned: During a drought in India years ago, several women grew food using Biointensive methods. Their production was double that of others who used single-dug row cropping practices. One woman got even higher yields than other Biointensive gardeners by using her available water, fertilizer, and seed on one growing area. Hoping for higher yields, the other had spread the same amount of resources over 7 to 15 times the area. The woman with the best results got more total production in one-seventh to one-fifteenth of the area. She had benefited by Alan Chadwick's observation, "Begin with one bed and tend it well! Then expand your growing area."

If these two goals are accomplished, both humus and nutrient levels of the soil can be replenished in a way that is sustainable. That is, the fertility of the soil can be maintained virtually indefinitely, since these practices do not rely on non-renewable resources directly (as in the case of chemical fertilizers which are produced from petroleum) or indirectly. Examples of practices that use nonrenewable resources are:

- the use of organic fertilizers which come from other soils, and

- the bringing in of organic matter from other soils— therefore, depleting nutrients from those soils. Many fertilizers used in organic agriculture are also finite.

These goals are lofty, but necessary if we are to think of long-term soil fertility. Some efforts, such as human waste recycling, may not be possible for you. The key is to be constantly asking oneself, "How sustainable is the way I produce food? What can I do to make it more sustainable?"

Unlike other fertilization strategies, GROW BIOINTENSIVE uses an overall approach instead of a case-by-case fertilization plan based on individual crops. Crops rotate throughout the garden over time and compost is created from the garden's production which is also distributed over the garden. These are reasons to create an overarching fertility plan instead of a specific crop plan.

Soil Testing

Ecology Action recommends that you test your soil for major nutrients and trace minerals, as well as pH (the acidity or alkalinity level of your soil), before choosing fertilizers. A **professional soil test** performed by a laboratory will provide you with the most complete evaluation. They are an excellent tool for analyzing deficiencies, excesses, and the relative balance of all nutrients in your garden's soil. Soil tests are an investment: they can save you a lot of money, since they all guard against over-application of fertilizers; allow you to account for nutrients already available in your soil for good plant growth; and increase yields. For professional soil testing, Ecology Action recommends the Timberleaf soil testing service.[1] This company specializes in testing for organic farmers and gardeners, and is familiar with Biointensive fertilitization practices. The service analyzes all soil and plant minerals and the soil's physical characteristics—24 different aspects, lets you know the level of each, describes how much amendment you need to add to correct deficiencies and imbalances, and tells you in normal English what it all means. Few testing services do this. They can also provide follow-up review and advice on your year's experience in the garden. Before having a professional soil test performed, inquire if the test includes organic fertilization recommendations.

If you are unable to arrange a professional soil test, purchase a home test kit. Ecology Action recommends the LaMotte kit.[2] With the home kit you will be limited to testing nitrogen, phosphorus, and potassium content, and pH. If you have difficulty growing healthy plants in your garden, a home test kit may not provide the solution. Plants grown in soil lacking any of the major or trace minerals show their deficiency in yellowed leaves, stunted plant growth, purple leaf veins, as well as a number of other ways.

WHAT A HOME SOIL TEST WILL *NOT* TELL YOU

A professional soil test is an excellent tool for analyzing deficiencies, excesses, and the relative balance of all plant nutrients in your garden's soil. A home test kit, however, is very limited and only points out pH level and deficiencies of nitrogen, phosphorus, and potassium.

Due to soil, weather, and other characteristics mentioned above, no standard added nutrient formula will work in all situations. The chart on page 74 should be considered a general guideline.

Taking a Soil Sample

To take a soil sample from your growing site, use a nonferrous trowel or a stainless steel spoon to dig a vertical soil slice from 8 inches below the surface. Take samples from 6 to 8 representative areas and mix them together well in a clean plastic bucket. Make sure you do not include residues, such as roots and surface organic litter, in the composite sample. Also, do not sample for 30 days after adding any fertilizers, manure, or compost to the area. The samples normally should be taken at the end of a growing season or immediately preceding one. You will need a total soil volume of one pound for professional testing or four heaping tablespoons for the home test kit.

To use the Timberleaf service, ship your composite sample as instructed in its soil test packet without drying the soil. Samples for a home kit should be dried in a small paper bag in indirect sunlight—

Fertility in Context: Ninety-six percent of the total amount of nutrients needed for plant growth processes are obtained as plants use the sun's energy to work on elements already in the air and water. Compost, soil, manure, wood ash, nitrogen from legumes, and nutrients from the growth of certain kinds of herbs and weeds in the beds (see Companion Planting chapter) supply only 4% of a plant's diet. Imagine: Plants do 96% of the work, and you are looking to enhance just 4%!

Soil Test		
Date Performed: _____		Performed by: _____

Test	Results	Recommendations per 100 square feet
Nitrogen		
Phosphorous		
Potassium		
pH (6.5 or slightly less acid is optimum)		
Remarks (including texture)		

not in the sun or an oven. When you are ready to begin testing, follow the instructions included with the kit.

Once you have completed the test, review the "Analysis of Recommended Organic Soil Amendments," which begins below and gives the key nutrient content of many commonly used organic fertilizers. In your calculations, it is not necessary to subtract the nutrients you add to the soil in the form of compost or composted manure.

The growth patterns of certain plants and presence of certain plants in an area can tell us valuable information about the nutrient availability. People used to learn about their soil's nutrient needs through observation of their fields and its vegetation. This skill is essentially lost. We recommend using John Beeby's *Test Your Soil with Plants* if this is an area of interest for you. Eventually, each of us could create living soil tests of plants grown to "read" and determine existing nutrient levels in the soil of a given area.

ANALYSIS OF RECOMMENDED ORGANIC SOIL AMENDMENTS[3]

Nitrogen, phosphorus, and potassium are the major nutrients that plants need. They are commonly known by their chemical symbols: N, P, K, respectively. According to law, any product sold as a fertilizer must provide an analysis upon request for these three minerals. Be aware that composition may vary for the same products from different sources. Be sure to check the analysis provided with the product.

Nitrogen is a key element in proteins, serves as a food source for microorganisms in the compost pile, and fosters green growth. **Phosphorus** gives plants energy and is necessary for the growth of flowers and seeds. **Potassium** aids in protein synthesis and the translocation of carbohydrates to build strong stems and roots which are the controlling part of the plant. Plants also need a good supply of **organic matter** to give them additional nitrogen, phosphorus, sulphur, copper, zinc, boron, and molybdenum, along with eight other nutrients. Only under *ideal conditions* do native soil minerals provide these nutrients naturally. Plants need a full meal of nutrients, and as good stewards of the soil we are responsible for providing them.

pH

A pH reading tells you the relative acidity or alkalinity of the soil water, generally called the **soil solution.** Nutrient availability for vegetable plants, soil microbial activity, and soil structure are all affected by pH. Most vegetables grow best in a slightly acidic soil with a pH of 6.8. A range of 6.0 to 7.0 is fine for most crops.

More important than the actual pH reading is the quality of the pH. This is determined by testing for the amount of plant-available potassium, magnesium, calcium, and sodium in your soil. Only a professional soil test can determine the soil's mineral balance. If possible, you should have this information before you apply pH modifiers to your soil. For instance, limestone is a common pH modifier. However, all limestone does not have the same mineral composition. An application of dolomitic instead of calcitic lime to a soil with high magnesium content could disrupt your soil balance and adversely affect plant growth.

Soil-applied organic matter and manure can alter the pH over time. Also, when adequate organic matter is used, we find crops will tolerate a wider pH range. Leaf mold, pine needles, and sawdust produce acidic compost that can lower the pH. Manures may be alkaline and raise the pH, although they may lower the pH one point in some instances. (For example, approximately 2 cubic feet (3 five-gallon buckets) of manure (50 pounds dry weight) applied per 100 square feet can lower the pH one point.) Compost can be either acidic or alkaline. Using the proper limestone with the correct mineral balance is the least expensive and most practical way to increase pH. Mined sulphur, a soil nutrient deficient in many soils, is an excellent amendment to lower the pH. Although you can use organic matter to alter pH, you will need to know your soil mineral structure, the existing soil pH, and the pH of the applied material in order to apply it accurately and in an effective amount.

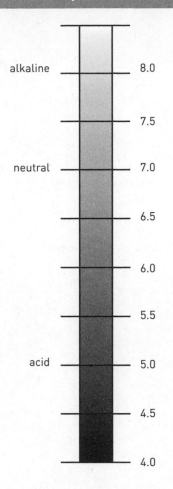

Soil pH Scale

alkaline — 8.0

— 7.5

neutral — 7.0

— 6.5

— 6.0

— 5.5

acid — 5.0

— 4.5

— 4.0

Note: We used to list many more organic fertilizers as nutrient sources. Over time, however, we noticed that many had semi-toxic, or toxic elements. For example, Oyster Shell Flour, an excellent source of calcium, often contains 2% lead.

Fertilization

Recommended Sources of Nutrients

NITROGEN

Alfalfa Meal

2% to 3% N, .7% P, 2.25% K. Lasts 3 to 4 months. Use $4^{1}/5$ to 21 pounds ($18^{1}/2$ quarts)/100 square feet. A quick-acting source of nitrogen and some potassium. (If not organic, it can contain methoxichlor pesticide residues.) Remember that too much nitrogen in your soil can cause the soil's all-important organic matter to break down too quickly.

PHOSPHORUS

Phosphate Rock

11.5% to 17.5% total P. Lasts 3 to 5 years. Use 4.5 to $13^{3}/5$ pounds ($1^{1}/3$ to 4 quarts)/100 square feet (see page 74). Very slow releasing.

SOFT PHOSPHATE (COLLOIDAL)

8% total P; 2% available P. Lasts 2 to 3 years. Use 9 to $27^{1}/5$ pounds ($1^{1}/3$ to 4 quarts)/100 square feet (see page 74). Its clay base makes it more available to plants than the phosphorus in phosphate rock, though the two are used interchangeably. It becomes available over two to three years.

POTASSIUM

Wood Ash

1% to 10% K. Lasts 6 months. Use a maximum of 1.5 pounds ($1^{3}/4$ quarts)/100 square feet. It becomes available over a six-month period. Ash from wood is high in potassium and helps repel maggots. Ash also has an alkaline effect on the soil, so use it with care if your soil pH is above 6.5. Black wood ash is best. Wood ash provides strength and plant essence, aids in insect control, and is a flavor enhancer for vegetables, especially lettuce and tomatoes. You can produce it with a controlled, soil-covered, slow-burning fire built during a soft drizzle or rain. This ash is higher in potassium and other minerals because they do not readily escape into the atmosphere as the wood is consumed by fire. Wood ash should be stored in a tight container until it is used;

exposure to air will destroy much of its nutrient value. Grey wood ash from a fireplace may be used if it is from wood and not from colored or slick paper.

Crushed Granite (Finely Ground)

3% to 5% K. It becomes available over a period of 10 years. Use 1½ to 8.5 pounds (0.6 to 3½ quarts)/100 square feet. It is not only a slow-releasing source of potassium, but also of trace minerals.

SOIL MODIFIERS

Dolomitic Lime

25% Ca (calcium) to 14% Mg (magnesium). A good source of calcium and magnesium to be used when both are needed. Do not use dolomitic lime in a soil with an adequate or high level of magnesium. Do not use lime to "sweeten" (neutralize the pH of) the compost pile; this will result in a serious loss of nitrogen. A layer of soil will discourage flies and reduce odors. 1 quart = about 3 pounds 8 ounces.

High-Calcium Lime (Calcite)

A good source of calcium when magnesium levels are too high for applying dolomitic lime. Oyster shell flour lime (34% to 36% Ca) is a good substitute if used in a limited way, but many sources are 2% lead. 1 quart = about 30 ounces.

Gypsum (Calcium Sulfate)

23% Ca, 19% S (sulfur). Used to correct excess levels of exchangeable sodium. Apply only when recommended by a professional soil test, because it causes the soil structure to be broken down and causes the soil to "plate." 1 quart = about 1 pound 4 ounces.

Dried Crushed Eggshells

High in calcium. Especially good for cabbage family crops. Eggshells help break up clay and release nutrients tied up in alkaline soils. Calcium also is instrumental in enabling other nutrients to be picked up more easily and effectively. Use up to 2 pounds (1¼ quart)/100 square feet. Dry them first.

Manure (All Types)

The nutrient levels in different manures will depend on proper management of the curing process and on the amount of straw or sawdust in the manure. Optimally, do no use more than 0.33 cubic feet per 100 square feet (one-half 5-gallon bucket) of aged manure per year (about 8.3 pounds dry weight.) It is best to use manure that contains little undecomposed sawdust.

Much aged or composted manure actually contains little nitrogen and may have a substantial amount of nitrogen-demanding sawdust. If you use a lot of manure containing large amounts of sawdust as a soil texturizer, you may want to add some additional nitrogen fertilizer, such as four extra pounds of alfalfa meal per 100 square feet. Manures that do not contain much sawdust or straw can contain excess salt and imbalanced rations of nitrogen, phosphorus, and potassium. The GROW BIOINTENSIVE method uses as much (or more) phosphorus and potassium as nitrogen. This results in stronger, healthier plants. It is a difference between the GROW BIOINTENSIVE method and the French intensive approach, which depended heavily on the use of horse manure, with about 3 parts nitrogen to 1 part phosphorus to 3 parts potassium. This ratio is unbalanced in favor of nitrogen, which at times results in weak and rank plant growth more susceptible to disease and insect attack. A ratio of 1 part nitrogen to 1 part phosphorus to 1 part potassium is better.

Composted manure is a microbial life stimulant and an animal and plant essence that has been "composted" both inside the animal and outside in the curing pile.

Using composted or aged manure is recommended as an alternative to compost only when compost is not available. One reason for this is that, in order to obtain a 1-inch layer of aged steer manure for use as compost on a 100-square-foot area, fodder for the animal to eat must be grown on a 500-square-foot area. This means an area 4 times as large as your growing area is being depleted of trace minerals and life-sustaining humus! Such a practice is not sustainable if used over a long period of time. When the proper compost crops are used instead, the compost materials for your 100-square-foot garden can be grown in just your 100-square-foot garden itself!

Compost

As discussed in the previous chapter, good compost is the most important part of the garden as it aerates soil, breaks up clay, binds together sand, improves drainage, prevents erosion, neutralizes toxins, hold precious moisture, releases essential nutrients, and feeds the microbiotic life of the soil, creating healthy conditions for natural antibiotics, worms and beneficial fungi.

GROW BIOINTENSIVE places heavy emphasis on compost for these reasons. In addition, as the demand for organic fertilizers increases, the supply available to each person in the world decreases. Soon, few fertilizers will be available at reasonable prices. The materials used to produce chemical fertilizers are becoming less available. Materials for GROW BIOINTENSIVE compost, on the other hand, are plants and soil, which can be produced in a sustained way by a healthy garden. While compost made from plants grown in a nutrient-poor soil will not contain nutrients that are not present; once the nutrients are introduced into the soil, compost "grown" in that soil recycles these nutrients. These compostable materials can be produced indefinitely if we take care of our soils and do not exhaust them.

Generally, use only a maximum of 4 cubic feet of cured compost, made from equal amounts by volume of mature (dry) material and immature (green) material and one-quarter part soil per 100 square feet, per 4- to 6-month crop to avoid using more than a sustainable amount of compost. (See page 53.) Four cubic feet of Biointensive compost made with soil is about one-sixth of a cubic yard. It will cover a 100-square-foot bed $1/2$ inch deep. Alternatively, use a maximum of 2 cubic feet (approximately $1^1/4$ inches) of cured compost made without soil. Both types of these composts—with and without soil—contain the same amount of organic matter.

Manures—Solids (approximate)			
Chicken—fresh	9–15% C	1.50% N	1.00% P	.50% K
Chicken—dry	Do not have data	4.50% N	3.50% P	2.00% K
Dairy Cow	7.28% C	.56% N	.23% P	.60% K
Horse	18.63% C	.69% N	.24% P	.72% K
Pig—fresh	6.5% C	.50% N	.32% P	.46% K
Sheep	19.6% C	1.40% N	.48% P	1.20% K
Steer	11.9% C	.70% N	.55% P	.72% K

Adding Fertilizers and Compost

The bed should be shaped before adding fertilizers and amendments. Add each of the chosen fertilizers and amendments one at a time. Avoid windy days, and hold the fertilizer close to the bed surface when spreading. Use the different colors to help you. The soil is dark, so sprinkle on a light-colored fertilizer (such as oyster shell flour) first, then a darker fertilizer (such as alfalfa meal), and so on (see illustrations below and opposite). It is better to underapply the fertilizers because you can go back over the bed afterward to spread on any left over, but it is difficult to pick up fertilizer if too much falls in one place. Aim for even distribution. Next, add compost. After all are applied, sift in the fertilizers and other amendments by inserting a spading fork 2 to 4 inches deep at a slant, then lifting it upward with a slight jiggling motion.

Several things should be noted about the nutrients added to the upper 2 to 4 inches of soil:

- The nutrients are added to the upper soil layer, as occurs in nature.

- The nutrients are relocated through the soil by the movement of larger soil organisms and when water flows downward.

- Organic fertilizers break down more slowly than most chemical fertilizers. By utilizing natural nutrient cycles, plant-available minerals are released over an extended period of time, and so are used more efficiently and benefit the plants for their entire life cycle.

More Sustainable Fertilization

Each gardener should strive to use less and less fertilizer brought in from outside his or her own garden area. Here are some ideas to create a more "closed-system" garden, to which few resources are imported:

1. Use most of the food you grow at home, so all the residues are returned to your soil. "Export" as little as possible of your valuable soil resource.

2. Grow some trees. Their deep root systems will bring up nutrients from far down in the subsoil into the topsoil and even into

Broadcasting fertilizers

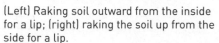
(Left) Raking soil outward from the inside for a lip; (right) raking the soil up from the side for a lip.

Casting fertilizer onto a bed's surface

Fertilization

Sifting in fertilizers with a spading fork. A "twist dig" is now being used to sift in fertilizers also. It is easier on the back and does not require bending over as far. This method requires 3 motions at once:

- a slight up-and-down motion with the left hand.
- a twist back and forth holding onto the D-handled spading fork with the right hand.
- a slight pushing in and out of the handle through the left hand with the right hand. Develop this skill by practicing. Do not rake the bed to smooth it out after sifting in fertilizers, as this usually creates irregular concentrations of fertilizers that were previously spread evenly.

the tree leaves. These nutrients would not otherwise become available for use as plant food.

3. "Grow" your own fertilizer by raising plants that produce good amounts of compost material, which concentrates the nutrients required in a form that plants can use. For beginning information on plants to use, see Ecology Action's *Growing and Gathering Your Own Fertilizers* (see Appendix 3), Bargyla and Gylver Rateaver's *Organic Method Primer*[4] and Ehrenfreid Pfeiffer's *Weeds and What They Tell*.[5] If everyone were to use organic fertilizers, there would be a worldwide shortage; eventually the key will be growing our own and recycling *all* wastes. The deep roots of alfalfa (as long as 125 feet) and comfrey (as long as 8 feet) also help bring up leached-out and newly released nutrients from the soil strata and rocks below.

4. Maintain at least 4% to 6% organic matter by weight in at least the upper 6 inches of soil in temperate regions and 3% organic matter in tropical ones. This will encourage microbial life growth, which can keep nutrients from leaching out of the soil.

5. Explore proper, safe and legal recycling of human waste. This subject remains much a taboo in many societies, however, research and establishment of best practices are critical for long-term sustainability. Most of the world's soils have been significantly depleted of their minerals as we harvest the nutrient-containing crops without returning the nutrients to the soil.

Nitrogen (N), Phosphorus (P), and Potassium (K)

Pounds of *pure nutrients*/fertilizer to add per 100 square feet. The goal is to reduce the nutrient deficiencies in the soil slowly over time. (If you add large amounts of readily available nutrients all at once, nutrients not in short supply in the soil may become unavailable.)

Existing Soil Nutrient Level (determined by soil test)	Very High[6]	High	Medium High	Medium	Medium Low	Low Very	Low
Pure Nitrogen	0.1	0.2	0.25	0.3	0.35	0.4	0.5
Alfalfa Meal	4.2	8.4	10.5	12.6	14.7	16.8	18.9
Pure Phosphorus	0.2	0.3	0.35	0.4	0.45	0.5	0.6
Phosphate Rock	4.5	6.8	8	9	10.2	11.4	13.6
Soft Phosphate	9	13.6	16	18	20.4	22.8	27.2
Pure Potassium	0.15	0.2	0.25	0.3	0.35	0.4	0.5
Wood Ash[7]	1.5	1.5	1.5	1.5	1.5	1.5	1.5
Crushed Granite[8]	1.5	2.5	3.5	4.5	5.5	6.5	8.5

ENDNOTES

1 Timberleaf, 39648 Old Spring Road, Murieta, CA 92563-5566. (951) 677-7510. www.timberleafsoiltesting.com. Based on our experience, Ecology Action recommends modifcation of Timberleaf's soil test results in the following areas: If gypsum is recommended, use two-thirds of the amount recommended. Compost built using Ecology Action's guidelines contains about 50% soil when cured. The Timberleaf compost recommendation assumes no soil. We recommend that the maximum sustainable amount of compost that should be applied is 4 cubic feet (including 50% soil). For nitrogen and phosphorus fertilizer recommendations, remember that in a GROW BIOINTENSIVE garden, fertilizers are used for the soil, not for particular crops; we recommend using the maximum amount of nitrogen and phosphorus fertilizer recommended by the Timberleaf test for all beds.

2 LaMotte Chemical Products, Box 329, Chestertown, MD 21620: Model STH. www.lamotte.com.

3 Ecology Action no longer uses nor recommends the use of many organic fertilizers because of potential problems with disease, pesticide residue, or heavy metal toxicity.

4 Rateaver, Bargyla and Gylver, *Organic Method Primer* (Pauma Valley, CA: Rateavers, 1973).

5 Pfeiffer, Ehrenfried, *Weeds and What They Tell* (Biodynamic Farming & Gardening Association, 1981).

6 Addition of nutrients at these levels is optional.

7 Wood ash application should be used with care for soils with a pH above 6.5. A maximum of 1.5 lbs should be used. 1.5 lbs contains .75 lbs potassium.

8 Finely ground.

OPEN-POLLINATED SEEDS, SEED PROPOGATION, CLOSE SPACING, AND SEED SAVING

Now that we know a little about the body and soul of our Earth, we are ready to witness the birth of seedlings. Just for a moment, close your eyes and pretend you are the seed of your favorite plant, tree, vegetable, fruit, flower, or herb. You are all alone. You can do nothing in this state. Slowly you begin to hear sounds around you. The wind, perhaps. You feel warmth from the sun, feel the ground underneath you. What do you need for good growth? Think like a seed, and ask yourself what a seed needs. It needs an entire microcosm of the world—air, warmth, moisture, soil, nutrients, and microorganisms. Plants need all these things, as do birds, insects, and animals.

Generally, the elements needed for growth fall into two categories: terrestrial (soil and nutrients) and celestial (air, warmth, moisture). The celestial elements cannot be completely categorized, however, since air, warmth, and moisture come from the heavens to circulate through the soil, and plants can take in air through their roots as well as through their leaves. Nutrients can also be borne upon air currents. In fact, citrus trees take in the important trace mineral zinc more readily by their leaves than by their roots. See chapter 7 for further information on the parts

Note: Seeds can germinate 2 to 7 times faster in a flat mix containing compost, because of the humic acids in the compost.

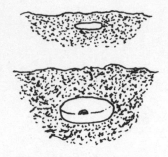

A seed is planted at a depth equal to its thickness.

that other elements in the plant and animal worlds play—other plants and insects, for example.

Seed Planting

Be sure to use open-pollinated seeds. They have stood the test of time, and that is why they are still available for us to use. Many have been used for a century or more and have been passed from generation to generation, because of their health, vigor, insect and disease resistance, and the beautiful color and taste of their edible portion! In addition, they are seeds that you can save this year, plant next year, and they will grow true to type. As you select them, you will be creating a new strain that has the characteristics you most appreciate and that best thrive in your climate and soil. For an incredible selection of seed varieties to choose from, see Kent Whealy's (ed.) *The Garden Seed Inventory*. It lists all open-pollinated seed varieties of vegetables commercially available in North America! You will be surprised at the number of varieties, colors and characteristics!

It only takes an average of 3% more growing area this year to grow the seeds that you will need next year—and you can begin

Hexagonal spacing: Leaf lettuce is spaced on 8-inch centers.

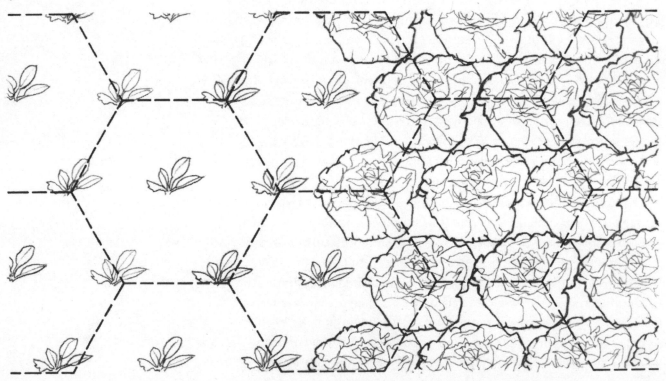

Open-Pollinated Seeds, Seed Propogation, Close Spacing, and Seed Saving

a wonderful seed exchange in your neighborhood! See "Growing to Seed," *Saving Seeds,* and *Seed to Seed* for more details. All are available from Bountiful Gardens, Ecology Action's nonprofit international gardening supply mail-order service.

Seeds should be planted at a depth equal to their thickness. Lima and fava beans may be planted on their sides. Their root systems, which emerge from an eye, can grow straight down. The seeds should be covered with humus-containing flat soil, which is similar to the soil with decomposed plant matter found over germinating seeds in nature. The compost stimulates the germination process. After spacing the seeds on the flat soil (described later in this chapter), cover seeds with a layer of flat soil equal to the height of the seed lying on the flat soil, and then water the flat evenly.

Seeds, whether they are planted in beds or in flats, should be planted in a diagonally offset or hexagonal spacing pattern with an equal distance between any two seeds. Refer to the Master Charts in chapter 8 to see how far apart to space different types of plants. The leaves of seedlings in the flat and of plants in the growing bed should barely touch. Appropriately spaced plants form a living mulch, which retards weed growth, aids in the retention of soil moisture by shading the soil, and creates the mini-climate under their leaves so essential to balanced, uninterrupted growth. When spacing seeds in flats, place the seeds far enough apart that the seedlings' leaves will barely touch when the seedlings are transplanting size. Try 1-inch to 2-inch spacings depending on the size of the seedling at its transplanting stage. In general, the plant spacings listed in the Master Charts for vegetables, flowers, and herbs are equal to the "within the row" spacings listed on the back of seed packets, or sometimes three-quarters of this distance. Disregard any "between row" spacings. The Master Charts list our best spacing determinations to date for these plants.

To make the placement of seeds in planting beds or flats easier, use frames with 1-inch or 2-inch mesh chicken wire stretched across them. The mesh is built on a hexagonal pattern, so the seeds can be dropped in the center of a hexagon and be on the proper center. Or, if a center greater than 1 inch is involved and you only have 1-inch mesh, just count past the proper number of hexagons before dropping the next seed.

When transplanting or planting seeds on spacings of 3 inches or more, try using measuring sticks cut to the required length to determine where each plant should be located. Transplant or sow a seed at each point of the triangulation process. You will eventually be able to transplant with reasonable accuracy without measuring!

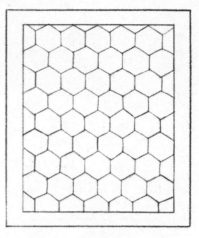

A spacing frame aids in placing seeds in flats. Place 1 seed in the center of each space.

Seeds

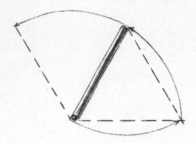

Use a spacing stick for placing seeds in beds; 3-inch to 36-inch sizes are used according to the crop planted. Triangulation is the way we plant most seeds and transplant seedlings.

Use a triangular spacing template for placing seeds in beds.

Use your digging board as a planting board to minimize compaction. As you move it along the bed, loosen the soil underneath with a hand fork.

Once you get the feel for plant spacing, you may want to practice broadcasting seeds by hand in flats for some crops, such as lettuce and flowers. Broadcasting was the method that Alan Chadwick and his apprentices used with flats. Be sure the seeds end up $1/4$ to $1/2$ inch apart in the first flat so the seeds can take advantage of their complete mini-climate for early growth stimulation and health. This method does, however, require more time to do 1 or more prick-outs. When these seedlings' leaves are barely touching, prick them out (transplant them) into other flats on 1-, $11/2$-, or 2-inch centers.

Cover the seeds in their flats with a layer of the flat soil mixture described later in this chapter. When broadcasting seeds onto a growing bed, gently "chop" them in afterward with a bow rake to a depth equal to their thickness (when they are lying flat on a surface). Be sure to chop the rake only up and down; do not pull it toward you. If you pull, seeds, fertilizers, and compost may concentrate irregularly over the bed rather than remain evenly spread. Or you may poke large seeds into the soil to their proper depth with your index finger. Fill the hole by pushing soil into it with your thumb and index finger.

Now that you have prepared your GROW BIOINTENSIVE bed and have spread the compost, you have a choice as to whether to sow seeds directly into the bed or to use seedlings.

Transplanting seedlings involves more advance planning and more time, but in a small garden, this has several advantages:

- Transplanted seedlings make better use of bed space. Seeds can take from 5 days to 12 weeks or more to reach transplanting size. If that growing is done in a flat, something else can be growing in the bed in the meantime.

- You can be reasonably sure that each transplanted seedling will grow into a healthy mature plant. Not all seeds germinate, so no matter how carefully you sow seeds directly in the bed, you can end up with gaps between plants and, therefore, bare soil that allows evaporation.

- Plants grow better if they are evenly spaced. Some seeds are sown by broadcasting, scattering them over the soil. Broadcast seeds—no matter how evenly you try to scatter them—will inevitably fall in a random pattern, with some closer and some farther apart than the optimal spacing for best plant growth. Plants that are too close together compete with each other for light, water, and nutrients. When plants are too far apart, the soil around them may become compacted, more water may evaporate, and space is wasted.

- The roots of evenly spaced transplanted seedlings can find nutrients and grow more easily, and their leaves will cover and protect the soil, creating a good mini-climate with better protection for the soil. Carbon dioxide is captured under the leaf canopy of closely spaced plants, where the plants need it for optimal growth.

- Transplanting stimulates growth. When you transplant a seedling into a double-dug, composted bed that is fluffy, aerated, and full of nutrients, you give it a second "meal" of nutrients, air, and moisture after its first meal in the flat. If the seeds are sown directly in the bed, the soil will begin to re-compact after its initial digging while the seeds are germinating and growing into seedlings. Therefore, the soil will not be as loose for the plants to grow in once the seedling stage is reached.

- Seedlings in a flat require much less water (a half-gallon per day) than seedlings in a bed (10 to 20 or more gallons per 100 square feet per day).

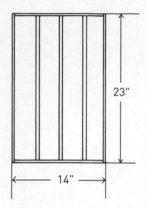

A bottom view of full-sized seedling flat construction. Leave 3/16 inch between board pieces for drainage. (All measurements given are internal dimensions.)

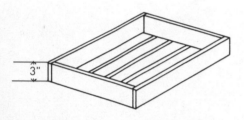

Seedling flats are made of redwood, or equivalent. A 3-inch-deep (internal dimension), full-sized flat with evenly moist flat soil and plants weighs about 45 pounds.

The leaves are roots in the air.

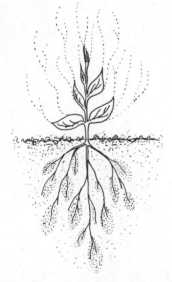

Roots are leaves in the ground.

Seedling Flats

The standard home-built flat size is 3 inches deep by 14 inches wide by 23 inches long (internal dimensions). For smaller gardens, half-sized flats may be more convenient. The depth is critical since an overly shallow flat allows the seedling roots to touch the bottom too soon. When this occurs, the plants believe they have reached their growth limit, and they enter a state of "premature senility." In this state the plants begin to flower and fruit even though they are only transplanting size. We have experienced this with broccoli and dwarf marigolds; the broccoli heads were the size of the nail on a little finger. The flat's length and width are not as critical. They should not become too large, however, or the flat will be hard to carry. If plants must remain in a container more than 4 to 6 weeks, use a half-sized flat that is 6 inches deep.

When planting seeds or seedlings, remember that the most important areas for the plant are the 2 inches above and the 2 inches below the surface of the flat or planting bed. The mini-climate created under the plants' leaves and the protection of the upper roots in the flat or the bed by the soil is critical. Without proper protection, the plants will develop tough necks at the point where the stem emerges from the soil. A toughened neck slows the flow of plant juices and interrupts and weakens plant growth. These few inches are also important because in a very real sense the *roots are leaves in the soil* and the *leaves are roots in the air*. The roots "breathe in" (absorb) gases in significant amounts as if they were leaves, and the leaves absorb moisture and nutrients from the air. Also, plant life activity varies above and below the ground according to monthly cycles. Root growth is stimulated more during the third quarter of each 28-day period, and leaf growth is stimulated more during the second quarter, in accordance with the phases of the moon. (See pages 86–89.)

The critical distance above and below the surface of the planting bed is not exactly 2 inches. Obviously it will be different for radishes than for corn, since their leaves begin at different heights from the soil surface and because their root systems have different depths. Generally speaking, though, the 2-inch guideline helps us develop a sensitivity to the plants' needs above and below ground. In particular, this mini-climate protects feeder roots and microbial life, which are both concentrated in the upper soil.

Once you have planted a flat, there are several locations—depending on the weather—where you can place it while the seeds germinate and grow:

- In a greenhouse or miniature greenhouse if the weather is cold.

- In a cold frame for 2 days when the seedlings are almost transplanting size as part of their *hardening off* (acclimatization to the cooler outside) for transplanting in cold weather.

- In the open for 2 more days to complete the hardening off process before transplanting.

- In the open under a 30% shade net during warm and hot weather.

- In the shade to slow down their growth in hot weather.

- You may want to build flat covers to protect seedlings from birds and mice. An easy way to do this is to build a flat similar to the ones the seedlings will be in, but *without* the wooden bottom. We use 1/2-inch galvanized wire fabric on the "bottom." Then we turn the unit upside down and place it on top of the flat to protect the seeds and seedlings.

A seedling flat

Note: Greenhouses are usually double glazed for maximum protection and are unheated or heated.

Note: Cold frames are single or double glazed; are open to the outside air, at least in part by being opened a little during the day; and are closed at night.

Flat Soil

You are now ready to prepare the soil in which to grow seedlings. *A good simple flat soil mix is 1 part sifted compost and 1 part bed soil* (saved from the first trench when you double-dug) by volume. "Old" flat soil, which has been used to raise seedlings, can be stored in a bin. Although some of the nutrients will have been depleted, it will still be rich in nutrients and organic matter, so it can be used to make a new flat mix. In this case, the recipe would be 1 part old flat soil, 1 part sifted compost, and 1 part bed soil. Compost for the flat soil mix should be passed through a sieve of 1/2-inch or 1/4-inch wire fabric. As your bed soil and your compost improve, your flat soil and seedlings also will improve.

Remember to completely fill your flat with soil, or even mound it slightly above the edge of the flat, so the seedlings will have as much depth as possible to grow in. If available, line the bottom of the flat with a 1/8-inch layer of oak leaf mold (partially decayed oak leaves) for drainage and additional nutrients. You may place crushed eggshells above the oak leaf mold for calcium-loving plants such as carnations and members of the cabbage family. Lightly sprinkle the eggshells to cover one-quarter of the total surface area.

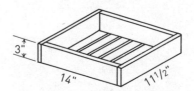

Half-sized flats are easier to carry. This shallow flat, with evenly moist flat soil and plants, weighs about 22 1/2 pounds.

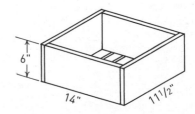

A half-sized deep flat (6 inches deep) ensures a manageable weight. This flat, with evenly moist flat soil and plants, weighs about 45 pounds. Note: All measurements given are internal dimensions.

Seeds

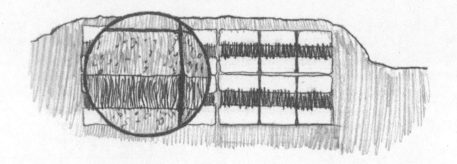

Turf loam compost pile

Alan Chadwick's classic planting mixture for starting seeds in flats is 1 part each by weight: evenly moist compost (sifted, if possible), sharp (gritty) sand, and turf loam. These 3 ingredients provide a fertile, loose-textured mixture. Turf loam is made by composting sections of turf grass grown in good soil. The sections of grass are composted by alternating grass sides together and soil sides together within the pile (see the illustration, on page 84). Good garden soil, from the first trench of a double-dug bed, for example, can be substituted for turf loam. Thoroughly mix the compost, sand, and garden soil or turf loam and, optionally, place them in the flat on top of oak leaf mold.

Some Causes of Poor Germination

When seeds fail to germinate or plants hardly grow at all after germination, some common causes are:

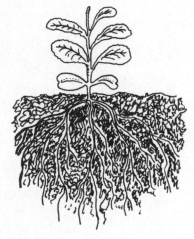

Loose soil with good nutrients enables roots to penetrate the soil easily, and a steady stream of nutrients flows into the stem and leaves.

- Using redwood compost. This compost is widely available as a mulch or soil conditioner but contains growth inhibitors that can keep seeds from germinating or plants from growing well. (This is how redwood trees reduce competition.)

- Planting too early or too late in the season. Seeds and seedlings wait for the right temperature and length of day to start and continue growth.

- Using weed killers or soil sterilizers. Many weed killers are short-lived, but they can limit growth in a garden long after they are supposed to degrade. Some people use them to minimize or eliminate yard care, but they can continue to have an effect for 2 years. There is never any reason to use these poisons in your yard. Also, dumping used motor oil can destroy valuable growing areas. Take it to a service station for recycling.

- Using old seeds. Check your source.

- Planting in soil that is too wet. Wet soil restricts oxygen, which is required for root growth. Plants can die in fertile soils when soil oxygen is too low to sustain growth.

Pricking Out Seedlings

The GROW BIOINTENSIVE method continually seeks to foster uninterrupted plant growth. Part of this technique is embodied in the "breakfast-lunch-dinner" concept that Alan Chadwick stressed. If seedlings are raised in very good soil—with good nutrients and a good structure—only to be transplanted into an area that has few nutrients and a poor structure, the plants will suffer root shock. Results are better when seedlings are pricked out from a flat with a good planting mixture "breakfast" into a second flat with a "lunch" consisting of fresh flat soil. The plant will forget the trauma of being pricked out when it tastes the delectable new lunch treats in the second flat. This process minimizes shock and even fosters growth. Finally, a splendid GROW BIOINTENSIVE "dinner" greets the plant in the growing bed! With this kind care and stimulated healthy plant growth, there is less likelihood of insect and disease damage. In the GROW BIOINTENSIVE method, pricking out and transplanting can stimulate growth rather than slowing it down.

Seedlings from broadcasted seed are ready to be pricked out after their cotyledons (the first "seed leaves" that appear, although they are not true leaves) have appeared and before their roots are too long to handle easily. You should do the second pricking out (if it is called for) when the seedlings' leaves have just begun to touch each other.

To prick out seedlings, fill a 3-inch- or 6-inch-deep flat with flat soil, and mound the soil slightly (remember to fill in the corners). Use a widger or kitchen knife to loosen the soil under the seedlings so you can lift out 1 seedling at a time, holding it by its cotyledons and keeping as much soil on the roots as possible.

Place the widger or kitchen knife into the soil of a second flat at a slight backward angle, just behind where the seedling should be, and pull the widger toward you to open a hole.

Let the seedling drop into the hole, placing it a little deeper than it was in the first flat. For many crops, lettuce and the cabbage family in particular, it is optimal for the seedling to be deep

Lift the first seedling out of the first flat.

Open the planting space in the new flat with a widger while . . .

. . . placing the seedling in the hole.

Gently sweep the soil into the hole.

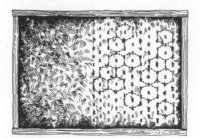

Evenly spaced pricked-out seedlings

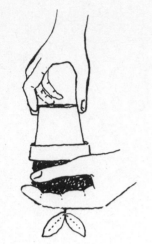

Unpot a seedling correctly.

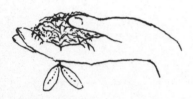

Spread root-bound plant roots out before transplanting them into a bed.

Note: Seedlings are transplanted when they are 2 to 3 inches high except for those marked "LG" in columns H and L of the Master Charts beginning on page 133. The LG seedlings are transplanted when they are 6 to 9 inches high.

For best bulb formation, do not plant onions too deeply; instead, plant as shown here.

enough so that its cotyledons are right at the level of the soil. Be sure not to bury the growing point.

Lift out the widger and let the soil fall around the seedling. It is often not necessary to spend time carefully pushing the soil up around the seedling; when you water the flat, the soil will settle in around the stem and roots. If the soil does need to be added to the hole into which the seedling is placed, just gently sweep the soil into the hole with a widger with one motion. Arrange the seedlings on offset, or hexagonal, centers to maximize the space in the flat and to optimize the mini-climate that will develop around the seedlings as they grow.

Transplanting

A Biodynamic gardener once had a row of broccoli plants. Only two plants had aphids, but both were quite infested. When they were dug up, the gardener discovered that the plants had experienced root damage during transplanting. The healthy broccoli, which had experienced uninterrupted growth, were untouched by the insects, while nature eliminated the unhealthy plants.[1]

When transplanting, it is important to handle the seedlings gently and to touch them as little as possible. Plants do not like their bodies to be handled, though they do like to have human companionship and to have dead leaves removed from their stems. You should hold them only by the tips of their leaves (if the plant must be touched) or by the soil around their roots. If you have grown the seedlings in a flat, use a hand fork to gently separate a 4-inch-square section of soil and plants from the rest. Using the fork, gently lift that section from the flat and place it on the ground. Then carefully pull away 1 plant at a time from the section for transplanting. If it is particularly dry, hot, or windy, place the section on a wet towel. Always keep as much soil around the roots as possible when transplanting.

If the seedling has been grown in a pot, turn the pot upside down, letting the plant stem pass between your second and third fingers, and tap firmly on the bottom of the pot with your other hand. Or tap the lip of the pot on something solid.

In all cases, if the plants are root-bound (the roots being so tightly grown together from having been kept in a starting flat or pot so long that with the soil they constitute a tight mass), gently spread the roots out in all directions. This process is important because the plant should not spend critical growth energy sending out a new, wide-ranging root system for eating and drinking when a good root system has already been produced. Instead, the plant's energy will go into the natural flow of continuous growth.

Be sure to place the seedling into a large enough hole so that the plant can be buried up to its first set of true leaves. Water the seedlings after transplanting to help settle the soil around the roots, to eliminate excess air spaces, and to provide an adequate amount of water for growth. As the soil is packed down under the pressure of watering, the final soil level will remain high enough to cover the upper roots. The plant's roots need firm contact with the soil to properly absorb water and nutrients. Press the soil firmly around the seedling, if necessary, but not too tightly. Tight packing will damage the roots and will not allow the proper penetration of water, nutrients, and air. Soil that is too loose will allow air and moisture to concentrate around the roots. This will cause root burn and decay.

Transplanting seedlings up to their first true leaves prevents them from becoming top-heavy and bending over during their early growth period. (This is especially true for members of the cabbage family.) If a plant bends over, it will upright itself, but will develop a very "tough neck" that will reduce the quality and size of the plant and crop. Onions and garlic, however, do better if the bulb does not have much soil weight to push up against.

Optimally, transplanting should be done in the early evening so the seedlings get settled into their new home during more moderate weather conditions. If transplanting is performed during the day, some temporary shading may be needed. In our hot summer weather, we shade newly transplanted seedlings with 30% shade-netting or Reemay, a row cover cloth, for several days to minimize transplanting shock and wilt.

Transplanting is preferable to directly sowing seeds. More importantly, transplanting improves plant health. Beds become compacted as they are watered and the soil will not be as loose for a seed that is planted directly in the bed. Some compaction will have occurred by the time the seed is a "child" a month later and, in some cases, so much so after 2 months, when it is likely to be an "adolescent," that its "adulthood" may be seriously affected. If, instead, you transplant the 1-month-old "child" into the growing bed, a strong adult root system can develop during the next 2 months, and a good adult life is likely. In fact, a study at the University of California at Berkeley in the 1950s indicated that a 2% to 4% increase in root health can increase yields 2 to 4 times.[2]

Most vegetables should be transplanted up to their first 2 true leaves.

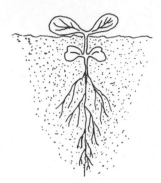

Proper

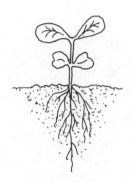

Improper

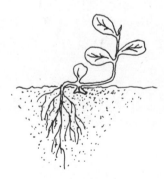

Result of improper transplanting

Tip: When the stems of cucumbers, melons, squash, pumpkin, and gourds grow into the path, turn the stems back into the bed's growing area to keep walkways clear. The stems prefer the more humid mini-climate in the growing area and will stay there.

Spotting

Some newly transplanted seedlings may die for various reasons or be eaten by animals or insects. Therefore, we usually save the surplus seedlings left in the flats after transplanting. We use these seedlings during the next 10 days to fill in the holes or "spots" in the mini-climate. This process has been named "spotting."

Planting by the Phases of the Moon

One of the most controversial aspects of the GROW BIOINTENSIVE method is Alan Chadwick's method of planting seeds and transplanting seedlings according to the phases of the moon. Short-germinating and extra-long-germinating seeds (which take approximately 1 month to germinate) are planted 2 days before the new moon, when significant magnetic forces occur, and up to 7 days after the new moon. Long-germinating seeds are planted at the full moon and up to 7 days afterward. Seedlings are transplanted at the opposite time (see chart on page 88). Both planting periods take advantage of the full sum of the forces of nature—which are greatest at the new moon—including gravity, light, and magnetism. The lunar gravitational pull that produces high tides in the oceans and water tides in the soil is very high at the new moon. And the moon, which is dark, gets progressively lighter. The exact day on which you plant or transplant is not as important as generally taking advantage of the impetus provided by nature.

If you place short-germinating seeds in the ground 2 days before the lunar tide forces are greatest, the seed has time to absorb water. The force exerted on the water in the seed helps create a "tide" that helps burst the seed coat in conjunction with the forces produced by the seed's swelling. No doubt you have wondered why one time beet seeds come up almost immediately and another time the germination process takes 2 weeks in the same bed under similar conditions. Temperature and moisture differences, pH changes, and humus levels may influence the seeds in each case, but the next time you note a marked difference in germination time, check your calendar to determine the phase the moon was in when you sowed the seeds. You may find the moon had an influence. Extra-long-germinating seeds are also planted at the new moon. They then germinate about a month later.

Looking at the drawing of the moon's phases, you can see that there are both increasing and decreasing lunar gravitational and light force influences that recur periodically during the lunar month. Sometimes the forces work against each other, and sometimes they reinforce one another. When the lunar gravitational pull decreases and the amount of moonlight increases during the first 7 days of the lunar cycle, plants undergo a period of balanced growth. The decreasing lunar gravity (and the corresponding relative increase in Earth's gravity) stimulates root growth. At the same time, the increasing amount of moonlight stimulates leaf growth.

During the second 7 days of the lunar cycle, the lunar gravitational force reverses its relative direction, and it increases. This pull slows down the root growth as Earth's relative gravitational pull is lessened. The moonlight, on the other hand, continues to a peak, and leaf growth is especially stimulated. If root growth has been sufficient during previous periods, then the proper amounts of nutrients and water will be conveyed to the above-ground part of the plant, and balanced, uninterrupted growth will occur. This time of increasing gravitational, moonlight, and magnetic forces gives seeds that have not yet germinated a special boost. Seeds that did not germinate at the time of the new moon should do so by the full moon. Alan Chadwick said that it is during this period that seeds cannot resist coming up, and mushrooms suddenly appear overnight.

During the third 7 days of the lunar cycle, the amount of moonlight decreases along with the lunar gravitational pull. As the moonlight decreases, aboveground leaf growth slows down. The root growth is stimulated again, however, as the lunar gravitational pull decreases. This is a good time to transplant, since root growth is active. This activity enables the plant to better overcome transplant shock and promotes the development of a good root system while leaf growth is slowed down. Then, 21 days later, when leaf growth is at a maximum, the plant will have a developed root system that can provide it with sufficient nutrients and water. This is also the time to plant long-germinating seeds that take approximately 2 weeks to germinate; they will then be ready to take advantage of the boost from the high gravitational pull of the new moon.

During the last 7 days of the lunar cycle, the lunar gravitational force increases, and root growth slows down. The amount of moonlight decreases and also slows down leaf growth. This period is one of a balanced decrease in growth, just as the first 7 days in the lunar month is a period of balanced increase in growth. The last 7 days, then, is a rest period that comes before the bursting forth of

Planting by the Phases of the Moon

2 days before new moon   **New moon**   **First 7 days**   **Second 7 days**

Plant short- and extra-long-germinating seeds (most vegetables and herbs) in flats and/or beds and transplant seedlings germinated from long-germinating seeds.

Balanced increase in rate of root and leaf growth.

Moonlight +
Lunar gravity -

Increased leaf growth rate.
Moonlight +
Lunar gravity +

Full moon   **Third 7 days**   **Fourth 7 days**   **New moon**

Transplant short- and extra-long-germinating seedlings from flats into beds and plant long-germinating seeds (most flowers) in flats and/or beds.

Increased root growth rate.

Moonlight -
Lunar gravity -

Balanced decrease in rate of root and leaf growth (resting period).

Moonlight -
Lunar gravity +

KEY

● New Moon   ◖ First Quarter   ○ Full Moon   ◗ Last Quarter

+ Increasing   – Decreasing

a period of new life. Short-, long-, and extra-long-germinating seed crops are listed in the Master Charts in chapter 8.

A planted seed bursts its seed coat around the 28th day of the lunar month and proceeds into a period of slow, balanced, and increasing growth above and below ground, passes into a period of stimulated leaf growth, then goes into a period of stimulated root growth (getting ready for the next period of stimulated leaf growth), followed by a time of rest. This plant growth cycle repeats itself monthly. Plants germinated from short- and extra-long-germinating seeds are transplanted at the full moon so they may begin their life in the growing bed during a time of stimulated root growth to compensate for the root shock that occurs during transplanting. (It is also vital that the plant's root system be well developed so it can later provide the leaves, flowers, vegetables, fruits, and seeds with water and nutrients.) The transplanted plant then enters a time of rest before beginning another monthly cycle. The workings of nature are beautiful.

Planting by the phases of the moon is a gardening nuance that improves the health and quality of plants. If you do not follow the moon cycles, your plants will still grow satisfactorily. However, as your soil improves and as you gain experience, each gardening detail will become more important and will have a greater effect. Try this one and see.

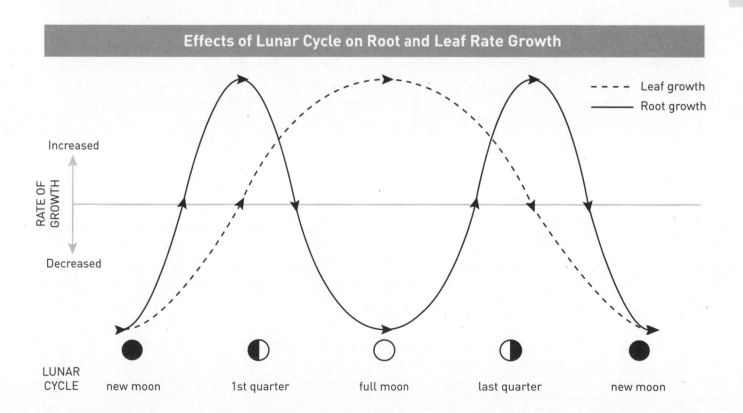

Effects of Lunar Cycle on Root and Leaf Rate Growth

- - - - Leaf growth
——— Root growth

Increased

RATE OF GROWTH

Decreased

LUNAR CYCLE

new moon   1st quarter   full moon   last quarter   new moon

Watering

When beds and flats are watered, the GROW BIOINTENSIVE method approximates rainfall as much as possible. The fine rain of water absorbs beneficial airborne nutrients as well as air, helping the growth process. For seeds and seedlings in flats, you can use a special English Haws watering can, which has fine holes in the sprinkler's "rose."[3] The rose points up so that when you water, the pressure built up in the rose first goes up into the air, where much of the pressure is dissipated as it flows through the air. The water then softly falls on the plants from above like rain, with only the force of gravity pulling the water down. When watering growing beds, you may employ the same method of spraying water into the air and letting it fall back down, using a water gun or a valve unit with a fan spray nozzle attached.[4] (If you use a water gun or a valve unit, you may need a heavy duty hose to contain the water pressure.) This gentle method of watering packs down the soil in the bed less, and the plants are not hit and damaged by a hard water spray. If you choose to point the fan downward, stand as far away from the plants as possible and/or keep the water pressure adjusted to a low point to minimize soil compaction and water damage.

Some plants, such as those in the cabbage family, like wet leaves. It is all right, and in fact beneficial, to water these plants from overhead. Other plants, such as tomatoes, peas, and members of the squash and melon families, can suffer from wilt and mildew, and their fruit may rot when their leaves are wet, especially in foggy or humid climates. Take care when watering these plants to water only the soil around them whenever possible. (In drier climates it probably will not matter.) To avoid spraying a plant's leaves, hold the fan just above the soil and point it sideways. A better method is to use a watering wand, which will allow you to more easily direct the water under the plant's leaves.

Water the beds sufficiently each day to keep them evenly moist. Daily watering washes the dust, grime, and insects from plant leaves and creates a deliciously moist atmosphere conducive to good plant growth and thriving microbial life. (Watering may be more or less frequent when the weather is warmer or cooler than normal.)

Water mature plants in beds when the heat of the day first subsides. This is about 2 hours before sunset during the summer and earlier during the winter. However, weather conditions, especially cloud cover, may necessitate earlier watering. The soil, warmed during the day, warms the cool water from the hose so it is more temperate by the time it reaches the plant roots. The roots suffer less shock,

English Haws watering can

Special upward-pointing Haws watering rose

Ross watering fan attached to a valve unit

Ross watering fan attached to a variable water pressure gun

and the soil and plants have more time to absorb water during the cooler, less windy night. Also, plants do a significant amount of their growing at night, and this ensures they will have plenty of water to do so. If you water early in the morning, much of the water will be lost in evaporation caused by the sun and wind, and the watering will be less effective. The loss will be even greater if you water at midday. If you water in the evening, the plants will be more susceptible to mildew and rust problems due to unevaporated water left on their leaves. By watering in the late afternoon, the water can percolate into the soil for 12 hours or more before the sun and wind reappear in strength. When they do, the bed will have a good reservoir of water from which the plants can draw before their next watering.

Seeds and seedlings in flats and immature plants in the growing beds may have to be watered in the morning and at noon as well as late in the afternoon. Until the living mulch effect occurs, the flats and beds dry out more rapidly. When the leaves grow closer together, less watering will be required.

To determine how much water to give a bed each day, strive for a 1/2- to 15-second "shiny."[5] When you first begin to water, a shiny layer of excess water will appear on top of the soil. If you stop watering immediately, the shiny layer will disappear quickly. You should water until the shiny layer remains for 1/2 to 15 seconds after you have stopped watering. The actual time involved will differ depending on your soil's texture. The more clayey the texture, the longer the time will be. A newly prepared bed with good texture and structure will probably have enough water when a 1/2- to 3-second shiny is reached. A newly prepared clayey bed may indicate that it has enough water with a 3- to 5-second shiny, since a clayey soil both retains more moisture and lets the water in less rapidly. A month-old bed (which has compacted somewhat due to the watering process) may require a 5- to 8-second shiny, and beds 2 to 3 months old may require more than that.

Eventually the watering process will become automatic, and you will not have to think about when the bed has received enough water; you will know intuitively when the point has been reached. (Remember to allow for the different natures of plants. Squash plants, for instance, will want a lot of water in comparison to tomato plants.) One way to determine whether you have watered enough is to go out the next morning and poke your finger into the bed. If the soil is evenly moist for the first 2 inches and continues to be moist below this level, you are watering properly. If the soil is dry for part or all of the first 2 inches, you need more shiny. If the soil is soggy in part or all of the upper 2 inches, you need less shiny.

A GROW BIOINTENSIVE bed

Watering tomato plants using a wand

Seeds

Note: It is important to realize that we are watering the soil, so that it may thrive as a living sponge cake. We are not watering the plants. The soil in turn then "waters" the plants. Keeping the soil alive will help retain water and minimize the water consumed.

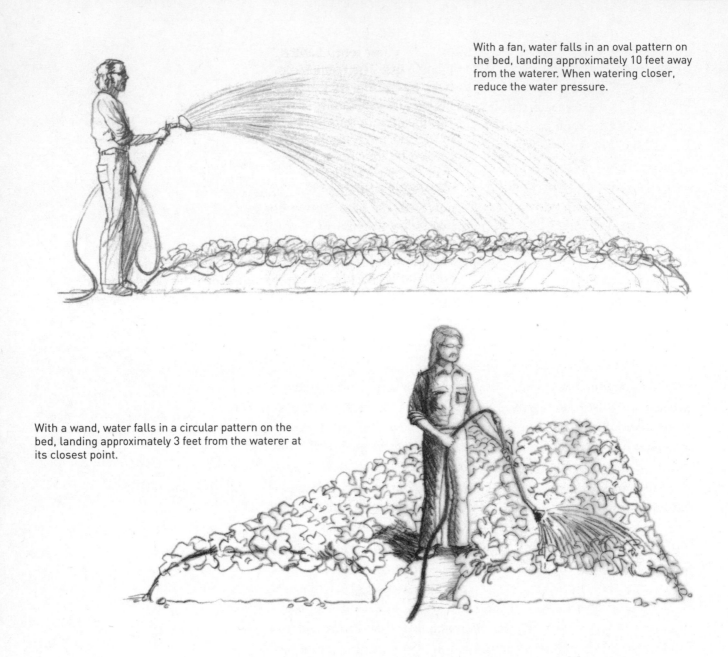

With a fan, water falls in an oval pattern on the bed, landing approximately 10 feet away from the waterer. When watering closer, reduce the water pressure.

With a wand, water falls in a circular pattern on the bed, landing approximately 3 feet from the waterer at its closest point.

Remember also to adjust your watering according to the weather. A bed may lose more moisture on a cloudy, windy, dry day than on a hot, clear, humid, and still one. And there are times when the flats and beds need no water or need watering twice a day. It is important to note these differences and to become sensitive to the soil's needs. You should water for good fruit, flower, and seed production, not just so the plant will stay alive. Be sure to water the sides and ends of the growing beds more than the middle. These areas, which many people miss or underemphasize, are critical because they are subject to more evaporation than the middle of the bed. Newly dug but still unplanted beds should be watered daily so they will not lose their moisture content. A transplant in a bed

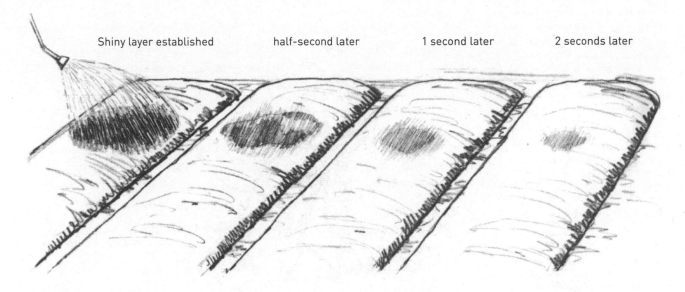

A newly prepared bed is properly watered when the shiny layer of excess water disappears within $1/2$ to 3 seconds after the watering stops.

that has a low moisture level (except in the recently watered upper 2 inches or so) will have difficulty growing well because of the dry pan below. If you wait until plants are wilting and drooping before you water them, they will revive but they will have suffered some permanent damage—an open invitation for pests and diseases. Slight drooping, however, is not usually a sign that you should water. Plants are just minimizing water loss (due to transpiration) when they droop on a hot day, and watering them at this time will increase water loss rather than lessen it. It will also weaken the plant through too much pampering.

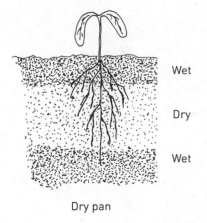

Wet

Dry

Wet

Dry pan

Shadenetting

After you have watered your newly planted bed, in hot weather you may want to consider covering this area with 30% shadenetting from approximately 10 a.m. to 5 p.m. Use shade netting that is 1 to 3 feet wider and 3 feet longer than your growing bed, so the netting can drape down around the edges to provide shade on the sides as well as the top. We generally insert 3-foot-long pieces of 1 by 1-inch wood on a 45-degree angle into the soil at the 4 corners of the bed and every 5 feet along and perpendicular to the sides. Headless nails are hammered partway into the top end of the sticks so the shade netting can be held in place. At 5 p.m. we unhook the netting from the long eastern side of the bed and hook its edges over the

Tip: To conserve water, raise your seedlings in flats until transplanting size (usually for the first 2 to 4 weeks). For many crops, 1 flat, which needs only about one-half gallon of water each day, will plant a 100-square-foot growing area. When planted, this growing area will need about 10 to 20 gallons of water daily during the main growing season. The water savings in 1 month (compared with direct sowing of seeds in the growing area) is about 285 to 585 gallons of water!

nails on the other side several times to secure the netting and keep it out of the paths and the bed. We reverse this process at 10 a.m. the next day. Make sure the nails do not jut into the path where they can be a hazard to you.

We also use shade netting to protect newly transplanted grains from birds in the fall and winter. In this case, we leave the shade-netting on for 10 days and use long pieces of 5/8-inch rebar to hold down the edges of the netting so birds cannot enter the growing area. We adjust the 1 by 1-inch sticks so the netting edges lie on the ground with the rebar along the edges. After 10 days, the shadenetting is removed because at this point the plants are less tasty and, therefore, are not attractive to the birds.

Mini-Greenhouses

A mini-greenhouse made from plastic sheeting and wood[6] can increase the temperature of the soil and the air surrounding plants and allow you to get an early start on the growing season in the spring and to lengthen the growing season in the autumn. Our design has double-walled construction, which can keep the inside temperature above the freezing point when the outside temperature falls as low as 20°F. This makes the unit a good season-extender for crops.

A mini-greenhouse.

Key Water Factors

The GROW BIOINTENSIVE method is especially important for areas with scarce water. Though much more experimentation is needed in this area, the information below should assist you.

- Seventy-five percent of the Earth's land surface where food is generally grown receives 10 inches of rainfall or more annually.

About one-half of this rainfall can be retained in soil properly prepared for plant use. To grow a good yield, 20 inches of rain are needed annually. In an area receiving only 10 inches of rainfall, the rain a growing area receives can be increased to 20 inches in the bent bed example illustrated below.

Sloped beds on flat ground (side view) can be used for water harvesting.

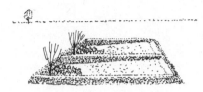

A Native American type of bent bed is used to capture rainfall effectively. This is a key water-harvesting technique.

- The GROW BIOINTENSIVE method uses an average of 10 gallons (a 5- to 20-gallon range) per day per 100 square feet, while commercial food-raising consumes an average of 20 gallons per day for the same area. *GROW BIOINTENSIVE has the potential to produce 4 times the food in the same area as commercial agricultural practices.*

- Research by academic institutions has shown that soil that has organic matter as 2% of its volume in the upper 11 inches can reduce the rainfall or irrigation required for poor soils by as much as 75%. (Poor soils have about .5% organic matter in the upper soil area.) GROW BIOINTENSIVE encourages maintaining more than 2% organic matter.

- Even under arid conditions, soil that is shaded can reduce evaporation up to 63%, depending on soil type. The mini-climate created by closely spaced plants provides good shading.

- Plants *transpire* water, which can be reduced by as much as 75% in soils that have sufficient and well-balanced nutrients in the soil water. The GROW BIOINTENSIVE method prepares the soil so it provides for a high level of fertility.

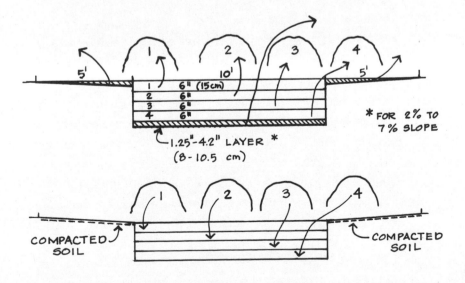

Preparation of a 5- by 20-ft bent bed for the concentration of rainwater in your growing area, assuming half the necessary amount of rainfall is available. To create a bent bed, soil is removed in 6-inch layers and placed in separate piles. (The lowest layer—layer 5—is not used in this bed.) The separated piles minimize unwanted mixing of soil strata. This is important because life-enhancing organic matter and microbial life are in higher concentrations in the upper layers. The slope range and soil compaction of that area encourages sufficient run-off into the loosened soil without erosion.

- If you combine the last 3 factors listed on page 95, water consumption can sometimes be reduced to one-thirty-second the level (one-quarter x one-half x one-quarter) plants normally require. We have found that GROW BIOINTENSIVE can reduce water consumption on average to one-eighth that of normal methods per pound of vegetable produced and to about one-third that of normal methods per pound of grain produced once the soil is in reasonable shape.

- Native people in some parts of Africa have been using a deeply prepared bed approach successfully with grains. They triple-dig the soil, incorporating a lot of organic matter into it just before the seasonal rains. Immediately after the rains stop, they plant their seeds. No more rain falls, yet crops are harvested at the end of the season. Others in the area reportedly are unable to grow crops well during this season.

Note: Twenty inches of rainfall over a 4-month growing season is an average of .167 inch per day.

- GROW BIOINTENSIVE techniques should produce at least 4 times the yield under natural rainfall conditions (when not irrigating) that would be obtained under the same conditions with commercial techniques. Let us know what works for you.

- Native Americans in the southwestern United States have used a number of approaches to grow food in limited rainfall areas. One method is to create large, diamond-shaped growing areas on a slight slope, with one point each being at the top and the bottom of the slope. Crops are planted in the bottom one-quarter to one-half of each diamond—depending on the amount of rainfall. (More water per unit of soil area is concentrated in the bottom part of the diamond.)

- With this method, use the following information to determine how much of the diamond to plant: Well-prepared soil needs to retain approximately 10 inches of water per unit of area (623 gallons per 100 square feet) to grow 1 complete crop during a 4-month growing season. To retain this much water, the soil needs about 20 inches of rainfall (1,246 gallons per 100 square feet) per season. If only 10 inches fall, you would have only one-half the water needed, and you would plant only the bottom one-half of each diamond. If you had only 5 inches of rain, you would only have one-quarter the water needed for a crop, and you would only plant the bottom one-quarter of the diamond (more or less). Experimentation will be required before you have optimum success. Be careful not to overplant. A completely dry soil does not rewet or absorb water easily, which will lead to erosion. To be on the safe side, start with a small area and plant one-quarter less crop than the above recommendations to ensure that the soil retains some moisture. Once you achieve success, you can increase the area under cultivation. Please share your experiences with us and others so this approach can be better understood.

- See John A. Widtsoe's *Dry Farming* for more information on dry farming.

Weeding

Intensively planted raised beds do not require weeding as often as other types of gardens due to the living mulch that the plants create. Usually, our beds only need to be weeded once, about a month after the bed is planted. A bed prepared in a new area may have to be weeded more often at first, however, since many dormant seeds will be raised to a place in the soil where they can germinate readily. Over time, as the soil becomes richer and more alive, you will probably have fewer weeds, since they tend to thrive more in poor and deficient soils than in healthy ones.

There really is no such thing as a "weed." A weed is just a plant that is growing in an area where you, the gardener, do not want it to grow. In fact, many so-called weeds, such as stinging nettle, are quite beneficial to the soil and to other plants. (This will be discussed in more detail in chapter 6.) Instead of weeding indiscriminately, you should learn the natures and uses of the different weeds so you can identify and leave some of the most beneficial ones in the growing beds. Until they are removed, weeds help establish a more quickly nourishing mini-climate for your current crop. Add the weeds you pull to the compost pile. They are rich in trace minerals and other nutrients and will help grow good crops next season.

Weeds are generally hardier than cultivated plants since they are genetically closer to their parental plant stock and nearer to the origin of the plant species. They tend to germinate before broadcasted cultivated plants. You should usually wait to remove these plants from the beds until the cultured plants catch up with the weeds in height or until the cultured plants become established (about transplanting size)—whichever comes first. Weeding before this time is likely to disturb the germinating cultured plant seeds or disturb the developing new root systems, causing interrupted

Appropriate posture can make weeding easier.

plant growth and weakened plants. However, be sure to remove any grass plants that develop in the beds after the first weeding. These plants put out incredibly large root systems that interfere with other plants in the competition for nutrients and water.

Planting in Season

Vegetables, flowers, and herbs—all plants for that matter—should be planted in season. This is a good way to love your plants. If they are forced (grown out of season), much of their energy is used up straining to combat unseasonable weather in the form of cold, heat, rain, or drought. Less energy is left for balanced growth, and a plant with limited energy reserves—not unlike people—is more susceptible to disease and insect attacks. Also, for the best crop health and yields, be sure to keep your plants harvested! To determine the best time to plant various crops, see chapter 9.

Satisfactory (and Optimal) Plant-Growing Temperature Ranges[7]			
Determine the Planting-Range Calendar for Your Area			
CROP SEASON	**TEMPERATURE RANGE**	**OPTIMAL TEMPERATURE RANGE**	**PLANT**
Cool-Season Crops[8]	30°F		Asparagus • Rhubarb
	40°–75°F	60°–65°F	Beet • Broad bean • Broccoli • Brussels sprouts • Cabbage • Chard • Collard • Horseradish • Kale • Kohlrabi • Parsnip • Radish • Rutabaga • Sorrel • Spinach • Turnip
	45°–75°F	60°–65°F	Artichoke • Carrot • Cauliflower • Celeriac • Celery • Chinese cabbage • Endive • Florence fennel • Lettuce • Mustard • Parsley • Pea • Potato
	45°–85°F	55°–75°F	Chicory • Chive • Garlic • Leek • Onion • Salsify • Shallot
Warm-Season Crops	50°–80°F	60°–70°F	Bean • Lima bean
	50°–95°F	60°–75°F	Corn • Cowpea • New Zealand spinach
	50°–90°F	65°–75°F	Pumpkin • Squash
	60°–90°F	65°–75°F	Cucumber • Muskmelon
Hot-Season Crops	65°–85°F	70°–75°F	Sweet peppers • Tomato
	65°–95°F	70°–85°F	Eggplant • Hot peppers • Okra • Sweet potato • Watermelon

Soil Temperature Conditions for Vegetable Seed Germination[9]				
CROP	**MINIMUM**	**OPTIMUM RANGE**	**OPTIMUM**	**MAXIMUM**
Asparagus	50°F	60°–85°F	75°F	95°F
Bean	60°F	60°–85°F	80°F	95°F
Bean, Lima	60°F	65°–85°F	85°F	85°F
Beet	40°F	50°–85°F	85°F	95°F
Cabbage	40°F	45°–95°F	85°F	100°F
Carrot	40°F	45°–85°F	80°F	95°F
Cauliflower	40°F	45°–85°F	80°F	100°F
Celery	40°F	60°–70°F	70°F*	85°F*
Chard, Swiss	40°F	50°–85°F	85°F	95°F
Corn	50°F	60°–95°F	95°F	105°F
Cucumber	60°F	60°–95°F	95°F	105°F
Eggplant	60°F	75°–90°F	85°F	95°F
Lettuce	35°F	40°–80°F	75°F	85°F
Muskmelon	60°F	75°–95°F	90°F	100°F
Okra	60°F	70°–95°F	95°F	105°F
Onion	35°F	50°–95°F	75°F	95°F
Parsley	40°F	50°–85°F	75°F	90°F
Parsnip	35°F	50°–70°F	65°F	85°F
Pea	40°F	40°–75°F	75°F	85°F
Pepper	60°F	65°–95°F	85°F	95°F
Pumpkin	60°F	70°–90°F	95°F	100°F
Radish	40°F	45°–90°F	85°F	95°F
Spinach	35°F	45°–75°F	70°F	85°F
Squash	60°F	70°–95°F	95°F	100°F
Tomato	50°F	60°–85°F	85°F	95°F
Turnip	40°F	60°–105°F	85°F	105°F
Watermelon	60°F	70°–95°F	95°F	105°F

*Daily fluctuation to 60°F or lower at night is essential.

Seeds

ENDNOTES

1 John and Helen Philbrick, *Gardening for Health and Nutrition* (New York: Rudolph Steiner Publications, 1971), p. 93.

2 Charles Morrow Wilson, *Roots: Miracles Below—The Web of Life Beneath Our Feet* (Garden City, NY: Doubleday, 1968), p. 105.

3 Available by mail order from many sources, including Walter F. Nicke, P.O. Box 433, Topsfield, MA 01983.

4 A Ross No. 20 is best.

5 A simple way to estimate the amount of water a bed is receiving is to first measure the gallons delivered per minute. Turn the hose on and point the spray into a 1-gallon jar or watering can. If, for example, it takes 15 seconds to fill the jar, then you know you are delivering 4 gallons per minute to the bed. Currently, in our moderately heavy clay, we find each 5 by 20-foot bed will take anywhere from 5 to 20 gallons daily (10 gallons on the average), depending on the weather, the type of plant, the size of the plants, and the tightness of the soil.

6 For plans and instructions, see *The Backyard Homestead, Mini-Farm and Garden Log Book* (Willits, CA: Ecology Action, 1993).

7 From James Edward Knott, *Handbook for Vegetable Growers* (New York: John Wiley & Sons, 1957), pp. 6–7.

8 Try these crops in shady areas in the summer. Remember, crops need at least 4 hours of direct sunlight to grow. Seven hours are preferred, and 11 hours are even better.

9 From James Edward Knott, *Handbook for Vegetable Growers* (New York: John Wiley & Sons, 1957), p. 8.

6

COMPANION PLANTING

Like people in relationships, certain plants like or dislike each other, depending on the specific natures involved. Seedlings of transplanting size begin to relate more and more with the plants around them. These relationships become especially important as adult plants develop distinct personalities, essences, and aromas. Green beans and strawberries, for example, thrive better when they are grown together than when they are grown separately. To get really good-tasting Bibb lettuce, 1 spinach plant should be grown for every 4 Bibb lettuce plants.

In contrast, no plants grow well near wormwood due to its toxic leaf and root excretions. However, wormwood tea repels black fleas, discourages slugs, keeps beetles and weevils out of grain, and combats aphids. So wormwood is not a totally noxious herb. Few plants are. Instead, they have their place in the natural order of things.

Weeds are often specialists and doctors in the plant community. They take very well to sick soil that needs to be built up and almost seem to seek it out. Where cultivated garden plants cannot manage, weeds are able to draw phosphorus, potash, calcium, trace minerals, and other nutrients out of the soil and subsoil and concentrate them in their bodies. Plants seem to have uncanny instincts.

Weeds can be used to concentrate nutrients for future fertilization or to withdraw noxious elements, such as unwanted salts, from the growing area. A deficient soil is often enriched by adding weeds to man-made compost or by returning their dead bodies to the soil as nature does.

Companion planting is the constructive use of plant relationships by gardeners, horticulturists, and farmers. A scientific definition of companion planting is "The placing together of plants having complementary physical demands." A more accurate, living, and spiritual description is "The growing together of all those elements and beings that encourage life and growth; the creation of a microcosm that includes vegetables, fruits, trees, bushes, wheat, flowers, weeds, birds, soil, microorganisms, water, nutrients, insects, toads, spiders, and chickens."

Companion planting is still an experimental field in which much more research needs to be performed. The age of the plants involved and the percentage of each of the types of plants grown together can be critical, as can be their relative proximity to one another. Companion planting should, therefore, be used with some caution and much observation. You may want to study the causes of some of these beneficial relationships. Are they due to root excretions, plant aroma, or the pollen of composite flowers that attracts certain beneficial insects? Companion planting is a fascinating field.

Some of the companion planting techniques you might try and experience are for health, crop rotation, nutrition, physical complementarity, and weed, insect, and animal relationships.

Health

Better growth—Growing green beans and strawberries together, and Bibb lettuce and spinach, has already been mentioned. On the other end of the spectrum, onions, garlic, chives, and shallots seriously inhibit the growth of peas and beans. In between the extremes, bush beans and beets may be grown together with no particular advantage or disadvantage to either plant. Pole beans and beets, however, do not get along well. The nuances are amazing. What is the difference between bush and pole beans? No one appears to know the scientific reason yet for this difference in behavior, but it can be observed.

Ehrenfreid Pfeiffer developed a method known as "crystallization," from which one can predict whether or not plants will be good companions. In this technique, part of a plant is ground up and mixed with a chemical solution. After the solution dries, a crystalline pattern remains. Different plants have distinct, representative patterns. When 2 plant solutions are mixed, the patterns increase, decrease, or stay the same in strength and regularity. Sometimes both patterns improve, indicating a reciprocal, beneficial influence. Or both patterns may deteriorate in a reciprocal negative reaction. One pattern may improve while another deteriorates, indicating a one-sided advantage. Both patterns may remain the same, indicating no particular companion advantage or disadvantage. And one plant pattern may increase or decrease in quality while the other undergoes no change. Two plants that suffer a decrease in quality on a 1 to 1 basis may show an increase in strength in a 1:10 ratio.

Spacing for better companions—Using GROW BIOINTENSIVE spacing with the plant leaves barely touching allows good companions to be better friends.

All-around beneficial influence—Certain plants benefit the entire plant community. These plants and their characteristics are:[1]

- Lemon balm (*Melissa officinalis*): Creates a beneficial atmosphere around itself and attracts bees. Part of the mint family.

- Marjoram (*Origanum majorana*): Has a "beneficial effect on surrounding plants."

- Oregano (*Origanum vulgare*): Has a "beneficial effect on surrounding plants."

- Stinging nettle (*Urtica dioica*): "Helps neighboring plants to grow more resistant to spoiling." Increases the essential oil content in many herbs. "Stimulates humus formation." Helps stimulate fermentation in compost piles. As a tea, it promotes plant growth and helps strengthen plants. Concentrates sulfur, potassium, calcium, and iron in its body.

- Valerian (*Valeriana officinalis*): "Helps most vegetables." Stimulates phosphorus activity in its vicinity. Encourages health and disease resistance in plants.

- Chamomile (*Chamaemelum nobile*): A lime specialist. "Contains a growth hormone which . . . stimulates the growth of yeast." In a 1:100 ratio, it helps the growth of wheat. As a tea, it combats

Note: Lemon balm, marjoram, oregano, dandelion, chamomile, stinging nettle, and valerian are perennials. They are traditionally planted in a section along an end of the bed so they need not be disturbed when the bed is replanted.

Stinging nettle and tomatoes are good garden companions.

diseases such as damping off in young plants. Concentrates calcium, sulfur, and potash in its body.

- Dandelion (*Taraxacum officinale*): Increases the "aromatic quality of all herbs." "In small amounts" it helps most vegetables. Concentrates potash in its body.

- Oak tree (*Quercus spp.*): Concentrates calcium in its bark (bark ash is 77% calcium). In a special tea, it helps plants resist harmful diseases. Its beneficial influence helps create excellent soil underneath its branches—which is a great place to build a compost pile, but keep the pile at least 6 feet from the tree trunk so the nearby environment will not be conducive to disease or attractive to harmful insects.

Soil life stimulation—Stinging nettle helps stimulate the microbial life, and this helps plant growth.

Soil improvement—Sow thistle (*Sonchus oleraceus*) brings up nutrients from the subsoil to enrich a depleted topsoil. After years of dead sow thistle bodies enrich the topsoil, heavier-feeding grasses return. This is part of Nature's recycling program, in which leached-out nutrients are returned to the topsoil, and it is a natural method for raising new nutrients to the upper layers of the soil. It has been estimated that 1 cereal rye plant grown in good soil produces an average of 3 miles of roots per day; that is 387 miles of roots and 6,603 miles of root hairs during a season. Plants are continuously providing their own composting program underground. In 1 year, plants put 800 to 1,500 pounds of roots per acre into the soil in a small garden, and red clover puts 1,200 to 3,850 pounds of roots into the soil in the same period of time.[2]

- Approximately, a minimum of 0.5 lb of nitrogen is needed per 100 sq ft of growing area annually. About half of this can come from a legume, such as vetch and/or cold-weather fava beans, such as the Banner variety that lives to 10°F., interplanted with a winter grain, such as wheat or cereal rye. This is a kind of **rotation in space.** The vetch and favas would be harvested while immature, when they are at 10% to 50% flower, so the nitrogen fixed in their nodules can remain in the soil. (If the legumes are allowed to go to seed, the nitrogen will be taken up and used in the formation of their seed.) The other half can come from a good and sustainable addition of compost.

Plant root systems improve the topsoil by bringing up nutrients from the subsoil.

- And/or **rotation over time** can also be used. This would be when you grow a grain, such as corn in the main season one year, and then grow a legume as a "catch crop" afterwards—and harvest it at 10% to 50% flower to keep the nitrogen in the soil.

Rotations

For many years Ecology Action often followed a heavy giver, heavy feeder, light feeder, low nitrogen lover type of crop rotation approach. However, we discovered that this process, while it was good for organizing one type of rotation program, was complicated and did not take everything into account. One example is potatoes, which are a "light feeder" crop according to the definitions involved, yet they, along with tomatoes, are in reality among the heaviest "heavy feeders."

Eventually, we began to research rotations and discovered that many rotation programs exist. However, it was difficult to find a repeating pattern in almost all of them. In addition, it has been observed that biologically intensive food raising, because of the diversity of crops it uses, produces genetically diverse compost piles. The use of the cured compost from these piles throughout the growing area, in turn, is itself a kind of "rotation." As a result of this and a lot of experience, we have developed the following simpler rotation guidelines:

- For **main-season crops,** with few exceptions, we try not to grow the same crop, or a member of the same family, in the same growing bed 2 years in a row. In areas where 2 or more crops can be grown in the same growing bed during the year, we do not grow the same crop, or a member of the same family, in that bed a second time during the year. In addition, we try to grow a quick-maturing 60+-day "catch crop" after the main-season crop whenever possible. Fast-maturing bean and amaranth varieties are examples of this. (A list of plant families is given on page 108.)

- In addition, for **non-main-season crops planted in the fall,** there are 3 possible approaches: a 3-year rotation and 2 types of 2-year rotations.

- There are some points to be noted in these 3 approaches. All begin with a planting for nitrogen accumulation to build up the soil before grains are grown to maturity. The second rotation system does this with a legume only and, therefore, provides the most nitrogen for the soil. The first rotation system has a third part, which grows a legume to maturity in order to provide a period of soil resting.[3]

- You may want to experiment with different combinations, depending on the quality of your soil and the type of climate you have. The important thing is to develop a combination that provides the nitrogen you need and that grows sufficient mature biomass and immature biomass to produce enough cured compost to maintain sustainable soil fertility while you grow food for yourself.

- In tropical areas, you will need to substitute warmer-weather crops that provide the same functions.

A 3-YEAR ROTATION

Year 1: The growing of a compost crop **interplanted mixture** (see Ecology Action's Self-Teaching Mini-Series Booklet 14) **with double the amount of seed of cold-weather grains** broadcasted (wheat or hull-less barley or hull-less oats or triticale, and cereal rye) and **legumes** (broadcasted vetch and a sown cold-weather fava bean). The entire crop is harvested when it is immature so a main-season crop can be planted in time to go to maturity. (Inoculation of the legumes with the relevant nitrogen-fixing bacteria for the crops involved will be needed if the soil does not already contain these microbes.)

Year 2: The transplanting of a **cold-weather grain** (wheat or hull-less barley or hull-less oats or cereal rye or triticale), with the entire crop being harvested at maturity. In areas with a long main growing season, a main-season hot-weather crop is planted afterward to go to maturity. In areas with a short main growing season, we try to grow a quick-maturing 60+-day "catch crop" after the grain harvest whenever possible. Fast-maturing bean varieties are examples of this. Or an immature compost crop, such as pearl millet, may be grown at this point.

Year 3: The transplanting of a **legume** (a cold-weather fava bean variety), with the entire crop being harvested at maturity. In addition, we try to grow a quick-maturing 60+-day "catch crop" after the legume harvest whenever possible. Amaranth is an example of this. Or an immature compost crop, such as pearl millet, may be grown at this point.

3-Year Rotation	
Year 1	Immature grain/legume combination for nitrogen in crop biomass & nodules
Year 2	Mature grain for calories and mature biomass
Year 3	Mature legume for soil nitrogen resting

A 2-YEAR ROTATION

Year 1: The transplanting of a **legume** (a cold-weather fava bean variety), with the entire crop being harvested when it is at 10% to 50% flower, so a main-season crop can be planted in time to go to maturity. (Inoculation of the legume with the relevant nitrogen-fixing bacteria for the crop involved will be needed if the soil does not already contain these microbes.)

    Year 2: The transplanting of a **cold-weather grain** (wheat or hull-less barley or hull-less oats or cereal rye or triticale), with the entire crop being harvested at maturity. In areas with a long main growing season, a main-season hot-weather crop is planted afterward to go to maturity. In areas with a short main growing season, we try to grow a quick-maturing 60+-day "catch crop" after the grain harvest whenever possible. Fast-maturing bean varieties are examples of this. Or an immature compost crop, such as pearl millet, may be grown at this point.

ANOTHER TYPE OF 2-YEAR ROTATION

Year 1: The growing of a compost crop **interplanted mixture** (see Ecology Action's Self-Teaching Mini-Series Booklet 14) with **double the amount of seed of cold-weather grains** broadcasted (wheat or hull-less barley or hull-less oats or triticale, and cereal rye) and **legumes** (broadcasted vetch and a sown cold-weather fava bean). The entire crop is harvested when it is immature, so a main-season crop can be planted in time to go to maturity. (Inoculation of the legumes with the relevant nitrogen-fixing bacteria for the crops involved will be needed, if the soil does not already contain these microbes.)

    Year 2: The growing of a compost crop **interplanted mixture** (see Ecology Action's Self-Teaching Mini-Series Booklet 14) of **legumes** (broadcasted vetch and a sown cold-weather fava bean) with **transplanted cold-weather grains** (a different grain from the one grown in Year 1, and cereal rye). The vetch and fava bean crops are removed when they are at 10% to 50% flower, and the entire grain crop is harvested when it is mature. In addition, we try to grow a quick-maturing 60+-day "catch crop" after the grain harvest whenever possible. Fast-maturing bean varieties are examples of this. Or an immature compost crop, such as pearl millet, may be grown at this point.

    Additional years: The same cycling as Year 1 and Year 2 above, with a different grain being used with cereal rye in each succeeding cycle.

2-Year Rotation	
Year 1	Immature legume for nitrogen in crop biomass & nodules
Year 2	Mature grain for calories and mature biomass

Another 2-Year Rotation	
Year 1	Immature grain / legume combination for crop biodiversity and nitrogen in crop biomass & nodules
Year 2	Mature grain for calories & immature legume combination for nitrogen in crop biomass & nodules

Companion Planting

Plant Families for Planning Rotations
(Avoid planting members of the same family in subsequent years.)

BEET FAMILY (Chenopodiaceae) beets / mangels / spinach / chard / orach / quinoa	**PARSLEY FAMILY (Umbelliferae, Apiaceae)** carrots / parsnips / celery / parsley / fennel / coriander / cilantro	**SUNFLOWER FAMILY (Compositae, Asteraceae)** lettuce / endive / sunflower / salsify / artichoke / cardoon / Jerusalem artichoke
ONION FAMILY (Amaryllidaceae, Alliaceae) garlic / onions / leeks / chives	**GRASS FAMILY (Gramineae, Poaceae)** corn / rice / barley / wheat / oats / rye / millet / sorguum	**TOBACCO FAMILY (Solanaceae)** tomatoes / potatoes / peppers / eggplant
PEA FAMILY (Fabaceae, Leguminosae) beans / peas / fava beans* / runner beans / cowpeas / lentils /garbanzos / peanuts	**SQUASH FAMILY (Cucurbitaceae)** cucumbers / gourds / melons, including watermelons / summer squash / winter squash / pumpkins	**COLE FAMILY (Brassicaceae)** broccoli / cabbage / cauliflower / kohlrabi / kale / collards / radish / rutabaga / turnip / mustard
MINT FAMILY (Labiatae, Lamiaceae) basil	**MORNING GLORY FAMILY (Convulvulaceae)** sweet potatoes	**MALO FAMILY (Malvaceae)** okra
AMARANTH FAMILY (Amaranthaceae) amaranth	**LILY FAMILY (Liliaceae)** asparagus	**BUCKWHEAT FAMILY (Polygonaceae)** buckwheat / rhubarb

*Caution: Some people of Mediterranean descent are *fatally allergic* to fava beans, even though the beans are very popular and widely eaten in that area. People on certain medications experience the same reaction. Check with your physician first.

Nourishing the Soil

Over time—Companion planting over time has been known for years as "crop rotation." A major form of this is given in the preceding pages. Another approach used by some is described below.

After properly preparing the soil, heavy feeders are planted. These are followed by heavy givers and then by light feeders. This is a kind of **agricultural recycling** in which people and plants participate to return as much to the soil as has been taken out.

Heavy feeders—most of the vegetables we like and eat (including corn, tomatoes, squash, lettuce, and cabbage)—take large amounts of nutrients, especially nitrogen, from the soil. In the GROW BIO-INTENSIVE method, after harvesting heavy feeders you can return phosphorus and potassium to the soil in the form of compost.

To return nitrogen to the soil, grow heavy givers. Heavy givers are nitrogen-fixing plants or legumes, such as peas, beans, alfalfa, clover, and vetch. Fava beans are also good for this purpose. Not only do they bring large amounts of nitrogen into the soil, they also excrete substances that help eradicate tomato wilt–causing organisms.

After heavy givers, plant light feeders (all root crops) to give the soil a rest before the next heavy feeder onslaught. Three vegetables are low nitrogen lovers: turnips (a light feeder), sweet potatoes (a light feeder), and green peppers (a heavy feeder of nutrients other than nitrogen). The 2 light feeders would normally be planted after heavy givers, which put a lot of nitrogen into the soil. You may find it useful to have them follow a heavy feeder instead. It would also be good to have green peppers follow a heavy feeder. (They normally come after a heavy giver and a light feeder.)[4] You should experiment with these out-of-sequence plantings.

In space—Companion planting of heavy feeders, heavy givers, and light feeders can be done in the same growing area, or space, at the same time. For example, corn, beans, and beets can be intermingled in the same bed. Just as with companion planting over time, you should proceed with care. In this combination, the beans must be bush beans, since pole beans and beets do not grow well together. Also, pole beans have been reported to pull the ears off corn stalks. Sometimes pole beans have been grown successfully with corn, however, and a vegetable such as carrots may be substituted for the beets so you can use the tall beans. When different plants are grown together, you sacrifice some of the living mulch advantage to companion planting "in space" because of the different plant heights. One way to determine the spacing for different plants grown together is to add their spacing together and divide by 2. If you grow corn and beets together, add 15 inches and 4 inches for a total of 19 inches. Divide by 2 and you get a per-plant spacing of 9$^{1}/_{2}$ inches. The beets, then, would be 9$^{1}/_{2}$ inches from each corn plant and vice versa. Each corn plant will be 19 inches from each corn plant and most beet plants will be 9$^{1}/_{2}$ inches from the other beet plants nearest to them. In the drawing below, note that each corn plant gets the 7$^{1}/_{2}$ inches in each direction that it requires for a total growing area with a diameter of 15 inches. Each beet plant, at the same time, gets the 2 inches it requires in each direction for a growing space with a 4-inch diameter.

A spacing example for 3 crops grown together—corn (a heavy feeder), bush beans (a heavy giver), and beets (a light feeder)—is given on page 111. You should note that this approach to companion planting in space uses more bush bean and beet plants than corn plants. Be sure to plant the corn and beet seedlings 2 weeks before the beans, or the beans will retard the others' growth.

An easier, and probably just as effective, method of companion planting in space is to divide your planting bed into separate

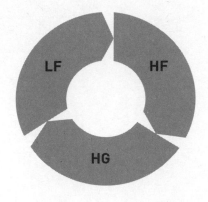

Agricultural recycling: To preserve the soil's nutrients, plant heavy feeders, then heavy givers, then light feeders.

Companion Planting

2-Crop Companion Planting

Circles show average root growth diameters.

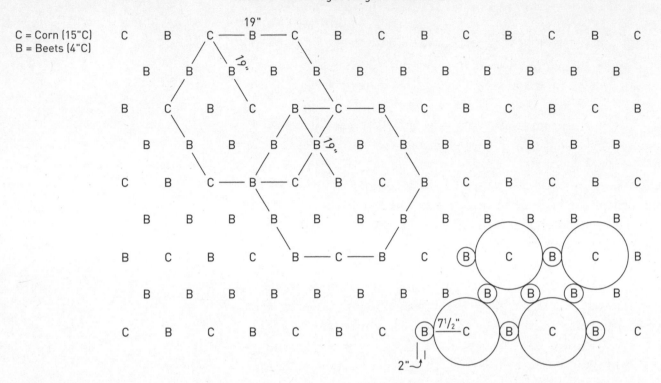

C = Corn (15"C)
B = Beets (4"C)

Multicrop Companion Planting in Space

corn	bush beans	beets	corn	bush beans	beets

Note: When interplanting corn with other crops (e.g. beans and squash), transplant the corn 2 weeks before the other crops, so the corn has time to establish itself first.

sections (or beds within a bed) for each vegetable. In this method, a grouping of corn plants would be next to a group of bush beans and a group of beets. In reality, this is a kind of companion planting over time, since there are heavy feeder, heavy giver, and light feeder sections within a bed. Roots extend 1 to 4 feet around each plant, so it is also companion planting in space. *We recommend you use this approach.* Additional spacing patterns no doubt exist and will be developed for companion planting in space.

Compromise and planning—You can see by now that companion planting involves selecting the combination of factors that works best in your soil and climate. Fortunately, the myriad details fall

Circles show average root growth diameters.

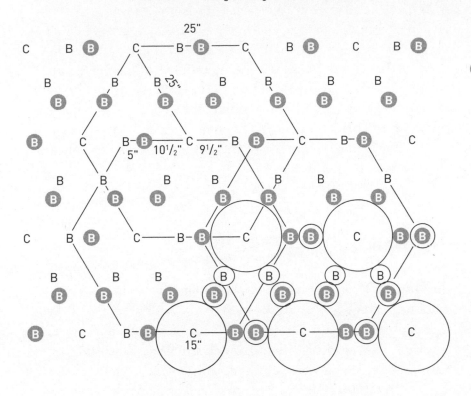

C = Corn (15"C)
B = Beets (4"C)
B = Bush beans (6"C)

into a pattern of simple guidelines. Within the guidelines, however, there are so many possible combinations that the planning process can become quite complex. Be easy on yourself. Do only as much companion planting as is reasonable for you and comes naturally. What you learn this year and become comfortable with can be applied next year, and so on. An easy place to start is with salad vegetables, since these are generally companions. Also, it is easier to companion plant over time rather than in space. Since you probably will not have enough area to use an entire bed for each crop, you might create several heavy feeder, heavy giver, and light feeder sections within each bed. You may want to grow a preponderance of crops from 1 group, such as the heavy feeders. (It is unlikely that you will want to grow one-third of each crop type.) Therefore, you will need to make adjustments, such as adding extra fertilizer and compost, when you follow one heavy feeder with another. Because of lack of space, you may have to grow some plants together that are not companions. If so, you may need to be satisfied with lower yields, lower-quality vegetables, and less-healthy plants. Or you might try to alter your diet so that it is still balanced but more in line with the balances of nature. At any rate, you can see it is useful to plan your garden in advance. You will need to know how many pounds of each vegetable you want during the year, how many plants are needed to grow the weight of vegetables you require, when to plant seeds in flats and in the ground, when and how to rotate your crops, and when to raise and transplant herbs so they will be at the peak of their own special influence. Use the Master Charts in chapter 8 to assist in this work. Herb plants should be reasonably mature when transplanted into a bed for insect control or general beneficial influence to have their optimum effect as companions. Try to plan your garden 12 months at a time, and always at least 3 months in advance.

Physical Complementarity

Note: Using the sun and shade technique is one way to make the most of your plants' physically complementary characteristics.

Lettuce plants can be nestled among other, larger plants for the partial shade they need.

Sun/Shade—Many plants have special needs for sunlight or a lack of it. Cucumbers, for example, are very hard to please. They like heat, moisture, a well-drained soil, and some shade. One way to provide these conditions is to grow cucumbers with corn. The corn plants, which like heat and sun, can provide partial shade for the cucumber plants. Having lettuce or carrot plants nestle among other plants for partial shade is another example. Sunflowers, which are tall and like lots of sun, should be planted at the north side of the garden. There they will receive enough sun for themselves but will not shade other plants.

Shallow/Deep rooting—One example is shallower-rooting beans interplanted with deeper-rooting corn. A dynamic process of improved soil structure occurs over time as plants with root systems of differing depths and breadths work different areas of soil in the planting bed.[5]

Fast/Slow maturing—The French intensive gardeners were able to grow as many as 4 crops in a growing bed at a time due to the staggered growth and maturation rates of different vegetables. The fact that the edible portions of the plants appeared in different vertical locations also helped. Radishes, carrots, lettuce, and cauliflower were grown together in 1 combination used by the French to take advantage of these differences.

Corn can provide the shade that cucumbers enjoy.

Vertical location of the plant's edible portion—See fast/slow maturing illustration, opposite.

Weed, Insect, and Animal Relationships

"Weed" control—The growth of beets, members of the cabbage family, and alfalfa is slowed down significantly by the presence of weeds. To minimize the weed problem for sensitive plants, you can grow other plants during the previous season that discourage "weed" growth in the soil in the current season. Two such plants are kale and rape. Another example is the Mexican marigold (*Tagetes minuta*).[6] "In many instances it has killed even couch grass, convolvulus (wild morning glory), ground ivy, ground elder, horsetail, and other persistent weeds that defy most poisons. Its lethal action works only on starch roots and has no effect on woody ones like roses, fruit bushes, and shrubs. Where it had grown, the soil was enriched as well as cleansed, its texture was refined, and lumps of clay were broken up."[7] Some care should be taken when using this marigold, however, since it might also kill vegetable crops and it does give off toxic excretions. Tests need to be performed to determine how long the influence of these excretions stays with the soil. But to cleanse a soil of pernicious weeds and thereby get it ready for vegetables, *Tagetes minuta* appears to be a useful plant.

Sow thistle grows with lettuce in one example of shallow/deep rooting symbiosis. Their roots do not compete with each other.

Insect and pest control—At least 2 elements are important in companion planting for insect control. First is the use of older plants with well-developed aroma and essential oil accumulations. You want the insects to know the plant is there. Second, it is important to use a large variety of herbs. Five different herbs help discourage the cabbageworm butterfly, although one herb may work better than another in your area. Testing several herbs will help you determine the ones that work best for you. The more "unpleasant" plants there are in the garden, the sooner harmful insects will get the idea that your garden is not a pleasant place to eat and propagate. Using a large number of herbs also fits in with the diversity of plant life favored by nature. Much more research needs to be performed to determine the optimum ages for control plants and the number of control plants per bed. Too few plants will not control an insect problem, and too many may reduce your yields. Some insect controls are:

- Whiteflies: Marigolds—but not pot marigolds (calendula)—and flowering tobacco. The first are supposed to excrete substances from their roots that the other plants absorb. When the whiteflies suck on the other plants, they think they are on a strong-tasting marigold and leave. The flowering tobacco plant has a sticky substance on the underside of its leaves to which whiteflies stick and die when they come for a meal.

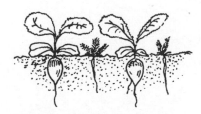

An example of using fast/slow maturing to advantage is to interplant carrots with radishes.

- Ants: Spearmint, tansy, and pennyroyal. Mint often attracts whiteflies, so you may want to grow a few marigolds for control, but not so many as to possibly impair the taste of the mint, and certainly not one of the more poisonous marigolds. This is another area for compromise. A few insects are probably less of a problem than mint with a strange taste.

- Nematodes and root pests: Mexican marigold (*Tagetes minuta*) "eliminates all kinds of destructive eelworms . . . wire worms, millipedes and various root-eating pests from its vicinity." The French marigold (*Tagetes patula*) eliminates some "plant-destroying nematodes . . . at up to a range of three feet . . . The beneficial . . . eelworms which do not feed on healthy roots were not affected."[8]

- Aphids: Yellow nasturtiums are a decoy for black aphids. They may be planted at the base of tomatoes for this purpose. Remove the plants and aphids before the insects begin to produce young with wings. Spearmint, stinging nettle, southernwood, and garlic help repel aphids.

- Tomato worms: Borage reportedly helps repel tomato worms and/or serves as a decoy. Its blue flowers also attract bees.

Gophers—Elderberry cuttings placed in gopher holes and runs reportedly repel these animals. Daffodils, castor beans, and gopher plant (*Euphorbia lathyrus*) are all poisonous to gophers. Be careful with the latter two, however, as they are also *very* toxic to children, especially infants.

Birds, bees, and other animals—Sow thistle attracts birds. Some birds are vegetarian, and some are omnivorous. The omnivorous birds may stay for a main course of insects after a seed snack. If you are having trouble with birds eating the berries in your berry patch, you could erect a wren house in the middle of it. Wrens are insectivores, and they will not bother the berries. But they will attack any bird, however large, that comes near their nest.

Hummingbirds are attracted to red flowers. They especially like the tiny, red, torchlike flowers of the pineapple sage in our garden. Bees may be attracted by hyssop, thyme, catnip, lemon balm, pot marjoram, sweet basil, summer savory, borage, mint, and blue flowers. Once in the garden they help pollinate.

Animals are good for the garden, too. Their manures can be used as fertilizers. Chickens are one of the few reliable controllers of earwigs, sow bugs, pill bugs, snails, grasshoppers, and maggots, though you may have to protect young seedlings from chickens pecking tasty plant morsels.

Companion planting in all its aspects can be a complex and often mind-boggling exercise—if you worry too much about the details. Nature is complex. We can only assist and approximate her in our creations. If we are gentle in relation to her forces and balances, she will correct our errors and fill in for our lack of understanding. As you gain more experience and develop a sensitivity and feeling for gardening, more companion planting details will become clear naturally. Do not let too much planning spoil the fun and excitement of working with nature!

Birds and plants can work together. The sonchus plant seeds attract the finch, which afterward eats aphids from the cabbage.

ENDNOTES

1 Helen Philbrick and Richard B. Gregg, *Companion Plants and How to Use Them* (Old Greenwich, CT: Devin-Adair Company, 1966), pp. 16, 57, 58, 60, 65, 84, 85, 86, 92; and Rudolf Steiner, *Agriculture—A Course of Eight Lectures* (London: Biodynamic Agricultural Association, 1958), pp. 93–95, 97, 99, 100

2 Helen Philbrick and Richard B. Gregg, *Companion Plants and How to Use Them* (Old Greenwich, CT: Devin-Adair Company, 1966), pp. 75–76.

3 Legumes fix atmospheric nitrogen in nodules on their roots during the first part of their growth. As the legume begins to flower and set seed, all of this nitrogen is transferred through the plant and goes into the seed to form protein. In this way, the growing of mature legumes provides a period of "soil nitrogen resting," since nitrogen in the soil is not needed for their growth, provided the appropriate bacteria are present in the soil.

4 This way of looking at crops was developed many years ago. It is based on how much nitrogen crops generally consume or produce. Actually, it is not always accurate. For example, potatoes, a root crop and therefore a light feeder, consume some of the largest amounts of nitrogen. As a result, they are functionally a heavy feeder. Nonetheless, this system can be a way to organize crop rotation. See: Francis Chaboussou, *Healthy Crops* (Charlbury, England: Jon Carpenter Publishing, Alder House, Ox7-3PH, 2004).

5 Also see Emanuel Epstein, "Roots," *Scientific American,* May 1973, pp. 48–58.

6 Illegal in California, where it is considered a noxious weed that aggressively takes over cattle lands and prevents fodder from growing. It is probably also toxic to cattle.

7 Audrey Wynne Hatfield, *How to Enjoy Your Weeds* (New York: Sterling Publishing, 1971).

8 Ibid, p. 17.

9 From *Organic Gardening and Farming,* February 1972, p. 54.

10 From *Organic Gardening and Farming,* February 1972, p. 52–53.

11 Plants in the gourd family.

Common Garden Vegetables, Their Companions, and Their Antagonists[9]		
VEGETABLES	**COMPANIONS**	**ANTAGONISTS**
Asparagus	Tomatoes, parsley, basil	
Beans	Potatoes, carrots, cucumbers, cauliflower, cabbage, summer savory, most other vegetables and herbs	Onions, garlic, gladiolus, chives
Beans, bush	Potatoes, cucumbers, corn, strawberries, celery, summer savory	Onions
Beans, pole	Corn, summer savory, sunflowers	Onions, beets, kohlrabi, cabbage
Beets	Onions, kohlrabi	Pole beans
Cabbage family (cabbage, cauliflower, kale, kohlrabi, broccoli)	Aromatic plants, potatoes, celery, dill, chamomile, sage, peppermint, rosemary, beets, onions	Strawberries, tomatoes, pole beans
Carrots	Peas, leaf lettuce, chives, onions, leeks, rosemary, sage, tomatoes	Dill
Celery	Leeks, tomatoes, bush beans, cauliflower, cabbage	
Chives	Carrots, tomatoes	Peas, beans
Corn	Potatoes, peas, beans, cucumbers, pumpkins, squash	
Cucumbers	Beans, corn, peas, radishes, sunflowers, lettuce	Potatoes, aromatic herbs
Eggplant	Beans, potatoes	
Leeks	Onions, celery, carrots	
Lettuce	Carrots and radishes (lettuce, carrots, and radishes make a strong team grown together), strawberries, cucumbers, onions	
Onions (and garlic)	Beets, strawberries, tomatoes, lettuce, summer savory, leeks, chamomile (sparsely)	Peas, beans
Parsley	Tomatoes, asparagus	
Peas	Carrots, turnips, radishes, cucumbers, corn, beans, most vegetables and herbs	Onions, garlic, gladiolus, potatoes, chives
Peppers	Basil, okra	
Potatoes	Beans, corn, cabbage, horse radish (should be planted at the corners of the patch), marigolds, eggplant (as a lure for the Colorado potato beetle)	Pumpkins, squash, cucumbers, sunflowers, tomatoes, raspberries
Pumpkins	Corn	Potatoes
Radishes	Peas, nasturtiums, lettuce, cucumbers	
Soybeans	Grows with anything, helps everything	
Spinach	Strawberries	
Squash	Nasturtiums, corn	
Strawberries	Bush beans, spinach, borage, lettuce (as a border), onions	Cabbage
Sunflowers	Cucumbers	Potatoes
Tomatoes	Chives, onions, parsley, asparagus, marigolds, nasturtiums, carrots	Kohlrabi, potatoes, fennel, cabbage
Turnips	Peas	

A Companionate Herbal for the Organic Garden[10]	
A list of herbs, their companions, and their uses, including some beneficial weeds and flowers.	
Basil	Companion to tomatoes; dislikes rue intensely; improves growth and flavor; repels flies and mosquitoes
Bee balm	Companion to tomatoes; improves growth and flavor
Borage	Companion to tomatoes, squash, and strawberries; deters tomato worms; improves growth and flavor
Caraway	Plant here and there; loosens soil
Catnip	Plant in borders; deters flea beetles
Chamomile	Companion to cabbage and onions; improves growth and flavor
Chervil	Companion to radishes; improves growth and flavor
Chives	Companion to carrots; improves growth and flavor
"Dead" nettle	Companion to potatoes; deters potato bugs; improves growth and flavor
Dill	Companion to cabbage; improves growth and health of cabbage; dislikes carrots
Fennel	Plant away from gardens; disliked by most plants
Flax	Companion to carrots and potatoes; deters potato bugs; improves growth and flavor
Garlic	Plant near roses and raspberries; deters Japanese beetles; improves growth and health
Henbit	General insect repellent
Horseradish	Plant at the corners of a potato patch to deter potato bugs
Hyssop	Deters cabbage moths; companion to cabbage and grapes; keep away from radishes
Lamb's quarters	An edible weed; allow to grow in moderate amounts, especially with corn
Lemon balm	Distribute throughout the garden
Lovage	Improves flavor and health of plants if planted here and there
Marigolds	A workhorse among pest deterrents; plant throughout the garden; discourages Mexican bean beetles, nematodes, and other insects
Marjoram	Plant here and there; improves flavor
Mint	Companion to cabbage and tomatoes; improves health and flavor; deters white cabbage moths
Mole plant	Deters moles and mice if planted here and there
Nasturtium	Companion to radishes, cabbage, and cucurbits[11]; plant under fruit trees; deters aphids, squash bugs, and striped pumpkin beetles; improves growth and flavor
Peppermint	Planted among cabbages to repel white cabbage butterflies

continued

Companion Planting

A Companionate Herbal for the Organic Garden, *continued*	
Petunia	Protects beans
Pigweed	Among the best weeds for pumping nutrients from the subsoil; good for potatoes, onions, and corn; keep weeds thinned
Pot marigold (Calendula)	Companion to tomatoes, but plant elsewhere also; deters asparagus beetles, tomato worms, and general garden pests
Purslane	This edible weed makes good ground cover among corn
Rosemary	Companion to cabbage, beans, carrots, and sage; deters cabbage moths, bean beetles, and carrot flies
Rue	Keep far away from sweet basil; plant near roses and raspberries; deters Japanese beetles
Sage	Plant with rosemary, cabbage, and carrots; deters cabbage moth and carrot fly; keep away from cucumbers
Southernwood	Plant here and there in the garden; companion to cabbage; improves growth and flavor; deters cabbage moths
Sow thistle	Plant in moderation with tomatoes, onions, and corn
Summer savory	Plant with beans and onions; improves growth and flavor; deters bean beetles
Tansy	Plant under fruit trees; companion to roses and raspberries; deters flying insects, Japanese beetles, striped cucumber beetles, squash bugs, and ants
Tarragon	Plant throughout the garden
Thyme	Plant here and there in the garden; deters cabbage worms
Valerian	Plant anywhere in the garden
Wild morning glory	Plant with corn
Wormwood	Plant as a border to deter animals
Yarrow	Plant along borders, paths, and near aromatic herbs; enhances essential oil production

AN INTERRELATED FOOD-RAISING SYSTEM: Creating and Caring for a Balanced Natural Ecosystem with Insect Life

Insects and people are only part of the complex, interrelated world of life. Both are important, integral parts of its living dynamism. Insects are an important part of the diet for many birds, toads, and frogs, and for some insects in nature's complex food chain. The GROW BIOINTENSIVE method reminds you that every time you relate to an insect you are relating to the whole system of life, and that if you choose to dominate the insect population, rather than work in harmony with it, part of the system dies. For example, we depend on insects to pollinate many of our vegetables, fruits, flowers, herbs, fibers, and cover crops. When we choose dominating, death-oriented control, then the scope and depth of our lives become narrower and smaller. We are actually detracting from our lives rather than adding to them. In trying to isolate an insect and deal with it separately out of relation to the ecosystem in which it lives, we work against nature, which in turn works against us in counterproductive results.

When an excess of insects appears in a garden, nature is indicating that a problem exists in the life of that garden. In each case, we need to become sensitive to the source of the imbalance. Observation and gentle action will produce the best results. In contrast, when a heavy-handed approach is taken and poisons are used, beneficial predators are killed as well as the targeted harmful insects. Spraying trees to eliminate worms or beetles often results in a secondary outbreak of spider mites or aphids because ladybugs and other predators cannot reestablish themselves as quickly as the destructive species.

Paying attention to the soil and to plant health, planning a varied environment, and leaving a few wild spaces for unexpected benefactors minimize pest losses more effectively than the use of poison. Also, in order to have beneficial insects in your food-producing area, you must provide food for them—which may be some of the harmful insects! If there are no harmful insects to feed them, then there will be few, if any, beneficial insects around to act as friendly guardians for your garden. This seeming paradox—the need for both kinds of insects for the healthiest garden—is symbolic of nature's balances. Not too much moisture, but enough. Not too much aeration, but enough. Not too many harmful insects, but enough. You find the need for these balances everywhere—in the compost pile, in the soil, in the mini-climate, and in the backyard microcosm as a whole.

In a small backyard garden ecosystem or mini-farm, it is especially important to welcome all life-forms as much as possible. Ants destroy fruit fly and housefly larvae and keep the garden cleared of rotting debris. Have you ever squashed a snail and watched how the ants come to whisk the remains away almost within a day? Earwigs are carnivorous and prey on other insects. Tachinid flies parasitize caterpillars, earwigs, tomato worms, and grasshoppers by laying their eggs in them. We've found cabbage worms immobilized and bristling with cottony white torpedoes the size of a pinhead—larvae of the braconid wasp, which will hatch and go in search of more cabbage worms. Toads eat earwigs, slugs, and other pests. Chickens control earwigs, sowbugs, and flies. Even the ancient and fascinating snails have a natural predator: humans!

The first step in insect control is to cultivate strong, vigorous plants by cultivating a healthy place where they can grow. Normally (about 90% of the time), insects only attack unhealthy plants. Just as a healthy person who eats good food is less susceptible to disease, so are healthy plants on a good diet less susceptible to plant disease and insect attack. The insect is not the source of the problem, but rather an unhealthy soil is. The soil needs your energy, not the insect. The uninterrupted growth that the GROW BIOINTENSIVE method stresses is also important to maintaining plant health. We are shepherds providing the conditions our plants need for healthy, vigorous growth.

Here are some elements to consider when caring for your garden's health:

- Did you dig the soil properly?

- Are the proper plant nutrients available in the soil?

- Did you use enough compost?

- Is the soil pH within reasonable limits for the plant being grown?

- Did you transplant the seedlings properly?

- Are you watering the plants properly?

- Are you weeding effectively?

- Are you maintaining the soil in a way that will enable it to retain moisture and nutrients?

- Are the plants receiving enough sun?

- Are you growing the plants in season?

Another factor that aids plant health and minimizes insect and disease problems is keeping a correct balance of phosphorus and potash in the soil in relation to the amount of nitrogen present. The optimal ratio among these elements is still to be determined. Research also needs to be completed to determine the minimum amounts of these elements (in pounds per 100 square feet) that should be in the soil. (Smaller amounts of organic fertilizer elements are required in comparison with soluble synthetic chemical fertilizers, since they break down more slowly and remain available to the plants for a longer period of time.)

Properly planning the garden can eliminate many insect and disease problems.

- Use seeds that grow well in your climate and soil.

- Use plant varieties that are weather hardy, insect resistant, and disease resistant. New strains, especially hybrids (whether developed for higher yields, disease resistance, or other reasons), should usually be avoided. Some hybrids produce foods of lower nutritive value in comparison with older strains, and often use up nutrients from the soil at a more rapid rate than a living soil can sustain over time. Hybrids also tend to be very susceptible to a few diseases even when they are greatly resistant to many prevalent ones.

- Companion plant. Grow vegetables and flowers together that grow well with each other.

- Avoid putting the same vegetable in the same growing bed each year. This practice invites disease.

- Rotate your crops; follow heavy feeders with heavy givers and then light feeders.

Natural Predators

Encourage natural insect control by enlisting the aid of Nature.

Birds—Some are vegetarians. Others are omnivorous. A bird that stops for a seed snack may remain for an insect dinner. A house wren feeds 500 spiders and caterpillars to her young in an afternoon; a brown thrasher consumes 6,000 insects a day; a chickadee eats 138,000 cankerworm eggs in 25 days; and a pair of flickers eats 5,000 ants as a snack. A Baltimore oriole can consume 17 hairy caterpillars in a minute. You can encourage the presence of birds with moving water, by planting bushes for their protection, by planting sour berry bushes for food, and by growing plants that have seeds they like to eat.

Toads, snakes, and spiders—They also eat insects and other garden pests. Toads eat as many as 10,000 insects in 3 months, including cutworms, slugs, crickets, ants, caterpillars, and squash bugs.

Ladybugs—These beetles are good predators in your garden since they eat a single particular pest, aphids, and do not eat beneficial insects. Ladybugs eat 40 to 50 insects per day, and their larvae eat even more.

Praying mantids—These predators should only be used in infestation emergencies, since they eat beneficial as well as harmful insects. They are not selective and even eat each other.

Trichogramma wasps—They lay their eggs in hosts, such as moth and butterfly larvae, that eat leaves. When they hatch, the wasp larvae parasitize the host larvae, which fail to reach maturity. Up to 98% of the hosts are rendered useless in this way.

Tachinid flies—These parasites help control caterpillars, Japanese beetles, earwigs, gypsy moths, brown-tail moths, tomato worms, and grasshoppers.

Syrphid flies—These parasites prey upon aphids and help pollinate crops.[1]

After you have done everything possible to provide a healthy, balanced garden for your plants, you may still have insect problems. If so, you should approach the unwanted insects with the idea of living control rather than elimination. If there is a problem, identify the pest and try to determine whether an *environmental change* can solve the problem. In our research garden, we have minimized (not eliminated, though) gophers by introducing gopher snakes.

The pocket Golden Guides *Insects and Insect Pests* are invaluable guides for getting to know the creatures that inhabit your garden. Out of the 86,000 species of insects in the United States, 76,000 are considered beneficial or friendly.[2] So, be careful! An insect that looks ugly or malicious may be a friend. If you can't seem to find an obvious culprit for your problem, try exploring at night with a flashlight. Many predators are active then.

Ask yourself whether the damage is extensive enough to warrant a policing effort. During 1972, we grew bush beans in one of our test beds. The primary leaves were almost entirely destroyed by the twelve-spotted cucumber beetle. But in most cases the damage was not so rapid as to prevent the development of healthy secondary leaves. The less tender secondary leaves were ultimately attacked and quite heavily eaten. About 80% of the secondary leaf area remained, however, and we harvested very tasty, unblemished beans. The yield in pounds was still 3.9 times the United States average! Recent tests have shown that leaf damage of up to 30% by insects can actually increase the yield in some crops. You may decide to sacrifice some yield for beauty; many destructive caterpillars become beautiful butterflies. To get the yield you want and/or to encourage the presence of butterflies, you can plant extra plants of the crops they like.

We often underestimate the ability of plants to take care of themselves. The damage done by insects often affects only a very small percentage of the edible crop. Because of this, many GROW BIOINTENSIVE gardeners plant a little extra for the insect world to eat. This practice is beautiful, mellow, and in keeping with life-giving forms of insect control. Furthermore, extensive research has shown that beneficial organisms found in soil and ocean environments can withstand stress, in the form of temperature, pressure, pH, and nutrient fluctuations, to a much greater degree in an organically fertilized medium than in a synthetically fertilized medium. I suspect researchers will come to a similar conclusion about plant resistance to insect attack.

Any time an insect or other pest invades your garden, there is an opportunity to learn more about nature's cycles and balances. Learn why they are there and find a *living control.* Look for controls that will affect only the harmful insect. Protect new seedlings from birds and squirrels with netting or chicken wire, trap earwigs in dry dark places, wash aphids off with a strong spray of water, or block ants with a sticky barrier of Vaseline, Tanglefoot Pest Barrier, or a tack trap. While you are doing this, continue to strive for a long-term natural balance in your growing area.

At our Common Ground Research Garden, only 3 pest problems have taken a lot of our energy: snails, slugs, and gophers. The first few years we primarily trapped gophers. A lot of time was spent checking and resetting traps and worrying about them, yet the gophers probably only damaged about 5% of our crop. We later found that, in addition to gopher snakes, they really do not like certain things placed in their holes (sardines, garlic juice, fish heads, male urine, and dead gophers). The gophers may also be blocked with strips of daffodils. Daffodils contain arsenic in their bulbs and can discourage them. Gopher snakes, of course, prevent a population explosion. A combination of approaches and gentle persistence paid off.

We have a simple routine for snails and slugs. At the end of the spring rains we go out at night with flashlights and collect gallons of them. We drop the snails in buckets of soapy water, which kills them. If we use soap that is quick to degrade, we can dump them on the compost pile the next day. We catch most of them in the first 3 nights. Going out occasionally over the next 2 weeks, we can catch new ones that were too small to get in the first sweep or that have just hatched from eggs laid in the soil. Such a concentrated cleanup can be effective for several months. The red-bellied snake eats large numbers of slugs. A sorghum mulch is reported to repel slugs as well.

Another kind of problem has been solved through observation. For example, one year a cherry tomato bed was wilting. Several people, including a graduate student studying insects, told us it was caused by nematodes. When we dug down into the soil to look for the damage, we discovered the real source. The soil was bone dry below the upper 8 inches. A good soaking took care of the problem, and we learned not to take gardening advice on faith, but to always check it out for ourselves—as we hope you will.

Other Initiatives

Here are some other living control approaches to try:

Hand-picking—You can pick the insects from plants once you are certain the insect involved is harmful and is the source of the problem. Some insects are only harmful in one stage and can even be beneficial in other stages.

Spraying—In general, insects may be divided into two categories—those that chew and bite plants and those that suck juices from them.

- Chewing or biting insects include caterpillars, flea beetles, potato bugs, cankerworms, cutworms, and grasshoppers. Aromatic and distasteful substances such as garlic, onion, and pepper sprays can discourage them.

- Sucking insects include aphids, thrips, squash bug nymphs, flies, and scale insects. Soap solutions (not detergents, which would damage the plant and soil as well as the insects), clear miscible oil solutions, and other solutions that asphyxiate the insects by coating their tender bodies and preventing respiration through body spiracles or breathing holes help control these insects.

Traps—Some traps, such as shredded newspaper in clay pots turned upside down on sticks in the garden, will attract earwigs during daylight hours. Snails, slugs, sowbugs, and symphylans can be trapped under damp boards or sweet potatoes cut in half lengthways. They retreat to these places in the heat and light of the day.

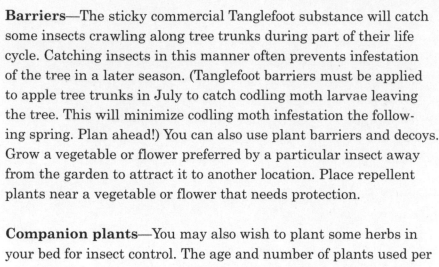

Barriers—The sticky commercial Tanglefoot substance will catch some insects crawling along tree trunks during part of their life cycle. Catching insects in this manner often prevents infestation of the tree in a later season. (Tanglefoot barriers must be applied to apple tree trunks in July to catch codling moth larvae leaving the tree. This will minimize codling moth infestation the following spring. Plan ahead!) You can also use plant barriers and decoys. Grow a vegetable or flower preferred by a particular insect away from the garden to attract it to another location. Place repellent plants near a vegetable or flower that needs protection.

Companion plants—You may also wish to plant some herbs in your bed for insect control. The age and number of plants used per 100 square feet determine the herb's effectiveness. A young plant does not have an aroma or root exudate strong enough to discourage harmful insects or to attract beneficial ones. Similarly, too few herbs will not control a pest or attract a needed predator. But too many herbs may retard vegetable growth and yield. Composite flowers, such as pot marigolds (calendulas) and sunflowers, are excellent attractants for predatory insects because their large supplies of pollen serve as predator food sources. A few (2 to 4) plants per 100-square-foot bed will probably suffice. We have not done many experiments with them yet, since accurate testing can take 2 to 3 years for 1 herb grown with 1 food plant to control 1 insect. You may wish to try some of these biodynamic observations, though. It's a lot of fun to try to see for yourself!

Probably the most important form of insect control with plants is just diverse cropping. The GROW BIOINTENSIVE method we use utilizes diverse cropping, and we have only experienced 5% to 10% crop loss due to pests. Biodynamic gardeners and farmers also use diverse cropping and have suggested planting 10% more area to make up for crop losses. In contrast, the monocropped acreage of today's commercial agriculture provides an ideal uniform habitat for widespread attack by pests that favor a single crop. Pesticides have been used to counteract the problem inherent in monocropping. Yet the Environmental Protection Agency estimated that in 1940, "American farmers used 50 million pounds of pesticides and lost 7% of their crop before harvest," and that by 1970, 12 times more pesticides were used, "yet the percentage of crops lost before harvest has almost doubled."[3] Today, about 30 times more pesticides are used than in 1940, and the percentage of crops lost to insects has been estimated to be as high as 37%. In fact, many pesticides targeted for a single pest species actually cause increases in numbers of nontargeted pests. By their action on the physiology of the plant, pesticides can make a plant more nutritionally favorable to insects, thereby increasing the fertility and longevity of feeding pests.[4]

Insect Pests and Plant Controls[5]	
INSECT PEST	**PLANT CONTROL**
Ants	Spearmint, tansy, pennyroyal
Aphids	Nasturtium, spearmint, stinging nettle, southernwood, garlic
Black flea beetle	Wormwood, mint
Blackfly	Intercropping, stinging nettle
Cabbageworm butterfly	Sage, rosemary, hyssop, thyme, mint, wormwood, southernwood
Colorado potato beetle	Eggplant, flax, green beans
Cutworm	Oak leaf mulch, tanbark
Flies	Nut trees, rue, tansy, spray of wormwood and/or tomato
Japanese beetle	White geranium, datura
June bug grub	Oak leaf mulch, tanbark
Malaria mosquito	Wormwood, southernwood, rosemary
Mexican bean beetle	Potatoes
Mosquito	Legumes
Moths	Sage, santolina, lavender, mint, stinging nettle, herbs
Plant lice	Castor bean, sassafras, pennyroyal
Potato bugs	Flax, eggplant
Slugs	Oak leaf mulch, tanbark
Squash bugs	Nasturtium
Striped cucumber beetle	Radish
Weevils	Garlic
Woolly aphids	Nasturtium
Worms in goats	Carrots
Worms in horses	Tansy leaves, mulberry leaves

Natural Ecosystem

It is evident that pesticides are not an effective solution for crop losses due to pests. Diverse cropping without pesticides may be able to reduce total pest losses more than monocropping with pesticides, even in large-scale agriculture. Using standard agricultural practices, Cornell University researchers, in a 5-year study completed in 1970, found that without pesticides the insect population could be cut in half when only 2 crops were grown together.[6] You can do this when you grow a diversity of plants in your backyard with life-giving techniques!

This introduction to insect control has emphasized philosophy and general approaches. Philbrick's *Companion Plants and How to Use Them,* Hunter's *Gardening Without Poisons,* and Philbrick's *The Bug Book* (see Insect Life and Balance section in online Bibliography at www.growbiointensive.org) have already vigorously explored the spectrum of organic insect control in detail. These books provide companion planting combinations, recipes for insect control solutions, and addresses for buying predatory insects.

I hope each person who reads this book will plant at least one small, 3 by 3-foot grow biointensive bed. You will find the experience fun and exciting beyond your wildest expectations!

ENDNOTES

1   Beatrice Trum Hunter, *Gardening Without Poisons* (New York: Berkeley Publishing Corp., 1971), pp. 31, 37, 42, 43, 48.

2   Ibid., p. 28.

3   James S. Turner, "A Chemical Feast: Report on the Food and Drug Administration" (Ralph Nader Study Group Reports) (New York: Grossman, 1970). Cited in Frances Moore Lappe and Joseph Collins, *Food First* (Boston: Houghton Mifflin Company, 1977), p. 49.

4   Francis Chaboussou, *Healthy Crops: A New Agricultural Revolution* (Charlsbury, UK: John Carpenter Publishing for The Gaia Foundation, 2004).

5   Helen Philbrick and Richard B. Gregg, *Companion Plants and How to Use Them* (Old Greenwich, CT: Devon-Adair Company, 1966), pp. 52–53. This book and others should be consulted for the proper use and application rates of these plant remedies. Improper use or application can cause problems and could be harmful to you, your plants, and animals.

6   Jeff Cox, "The Technique That Halves Your Insect Population," *Organic Gardening and Farming,* May 1973, pp. 103–104.

MASTER CHARTS AND PLANNING

The Master Charts that follow should help your gardening
efforts. The charts for grains, compost crops, trees, and other
crops provide a picture of what you can accomplish in your
own backyard or small farm-holding. (Also see Ecology Action's *The
Backyard Homestead, Mini-Farm and Garden Log Book.*) Additional information about special seed sources and harvesting, clean-
ing, grinding, storing, and preserving these crops will be included
in the future. The charts are largely based on our many years of
experience and are generally complete and accurate.

Ecology Action continues to study the spacings and other growing information for grains, fodder crops, fibers, bush and dwarf
fruit trees, other tree crops, berries and grapes, and compost crops.
As testing continues, the information is revised and the chance
of error reduced. (A good explanation of the information in these
charts is given in the planning section of *The Sustainable Vegetable
Garden.*)

It should be noted that:

- You may not reach maximum yields in the first year. Also,
  1 plant grown alone will probably not produce as large a yield

Note: Microbial life-forms thrive and greatly increase in activity when the nighttime air temperature reaches a minimum of 60°F. The next time you go out in the morning early in the season and notice that your garden has grown a foot overnight and is a darker, lush green, check the previous night's temperature. You may be surprised!

Other Key Air Temperatures

32°F:	Nitrogen release begins in the soil.
50°F:	Significant nitrogen release occurs in the soil.
86°–95°F:	The maximum nitrogen release point is reached in the soil.
90°F:	The pollination process begins to decrease.
95°–104°F:	A significant decrease in nitrogen release occurs in the soil.
131°F:	Nitrogen release stops in the soil.

as 1 plant grown among several plants under mini-climate conditions.[1]

• Seeds grown out of season will take longer to germinate and/or may decompose before they do germinate unless grown under special mini-greenhouse or shade netting conditions.

• Closer spacing may be needed during the winter to make up for slower plant growth during this period and to create a balanced winter mini-climate. (Try three-quarters or one-half the usual spacing with lettuce in the winter.) Closer spacing can also promote faster, balanced growth by more rapidly creating a mini-climate. Thin any extra plants to make room for larger plants. (Baby carrots and beets are a delicacy.)

• You may need wider spacings in the humid tropics during the wetter months.

One of the exciting things about the GROW BIOINTENSIVE method is its emphasis on the soil. Once you know how to prepare soil well for vegetables, a whole world of crops becomes available to you. The bed preparation, fertilization, and watering approaches remain essentially the same—only the plant spacings are different!

These charts will help you expand from growing only vegetable crops to including plants from the following broad groups:

• Grains, protein sources, and vegetable oil crops.

• Compost, organic matter, and fodder crops. Some compost crops, such as pearl millet, sorghum, and corn, can produce very high yields of biomass and should be fully recycled through composting whenever possible to minimize the potential for soil depletion.

• Energy, fiber, paper, and miscellaneous crops.

• Tree and cane food crops.

Eventually, we hope to add tree crops for fuel and building materials. If you seek more information than is contained in these detailed charts, refer to the books listed on the Ecology Action website.

There is a convenient soil improvement succession that is good to know. Vegetables from one year improve soil for grains the next year, and this leads to soil that supports more permanent tree crops the third year. If you want to study this process more closely, see Ecology Action's *The Backyard Homestead, Mini-Farm and Garden Log Book* for vegetable, grain, fodder, and tree crops, and read our *One Crop Test Booklet: Soybeans* (Booklet 2).

The importance of the soil is especially apparent with a permanent crop-growing system. Even biological and tree cultivation systems can be environmentally unsound if improperly used. Dr. Hans Jenny, soil scientist emeritus at the University of California, Berkeley, pointed to this in *Science* magazine:

> "At the turn of the century, farsighted agricultural experiment stations set up permanent cultivation plots and monitored for decades the nitrogen and carbon balances. Stirring soil and removing crops initiated profound declines in nitrogen, carbon, and humus substances and caused deterioration of soil structure. Under these circumstances water infiltration is reduced and runoff and sheet erosion are encouraged. Crop yields suffer. While applications of nitrogen fertilizers boost yields, they have not restored the soil body. In central Europe, farmers used to remove forest litter and put it on their fields for manuring. Tree production declined markedly, documented by Aaltonen.[2]
>
> I am arguing against indiscriminate conversion of biomass and organic wastes to fuels. The humus capital, which is substantial, deserves being maintained because good soils are a national asset. The question will be raised, How much organic matter should be assigned to the soil? No general formula can be given. Soils vary widely in character and quality."

Growing crops must be approached, then, with a sensitivity to how the way they are being grown affects the sustainability of the soil's vitality and health. Understanding this proper relationship will take time and eventually will involve growing many different crops, including a large number of trees. Trees beneficially modify our climate, bring up and make available nutrients from deep down in the soil, protect the soil from erosion, help maintain healthy water tables, and provide us with food and building materials.

Food value columns have been added to the Master Charts for protein, calories, and calcium for each crop. These are important, but so are many other food values—including iron, vitamins, and amino acids. See the reference books listed in the bibliography if you want to pursue this further. Be sure to explore growing compost crops in between your trees to increase the soil's friability and its nitrogen and organic matter content. Try medium red clover. It has beautiful red flowers.

Note: GROW BIOINTENSIVE techniques can be used to grow important protein crops. Experiments with wheat, soybeans, grains, beans, and other seeds have worked well. For information on how to grow your own open-pollinated seeds in the smallest area while preserving genetic diversity, see Ecology Action's Self-Teaching Mini-Series, Booklet 13, *Growing to Seed*.

Note: Wheat can be threshed easily with a mini-thresher[3] made available by a public organization in your area.

Master Charts

Increasingly, more people want to grow food. One hundred square feet of grain may yield 4, 8, 12, or more pounds of edible seed. If you are in a cooler climate and wish to grow beans for eating, try varieties such as the peanut, yellow-eye, and cranberry beans available from the Vermont Bean Seed Company. Dwarf fruit trees, if nurtured properly, can yield 50 to 100 pounds of fruit annually at maturity. Two trees on 8-foot centers in 100 square feet can have a combined yield of up to 200 pounds, and the average person in the United States eats only about 162 pounds of tree fruit per year. Fava beans may yield the greatest amount of organic matter. Alfalfa and clover are also fun to raise as nitrogen-fixing legumes to improve your soil's fertility.

Our goal with wheat is to eventually get two 26-pound crops in an 8-month period. This would yield one 1-pound loaf of bread for every week in the year from only 100 square feet! Then we could literally raise our own bread in our backyards. Sound impossible? Yields close to this are already occurring in some parts of the world. Our highest wheat yield to date is at the rate of about 21 pounds per 100-square-foot bed, using about 10 inches of water for the whole season, with compost we grew ourselves for fertilizer and a small amount of purchased organic fertilizer. The Zulus in South Africa use a technique similar to the GROW BIOINTENSIVE method and grow grains with natural rainfall. See what you can do! Let us know if you get to 26 pounds—and tell us how you do it!

When planning your garden, remember to look closely at all the factors involved. For example, sesame seeds are very high in nutrition, but they usually have low yields (compared with other protein crops), are somewhat difficult to harvest, and exhaust the soil. So on a per-square-foot, sustainable-nutrition yield basis, sesame seeds are not particularly superior to other protein sources, even though they are great nutritionally and good to eat. A large harvest of sesame seeds would also require a very large growing area. It is important to examine each crop's total practicality.

When you begin to produce intermediate yields, another factor to consider is the quantity of nutrients each crop takes from the soil. Many legumes, which fix nitrogen in the soil, can exhaust the soil of other nutrients over time. Soybeans are such plants, and continuous cropping of them has been demonstrated to wear out the soil. It is important to develop and work within natural sustainable cycles.

Note: In Column Z of the Master Charts additional information is indicated, including an expected "refuse" percentage. For instance, it is 12% for green beans and 25% for leeks. If you harvest these in the most timely way, there need be virtually not refuse. Do keep the potential refuse factor in mind, as personal preferences may involve some refuse in the preparation of the food, and even more than the amount indicated. It is interesting to realize that "Irish" potatoes have most of their vitamins and minerals in and just underneath the skin, so if you "peel" the potatoes, which have a 19% refuse percentage, you will have a disproportionate amount of nutrients lost compared to the weight of the peels.

Letter Codes

A	Approximate germination rate as sold by seed companies. No known minimum legal germination rate. Can be higher or lower.	**R**	Replant at points where germination fails. We call this "spotting."
AA	Each "seed" contains about 3 seeds, of which half germinate.	**S**	Short-germinating seed (1 to 7 days).
AC	Harvest alfalfa and clover 2 to 4 inches above the growing crown (sheep shears work well for this), loosen the soil with a border fork, water the bed, and cover the growing area with shade netting cloth for 1 to 2 weeks.	**SN**	During hot weather, cover with shade netting cloth between approximately 10 a.m. and 5 p.m. for better results.
		SP	Spring.
B	In beds.	**SU**	Summer.
BB	Soak seeds overnight for best germination.	**T**	Tablespoon.
BC	Broadcast.	**t**	Teaspoon.
C	Centers.	**TO**	18 inches for cherry tomatoes; 21 inches for regular tomatoes; 24 inches for large tomatoes. Sequential information in columns D, H, and I should be used according to spacing chosen.
c	Cups.		
CA	Cantaloupe.		
D	Do not know yet.	**U**	One 1-pound loaf of bread requires 2/3 pound flour (2 1/2 cups).
E	Spacing increases with warmth of climate.		
EL	Extra-long-germinating seed (22 to 28 days).	**V**	Approximate minimum.
F	In flats.	**W**	12 or 15 inches for midget varieties; 18 inches for 5- to 7-pound varieties; 21 inches for 10- to 15-pound varieties; 24 inches for largest varieties.
FA	Fall.		
G	"Seed" is a seed packet of 2 to 6 seeds, of which approximately 1.62 germinate.	**WI**	Winter.
		Y	Estimate.
H	Honeydew.	**Z**	Based on Ecology Action experience, half of the garlic cloves are large enough to use, on the average.
I	Transplant into a 1- to 5-gallon container as appropriate. Raise sapling until 1 year old. Then transplant into soil.		
		*	Digestible protein for animals.
J	Germination average in a laboratory.	******	Depending on variety selected.
K	Straw weight is generally 1 to 3+ times harvested and cleaned seed weight for GROW BIOINTENSIVEly grown grains, 1 to 2 times for grains grown with commercial agriculture (Roger Revelle, "The Resources Available for Agriculture," *Scientific American,* September 1976).	**—**	Not applicable.
		#	First set of figures: summer sowing in a shade netting house for fall set out, or winter sowing in areas with a less cold winter and in a greenhouse for spring set out. (A shade netting house is an area generally covered with 30% shade netting to provide a cooler, more humid area for the protected raising of fall seedlings during hot weather.) 　　Second set of figures: winter sowing in a good greenhouse or a miniature greenhouse in areas with very cold winters for spring set out. 　　Harden off for 2 days outside in flat before transplanting into bed.
L	Long-germinating seed (8 to 21 days).		
LG	Transplant seedling when larger—about 6 to 9 inches tall.		
M	Cook to minimize oxalic acid, which ties up calcium.		
N	Narrow bed (2 feet wide) will produce better yields due to improved pollination.		
P	Perennial.		
Q	Celery is pricked out into a third flat, 6 inches deep, on 2-inch centers, where it grows for a further 4 to 6 weeks until it is ready to be transplanted. The seedlings may be 4 inches tall. Overall, it takes 3 to 4 months from sowing until transplanting.	**##**	If direct sowing on centers, rather than broadcasting, plant 2 seeds per center to compensate for low germination rate.
		+	Yield may be significantly higher.
		++	Given harvest time in column O.
qt	Quarts.	**+++**	Overall yields similar, but highest dry biomass and seed yields on *smallest* center. Largest seed, which is easiest to dehull, is on largest center.

Visit growbiointensive.org/footnotes/ for downloadable pdfs of this page and pages 177–179. If you print them doublesided and laminate them, the result is a Master Chart Bookmark set that can be used to quickly and easily access the codes and footnotes.

Master Charts

CROP	A — Approx. No. Seeds per Ounce[4] (Range: larger–smaller seed)	B — Minimum Legal Germination Rate[5]	C — Ounces / Volume Seed per 100 Square Feet (adj. for germ. rate, offset spacing, and curv. surf.)[6,7,8]	D — Short/Long/Extra-Long Germination Time	E — Plant Initially in Flats/Beds; Space in First Flat (in order of preference)	F — Approx. No. of Plants per Flat (adj. for germ. rate)[14]	G — No. First Flat(s) per 100 Sq Ft	H — Approx. No. Weeks in First Flat[16]	I — Depth of Second Flat and Spacing (Inches)	J — No. Plants in Second Flat[14]	K — No. Second Flats per 100 Sq Ft	L — Approx. No. Weeks in Second Flat[16]	M — In-Bed Spacing (Inches)	N — MAXIMUM No. Plants per 100 Square Feet[7]
1 Artichoke, Jerusalem	Sprouted 2 oz tuber pieces	—	10.5 lbs / —	L	F/B–use 6" deep flat. Put tubers as close as possible.	Put tubers as close as possible.	3	3–4	—	—	—	—	15 (centers) / 6 (depth)	84
2 Artichoke, Regular	From divided roots or seeds	Seeds: .70[A]	3 roots / —	L	Seeds: F Roots: B Seeds 1	Seeds 175	Small part of 1 flat	Seeds 3–4	6 / 2	60	Small part of flat	12–16	72	3
3 Asparagus	875–1,250	.70	.32 / 1 t or 159 roots	L	Seeds: F 1 Roots: B	175	0.9	D	6 / 2	60	2.65	D	12	159
4 Basil	12,000	.60	.09 / 1 t	L	F:BC	175	0.9	1–2	3 / 1.5	111	5.6	3	6	621
5 Beans, Lima, Bush	Baby: 75–90 Regular: 25–38	.70	Regular: 35.5–23.3 / $6\frac{3}{16}$–$3\frac{3}{4}$ c	S	F 1	175	3.5	1–2	—	—	—	—	6	621
6 Beans, Lima, Pole[N]	Baby: 35–90 Regular: 25–38	.70	Regular: 18.3–12 / $3\frac{3}{16}$–2 c	S	F 1	175	1.8	1–2	—	—	—	—	8	320
7 Beans, Snap, Bush	100–125	.70	8.8–7.0 / $1\frac{1}{2}$–$1\frac{1}{8}$ c	S	F 1	175	3.5	1–2	—	—	—	—	6	621
8 Beans, Snap, Pole[N]	100–125	.70	8.8–7.0 / $1\frac{1}{2}$–$1\frac{1}{8}$ c	S	F 1	175	3.5	1–2	—	—	—	—	6	621
9 Beets, Cylindra	1,500–1,625	.65[G]	1.4–1.3 / 6 T[AA]	S	F 1	162	8.2	3–4	—	—	—	—	4	1,343
10 Beets, Regular	1,500–1,625	.65[G]	1.4–1.3 / 6 T[AA]	S	F 1	162	8.2	3–4	—	—	—	—	4	1,343

NOTES

NUTRITION

PLANNING

TIMING

YIELD

CROP

Master Charts

CROP	O — Possible GROW BIOINTENSIVE Yield in Pounds per 100-Square-Foot Planting[9]	P — Average U.S. Yield in Pounds per 100 Square Feet[12,13]	Q — Approx. Maximum Pounds Seed Yield per 100 Square Feet[19]	R — Approx. No. of Weeks to Maturity in Ground[17]	S — Approx. No. Weeks in Harvesting Period	T — Time of Year to Plant (SP, SU, FA, WI)	U — Crop Procedures	V — Pounds Consumed per Year by Average Person in U.S.[13,18]	W — Protein Content per Pound in Grams (454 g per pound)[25]	X — Calorie Content per Pound[25,50]	Y — Calcium Content per Pound in Milligrams (mg)[25]	Z — Notes
1 Artichoke, Jerusalem	Tubers: 100 / 206 / 460+ Biomass, air-dry: ~7.5 / -15 / -30	D	Tubers: 420+	17–26	—	SP	Plant tubers 1 week after last hard frost. Try 90-day varieties. Harvest after flowers die.	D	7.2	345	44	:Raw. 31% refuse. Used in alcohol production for gasohol. Good source of organic matter.
2 Artichoke, Regular	D	28.3	D	D, P	8	FA	Harvest artichokes when fully plump but before they become fibrous. Cut down stalks after they begin to dry. Resprouts from root.	D	5.3	213	93	:Raw.
3 Asparagus	9.5 / 19 / 38	7.3	8.7	Seeds: 4 yrs. Roots: 1 yr.	8	SP	Grow from roots or seed. From seed: Let plants go to seed without harvesting first and second year, so plants build strong roots; cut down dry stalks; harvest small shoots third year; harvest full-sized shoots fourth year. From roots: Let go to seed first year, harvest second year.	1.1 (fresh) .2 (canned) .1 (frozen)	6.4	104	56	:Raw. 44% refuse.
4 Basil	35 / 75 / 150	D	D	6–8	12	SU	Transplant when seedlings have 2 sets of true leaves and a third one coming; set down to cotyledons. After approx. 6 growth nodes appear on plant or when it begins to flower, cut back to 2 nodes. Cut branches back to 1 node.	D	12	123	385	
5 Beans, Lima, Bush	Dry: 11.5 / 17.2 / 23	5.9	23.0	9–11	12	SU	Transplant when seedlings have 2 true leaves but before seedlings reach 3–4 inches tall; bury up to half of stem up to cotyledons.	"1.3"	92.5	1,533	327	:Dry seeds. (Lima beans contain a small amount of cyanide.)
6 Beans, Lima, Pole[N]	Dry: 23+ / 34.4+ / 46+	11.8+	23.0+	11–13	12	SU	Snap and shell beans: Harvest regularly (every other day) for higher yields. Some varieties produce all at once; others continue to produce over a longer period.					
7 Beans, Snap, Bush	30 / 72 / 108	17.6	17.0	8	12	SP, SU		2.0 (fresh) 3.7 (canned) 1.9 (frozen)	7.6	141	124	:Raw. 12% refuse.
8 Beans, Snap, Pole[N]	30+ / 72+ / 108+	17.6+	29.7	8–9	12	SP, SU	Dry beans: pick when beans are bulging through pods so plants will set more beans.					
9 Beets, Cylindra	Roots: 110 / 220 / 540 Greens: 55 / 110 / 270	"68.0" D	30.6	8–9	4+	SP, SU, FA	Each seed produces 1–3 seedlings. Transplant only 1 seedling from a cluster to enhance genetic diversity. For optimum yield, harvest bulbs and greens when bulbs have reached maximum size without becoming fibrous and when greens are still succulent.	"1.9"	Roots: 5.1 Tops: 5.6	Roots: 195 Tops: 100	Roots: 51 Tops: 302 M	:Roots, raw. 33% refuse. Excellent tops often mean too much nitrogen fertilizer and poor root growth. Cylindra variety twice the weight of regular beets. :Greens, raw.
10 Beets, Regular	Roots: 55 / 110 / 270 Greens: 55 / 110 / 270	"34.0" D	30.6	8–9	4+	SP, SU, FA						

CROP	A — Approx. No. Seeds per Ounce[4] (Range: larger–smaller seed)	B — Minimum Legal Germination Rate[5]	C — Ounces / Volume Seed per 100 Square Feet (adj. for germ. rate, offset spacing, and curv. surf.)[6,7,8]	D — Short/Long/Extra-Long Germination Time	E — Plant Initially in Flats/Beds; Space in First Flat (in order of preference)	F — Approx. No. of Plants per Flat (adj. for germ. rate)[14]	G — No. First Flat(s) per 100 Sq Ft	H — Approx. No. Weeks in First Flat[16]	I — Depth of Second Flat and Spacing (Inches)	J — No. Plants in Second Flat[14]	K — No. Second Flats per 100 Sq Ft	L — Approx. No. Weeks in Second Flat[16]	M — In-Bed Spacing (Inches)	N — MAXIMUM No. Plants per 100 Square Feet[7]
11 Broccoli	9,000	.75	.01 / 1/24 t	S	F 1	187	0.45	2-3# / 3-4	6 / 2	60	1.4	3-4# / 5-6 LG	15	84
12 Brussels Sprouts	9,000	.70	.01 / 1/24 t	S	F 1	175	0.3	2-3# / 3-4	6 / 2	60	0.9	3-4# / 5-6 LG	18	53
13 Burdock	1,700	.60	1.3 / 4 T	S	F 1	150	8.9	3-4+	—	—	—	—	4	1,343
14 Cabbage, Chinese	9,000	.75	.03 / 1/8 t	S	F 1	187	1.1	2-3# / 3-4	6 / 2	60	3.35	3-4# / 5-6 LG	10	201
15 Cabbage, Regular	9,000	.75	.023 / .012 / .007 / 1/24 t	S	F 1	187	0.85 / 0.45 / 0.3	2-3# / 3-4	6 / 2	60	2.6 / 1.4 / 0.9	3-4# / 5-6 LG	12 / 15 / 18**	159 / 84 / 53
16 Carrots	18,750–25,000	.55	.2 / 1 1/4 t BB	S	F:BC/B##:BC	137	6.1	3-4	—	—	—	—	3	2,507
17 Cauliflower	9,000	.75	.01 / 1/24 t	S	F 1	187	0.45	2-3# / 3-4	6 / 2	60	1.4	3-4# / 5-6 LG	15	84
18 Celery	72,000	.55	.016 / 1/4 t	L/EL	F:BC	137	1.1	4-6	3 / 1	250	2.5	4-6 LG	6	621
19 Chard, Swiss	1,500	.65 G	.4 / 2 T AA	S	F 1	162	2	3-4	—	—	—	—	8	320
20 Collards, Annual & Perennial	9,000	.80	.022 / 1/8 t	S	F 1	200	0.8	2-3# / 3-4	6 / 2	60	2.6	3-4# / 5-6 LG	12	159

CROP	YIELD			TIMING			CROP PROCEDURES	PLANNING	NUTRITION			NOTES
	Possible GROW BIOINTENSIVE Yield in Pounds per 100-Square-Foot Planting [9]	Average U.S. Yield in Pounds per 100 Square Feet [12, 13]	Approx. Maximum Pounds Seed Yield per 100 Square Feet [19]	Approx. No. of Weeks to Maturity in Ground [17]	Approx. No. Weeks in Harvesting Period	Time of Year to Plant (SP, SU, FA, WI)		Pounds Consumed per Year by Average Person in U.S. [13, 18]	Protein Content per Pound in Grams (g) (454 g per pound) [25]	Calorie Content per Pound [25, 50]	Calcium Content per Pound in Milligrams (mg) [25]	
	O	P	Q	R	S	T	U	V	W	X	Y	Z
11 Broccoli	Heads: 26 / 39 / 53; Leaves: 52+ / 78+ / 106+	33.9 / D	5.5	8–9	4–6	SP, FA	See Cabbage for prick-out and transplanting. Heads grow very fast. Harvest before flowering begins. Can produce secondary heads for additional good harvest.	5.7 [fresh] / 2.6 [frozen]	12.7 / 13.6	127 / 127	364 / 1,189	:Head, raw. 22% refuse. :Leaves, raw. Contain more nutrition than heads.
12 Brussels Sprouts	71 / 106 / 142	"36.7"	2.8	11–13	12	SP, FA	Does better in fertile soil. See Cabbage for prick-out and transplanting. When sprout node begins to bulge, remove leaf below it for best growth. Harvest when sprouts are at maximum plumpness, before outer leaves become fibrous and sprout becomes bitter.	".3"	20.4	195	150	:Raw. 8% refuse.
13 Burdock	75 / 150 / 300	D	D	Up to 42	8–12	FA	Harvest after about 10 months when roots have reached maximum size and before they become fibrous.	D	6.9	327	186	Sow Watanabe in spring for summer harvest and Takinogawa in spring or fall for late summer or following spring harvest.
14 Cabbage, Chinese	96 / 191 / 383	"69.4"	6.1	7–11**	—	SP, FA	Harvest at peak of size and succulence, before leaves begin to yellow and plants go to seed.	D	5.3	59	189	:Raw. 3% refuse.
15 Cabbage, Regular	96 / 191 / 383	"69.4"	3.6	9–16**	2–4+	SP, FA	For prick-out, set seedlings down to cotyledons. For transplant, set seedlings deep, leaving 1–3 leaves above the soil. Harvest heads before top turns yellow or top leaves begin to split.	7.5 [fresh] / 1.1 [kraut]	5.3 / 8.2	113 / 113	200 / 171	:Green, raw. 10% refuse. :Red, raw. 10% refuse.
16 Carrots	Roots: 100 / 150 / 400+	Fresh: 72.5 / Processing: 97.2	17.8	9–11	4+	SP, SU, FA	Transplant when seedlings have 2 true leaves, a third one coming, and a good root not more than 3 inches long; be careful to keep the root straight. Harvest at maximum diameter while they are still sweet.	8.8 [fresh] / 1.6 [canned] / 1.5 [frozen]	4.1	195	134	:Raw, without tops. 18% refuse. Excellent tops often mean too much nitrogen fertilizer and poor root growth.
17 Cauliflower	44 / 100 / 291	38.5	1.0	8–12**	—	SP, FA	See Cabbage for prick-out and transplanting. Cauliflower head often develops in just a few days. Harvest at full size before it begins to yellow.	1.7 [fresh] / .4 [frozen]	12.2	113	113	:Raw.
18 Celery	240 / 480 / 959+	160.7	9.9	12–16	3–4 to 26[52]	SP, FA	Transplant when seedlings are about 4 inches tall. For maximum yield, harvest outer stalks sequentially by pulling down and twisting while holding the plant; leave a minimum of 6–8 significant stalks per plant; outer stalks will get bigger as plants mature.	6.1	5.3	73	189	:25% refuse.
19 Chard, Swiss	200 / 405 / 810	D	29.0	7–8	44	SP, SU, FA	For transplanting, see Beets. Harvest sequentially as leaves mature, 1–2 outer stalks per plant; be sure to leave a minimum of 5 significant stalks per plant.	D	10.0	86	367 M	:Raw. 8% refuse. Good organic matter crop at high yields.
20 Collards, Annual & Perennial	96 / 191 / 383	D	D	12	24	SP, FA	For prick-out and transplanting, see Cabbage. Harvest sequentially as leaves mature, 1–2 leaves per plant; be sure to leave at least 5 significant leaves per plant/stem.	D	16.3	136	921	:Leaves and stems, raw.

Letter codes on page 133, notes on pages 177–179

Vegetable and Garden Crops

CROP	A: Approx. No. Seeds per Ounce[4] (Range: larger–smaller seed)	B: Minimum Legal Germination Rate[5]	C: Ounces / Volume Seed per 100 Square Feet (adj. for germ. rate, offset spacing, and curv. surf.)[6,7,8]	D: Short/Long/Extra-Long Germination Time	E: Plant Initially in Flats/Beds; Space in First Flat (in order of preference)	F: Approx. No. of Plants per Flat (adj. for germ. rate)[14]	G: No. First Flat(s) per 100 Sq Ft	H: Approx. No. Weeks in First Flat[16]	I: Depth of Second Flat and Spacing (Inches)	J: No. Plants in Second Flat[14]	K: No. Second Flats per 100 Sq Ft	L: Approx. No. Weeks in Second Flat[16]	M: In-Bed Spacing (Inches)	N: MAXIMUM No. Plants per 100 Square Feet[7]
21 Corn, Sweet	112–156	.75	1.0–.72 / 2–1²/5 c	S	F 1	187	0.45	3–5 days	—	—	—	—	15	84
22 Cucumbers	938–1,000	.80	.2 / 1¼ T	S	F 2	48	3.3	2–3# / 3–4	—	—	—	—	12	159
23 Eggplant	6,500	.60	.014 / 1/12 t	L/EL	F 1	150	0.35	2–3	6 / 2	60	0.9	3–4# / 5–7 LG	18	53
24 Garlic	Cloves: 12	.5 z	20 lbs / 10 qt bulbs	L	B	—	—	—	—	—	—	—	4	1,343
25 Horseradish	Live roots used	—	159 roots / —	L	B	—	—	—	—	—	—	—	12	159
26 Kale	9,000	.75	.01 / 1/24 t	S	F 1	187	0.45	1–2# / 3–4	6 / 2	60	1.4	3–4# / 5–6 LG	15	84
27 Kohlrabi	9,000	.75	.20 / 1/16 t	S	F 1	187	7.2	2–3# / 3–4	—	—	—	—	4	1,343
28 Leeks	12,500	.60	.1 / 3/8 t	S	F:BC	150	2.1	6	6 / 1.5	111	5.6	6	6	621
29 Lettuce, Head	25,000	.80	.008 / 1/8 t	S	F:BC	200	0.2	1–2	3 / 1.5	111	1.4	2–3	12	159
30 Lettuce, Leaf	25,000	.80	.016 / .012 / 1/4 t	S	F:BC	200	0.4 / 0.31	1–(2)	3 / 1.5	111	2.9 / 2.2	2–3	8 WI / 9 SP–FA	320 / 248

CROP	YIELD			TIMING			CROP PROCEDURES	PLANNING	NUTRITION			NOTES
	O: Possible GROW BIOINTENSIVE Yield in Pounds per 100-Square-Foot Planting[9]	P: Average U.S. Yield in Pounds per 100 Square Feet[12,13]	Q: Approx. Maximum Pounds Seed Yield per 100 Square Feet[19]	R: Approx. No. of Weeks to Maturity in Ground[17]	S: Approx. No. Weeks in Harvesting Period	T: Time of Year to Plant (SP, SU, FA, WI)	U	V: Pounds Consumed per Year by Average Person in U.S.[13,18]	W: Protein Content per Pound in Grams (g) (454 g per pound)[25]	X: Calorie Content per Pound[25,50]	Y: Calcium Content per Pound in Milligrams (mg)[25]	Z
21 Corn, Sweet	Shelled, wet: 17 / 34 / 68 Biomass, air-dry: 12 / 24 / 48	27.0 / 0	22.6	9–13**	—	SU	To check maturity, pull the husk open and pierce a kernel with a thumbnail. Harvest when the juice is halfway between clear and milky. Wait an additional 30 days to harvest plants for optimum compost pile biomass.	Shelled, wet: 9.7 (fresh), 9.0 (frozen), 8.3 (canned)	8.7	400	7	Raw, 45% refuse (cob).
22 Cucumbers	158 / 316 / 581	Fresh: 39.3 Picking: 25.0	4.1	7–10	7–14	SU	Transplant when seedlings have 3 large true leaves. Harvest when approx. 6–8 inches long; fruit should be smooth, with no ridges, just beginning to turn lighter green; cut stem about 1/2 inch from plant.	Reg: 6.1, Pickles: "4.4" (fresh) 3.6 (canned)	3.9	59	108	Raw, whole. 5% refuse.
23 Eggplant	54 / 108 / 163	"55.1"	.6	10–11	13	SU	Transplant when seedlings are about 6 inches tall. Harvest when fruit is beginning to soften.	".5"	4.4	118	44	Raw, 19% refuse.
24 Garlic	60 / 120 / 240+ Hardneck: biomass, air-dry: 7.5 / 15 / 30+[54]	40.9	Bulbs: 240	17–44	—	SP, FA	Separate bulbs into cloves; plant only the largest cloves 1–2 inches below the soil. Most bulb growth occurs in last 45 days. Harvest when plants have 6–7 green leaves. Dry well in shade. Softneck: braid or cut off stems 2 inches from bulb. Hardneck: cut off stems 2 inches from bulb.	2.8	24.8	676	116	12% refuse. Contains antibiotics. Amount of seed depends on size of bulbs and cloves.
25 Horseradish	D	D	D	26	—	SP, FA	Transplant root pieces after last hard frost. Dig up roots after 6 months or when leaves begin to die back. Perennial in warmer climates.	D	10.6	288	464	Raw, 27% refuse.
26 Kale	76 / 114 / 153	"16.0"	3.8	8–9	17	SP, FA	For prick-out and transplanting, see Cabbage. For harvest, see Chard.	D	14.1	227	601	Raw leaves and stems. 26% refuse. Good vitamin and mineral content.
27 Kohlrabi	67 / 135 / 270	D	20.1	7–8	4–8	SP, FA	For prick-out and transplanting, see Cabbage. Harvest as soon as leaves begin to become less green and dull and bulbs stop increasing in size.	D	6.6	122	136	Raw, 27% refuse.
28 Leeks	240 / 480 / 960 biomass, air-dry: 7.5 / 15 / 30	D	9.8	19	4–8	SP, FA	Transplant after 8–12 weeks in flat, when seedlings are as big around as a No. 2 pencil. Harvest after approx. 5+ months.	D	5.2	277	123	Raw, 25% refuse.
29 Lettuce, Head	75 / 150 / 300	85.8	D	11–13	1–3	SP, FA	Transplant when seedlings are about 2–3 inches tall. Harvest in very early morning for best taste, when outer leaves are still green and shiny.	21.4	3.9	59	86	Raw, 5% refuse.
30 Lettuce, Leaf	135 / 202 / 540	56.1	4.0	6–12**[26]	1–3	SP, SU, FA, WI	Transplant when seedlings are about 2–3 inches tall. Harvest in very early morning for best taste, when plant is at maximum fullness and before it begins to bolt or become bitter. Winter growing in double-walled mini-greenhouse.	9.5	3.8	82	197	Raw, 36% refuse.

Master Charts

CROP	A — Approx. No. Seeds per Ounce[4] (Range: larger–smaller seed)	B — Minimum Legal Germination Rate[5]	C — Ounces / Volume Seed per 100 Square Feet (adj. for germ. rate, offset spacing, and curv. surf.)[6,7,8]	D — Short/Long/Extra-Long Germination Time	E — Plant Initially in Flats/Beds; Space in First Flat (in order of preference)	F — Approx. No. of Plants per Flat (adj. for germ. rate)[14]	G — No. First Flat(s) per 100 Sq Ft	H — Approx. No. Weeks in First Flat[16]	I — Depth of Second Flat and Spacing (Inches)	J — No. Plants in Second Flat[14]	K — No. Second Flats per 100 Sq Ft	L — Approx. No. Weeks in Second Flat[16]	M — In-Bed Spacing (Inches)	N — MAXIMUM No. Plants per 100 Square Feet[7]
31 Mangels	1,600	.65	.41 / 3 2/5 TAA	S	F 1	162	2.7	3-4+	—	—	—	—	7	432
32 Melons	1,000–1,250	.75	.1-09 / ½ t	S	F 2	45	1.86	3-4 LG	—	—	—	—	15	84
33 Mustard	15,000	.75	.055 / ¼ t	S	F 2	187	3.3	3-4	—	—	—	—	6	621
34 Okra	500	.50	.64 / 3½ t	L	F 1	125	1.3	6-8	6 / 2	60	2.6	3-4	12	159
35 Onions, Bunching	11,250–12,500	.70	.32-29 / 3¾ T	S	F:BC	175	7.2	6-8	—	—	—	—	3	2,507
36 Onions, Regular	8,125	.70	.2 / 2½ T	S	F:BC	175	3.8	6-8# / 8-10	—	—	—	—	4	1,343
37 Onions, Torpedo	8,125	.70	.2 / 2½ T	S	F:BC	175	3.8	6-8# / 8-10	—	—	—	—	4	1,343
38 Parsley	18,000	.60	.08 / 1 t	L / EL	F:BC	150	2.8	2-3	6 / 2	60	13.9	6-8	5	833
39 Parsnips	4,900	.60	.47 / 1⅔ c	L	F 1	150	9	3-4	—	—	—	—	4	1,343
40 Peas, Bush	94–156	.80	2-1.25 lbs / 2-1¼ c	S	F 1	200	12.5	1-2	—	—	—	—	3	2,507

CROP	YIELD			TIMING			CROP PROCEDURES	PLANNING	NUTRITION			NOTES
	O	P	Q	R	S	T	U	V	W	X	Y	Z
	Possible GROW BIOINTENSIVE Yield in Pounds per 100-Square-Foot Planting[9]	Average U.S. Yield in Pounds per 100 Square Feet[12, 13]	Approx. Maximum Pounds Seed Yield per 100 Square Feet[19]	Approx. No. of Weeks to Maturity in Ground[17]	Approx. No. Weeks in Harvesting Period	Time of Year to Plant (SP, SU, FA, WI)		Pounds Consumed per Year by Average Person in U.S.[13, 18]	Protein Content per Pound in Grams (g) (454 g per pound)[25]	Calorie Content per Pound[25, 50]	Calcium Content per Pound in Milligrams (mg)[25]	
31 Mangels	Roots: 200 / 400 / 800+ Greens: 100 / 200 / 400+	Roots: "68.0" Greens: D	20.0+	8–12+	4+	SP, SU, FA	See Beets.	D	D	D	D	See Beets.
32 Melons	50 / 72 / 145	51.9H 59.0CA	2.9	12–17**	13	SU	Transplant when seedlings have 3 large true leaves. Harvest when the outer skin begins to change color and the blossom end begins to soften.	10.8CA 2.2H	1.6 2.3	68 159	32 32	:Cantaloupe. 50% refuse. :Honeydew. 37% refuse.
33 Mustard	180 / 225 / 270	D	5.7	5–6	8–30	SP, FA	Transplant when seedlings have 3–4 good true leaves. Harvest outer leaves regularly, leaving 3 good leaves in the center.	D	9.5	118	73	:Raw. 30% refuse.
34 Okra	30 / 60 / 120	D	9.3	7–8	13	SU	Prick out when seedlings are 2 inches tall. Transplant when seedlings are about 6 inches tall. Harvest when the pods are succulent, before they become tough.	D	9.4	150	359	:Raw. 14% refuse.
35 Onions, Bunching	100 / 200 / 540	D	39.6	8–17	–	SP, SU, FA	Transplant when the seedlings are about the thickness of ordinary pencil lead. Harvest when the plants are slightly thicker than your little finger, or as desired. Root length for planting 1" (trim). Harvest when 1/8"–3/16" in diameter 1" above start of roots.	D	6.5 1.8	145 76	222 67	:Raw. Bulb and entire top. 4% refuse. :Raw. Bulb and white portion of top. 63% refuse.
36 Onions, Regular	100 / 200 / 540	101.4	10.3	14–17	–	SP, FA	Transplant when the seedlings are about the thickness of ordinary pencil lead. Harvest: when a significant number of tops have fallen down, push down the rest and continue to water for 1 week; stop watering and let onions begin to cure in the ground for 1–2 weeks; loosen the soil under the onions and lift them out. Put them in single layer in a shady, well-ventilated area to dry thoroughly. Eat first any onions that do not dry well. Root length for transplanting: trim to 2".	19.2	6.2	172	111	:Dry. Raw. 9% refuse.
37 Onions, Torpedo	200 / 400 / 800+	101.4	10.3	14–17	–	SP, FA		19.2	6.2	172	111	:Dry. Raw. 9% refuse.
38 Parsley	45 / 91 / 182 (4- to 6-mo. harvest)	D	24.8	10–13	17–26	SP, FA	Prick out when seedlings have 1 true leaf. Transplant when seedlings are about 3 inches tall. Plants are sensitive to inappropriate handling. Choose best seedlings to transplant: white forking roots, dark green leaves. Harvest outer stalks carefully, leaving 3–5 large stalks per plant; remove inedible stalks and compost them.	D	16.3	163	921	:Raw.
39 Parsnips	119 / 238 / 479	D	24	15	4–8+	SP, FA	Slow to germinate and grow. Transplant when seedlings have 3–4 good true leaves. Be patient! Harvest when mature or after frost for sweetest flavor.	D	6.6	340	193	:Raw. 15% refuse.
40 Peas, Bush	Fresh: 25 / 53 / 106 Dry: 4 / 10 / 24	Fresh: 9.2 Dry: "4.4"		8–10	12	SP, FA	Timing is important: transplant approx. 1 week after last hard frost or after last soft frost in areas with a cool growing season. Harvest when seeds are bulging in the pods. Pole peas in 2' wide beds generally yield better due to improved pollination.	"4.1" (fresh) 1.3 (canned) 1.9 (frozen)	10.9 109.4	367 1,542	45 290	:Green, without pods. 62% refuse (pods). :Dry. Try sugar snap edible variety.

Vegetable and Garden Crops

	SEED				PLANTING	FLATS							BEDS	
CROP	A — Approx. No. Seeds per Ounce[4] (Range: larger–smaller seed)	B — Minimum Legal Germination Rate[5]	C — Ounces / Volume Seed per 100 Square Feet (adj. for germ. rate, offset spacing, and curv. surf.)[6,7,8]	D — Short/Long/Extra-Long Germination Time	E — Plant Initially in Flats/Beds; Space in First Flat (in order of preference)	F — Approx. No. of Plants per Flat (adj. for germ. rate)[14]	G — No. First Flat(s) per 100 Sq Ft	H — Approx. No. Weeks in First Flat[16]	I — Depth of Second Flat and Spacing (Inches)	J — No. Plants in Second Flat[14]	K — No. Second Flats per 100 Sq Ft	L — Approx. No. Weeks in Second Flat[16]	M — In-Bed Spacing (Inches)	N — MAXIMUM No. Plants per 100 Square Feet[7]
41 Peas, Pole[N]	94–156	.80	1.1 lbs–10.7 oz / 1 1/10–2/3 c	S	F 1	200	6.7	1–2	—	—	—	—	4	1,343
42 Peppers, Cayenne	4,500	.55	.064 / 3/8 t	L / EL	F 1	137	1.2	2–3	6 / 2	60	2.6	3–4# 5–7LG	12	159
43 Peppers, Green	4,500	.55	.064 / 3/8 t	L / EL	F 1	137	1.2	2–3	6 / 2	60	2.6	3–4# 5–7LG	12	159
44 Potatoes, Irish	—	—	31–23.25 lbs / 16–12 qt	L	Note 31	—	—	—	—	—	—	—	9 centers 6 to 9 depth[49]	248
45 Potatoes, Sweet	—	—	12 lbs / 6 qt	L	Note 32	60	—	4–6	—	—	—	—	9 centers 6 to 9 depth[49]	248
46 Pumpkin	94–250	.75	.75–.07 / 1/10 T	S	F 2	45	1.2/0.3	3–4LG	—	—	—	—	18 / 30**	53 / 14
47 Radishes	2,500–3,125	.75	1.3–1 / 1 3/4 T	S	B:BC	—	—	—	—	—	—	—	2	5,894
48 Rhubarb	1,700[Y]	.60[Y]	.025 / 2/3 t	L	Seeds: F 1 Roots: B	150	0.18	D	6 / 2	60	0.4	D	24	26
49 Rutabagas	9,375–11,875	.75	.09 / 1/4 t	S	F 1	187	3.3	3–4	—	—	—	—	6	621
50 Salsify	1,900	.75	1.7 / 1/2 c	S	F 1	187	3.2	3–4	—	—	—	—	3	2,507

CROP	YIELD			TIMING			CROP PROCEDURES	PLANNING	NUTRITION			NOTES
	O — Possible GROW BIOINTENSIVE Yield in Pounds per 100-Square-Foot Planting[9]	P — Average U.S. Yield in Pounds per 100 Square Feet[12,13]	Q — Approx. Maximum Pounds Seed Yield per 100 Square Feet[19]	R — Approx. No. of Weeks to Maturity in Ground[17]	S — Approx. No. Weeks in Harvesting Period	T — Time of Year to Plant (SP, SU, FA, WI)	U	V — Pounds Consumed per Year by Average Person in U.S.[13,18]	W — Protein Content per Pound in Grams (g) (454 g per pound)[25]	X — Calorie Content per Pound[25,50]	Y — Calcium Content per Pound in Milligrams (mg)[25]	Z
41 Peas, Pole[N]	Fresh: 25+ / 53+ / 106+ Dry: 4 / 10 / 24	Fresh: 9.2 Dry: "4.4"	24	10–11	12	SP, FA	Timing is important: transplant approx. 1 week after last hard frost or after last soft frost in areas with a cool growing season. Harvest when seeds are bulging in the pods.	"4.1" (fresh) 1.3 (canned) 1.9 (frozen)	10.9 / 109.4	367 / 1,542	45 / 290	:Green, without pods. 62% refuse (pods). :Dry. Try sugar snap edible-pod variety.
42 Peppers, Cayenne	Dry: 5 / 10 / 20	D	.1	9–11	17	SU	Transplant when seedlings are about 6 inches tall and the soil is warm. Use a mini-greenhouse or a row cover in areas with a short growing season.	D	45	1,470	681	:Dry (including seeds). 4% refuse.
43 Peppers, Green	68 / 136 / 204	68.7	.3	9–12	17	SU	Harvest when fully mature and before fruit begins to discolor.	7.0	4.5 / 5.1	82 / 122	33 / 47	:Green. 18% refuse. :Red. 20% refuse.
44 Potatoes, Irish	100 / 200 / 780	84.2	Tubers: 780	9–17	—	SP, SU	See note 31. After tops die, stop watering, wait 2 weeks, dig up carefully. Put in single layer in shade to cure for 2–3 days. Store in a cool, dark, well-ventilated place.	47.2 (fresh) 57.2 (frozen)	7.7	349 avg. Red: 327 Russet: 358 White: 318	26	:Raw. 19% refuse. Green parts poisonous. See above. Δ
45 Potatoes, Sweet	82 / 164 / 492	39.5	Tubers: 492	13–17 (3-mo var.) 26–34 (6-mo var.)	—	SU	See note 32. It is also possible to buy slips to plant. Harvest when tops are dead.	4.7	6.6 / 6.2	375 / 430	118 / 118	:Jewel (firm). 19% refuse :Puerto Rican (soft). (peelings) See above. Δ
46 Pumpkin	Whole: 48 / 96 / 191 Seeds without hulls: 1 / 2 / 4	D	5.1	14–16	—	SU	For transplanting, see Cucumbers. For harvest, see Winter Squash.	".6"	3.2 / 131.5	118 / 2,454	67 / 231	:Raw fruit. 30% refuse. :Seeds. Hulls 30% of unhulled weight.
47 Radishes	Roots: 100 / 200 / 540	D	20.6	3–9**	1	SP, FA	Small radishes: Broadcast directly in bed (use seed amount in Col. D), or use chicken wire to space seeds 1 inch apart in the bed (will require 4 times the seed). Chop seeds in lightly with rake. Harvest after about 3–4 weeks in the ground and before the bulb becomes too hot and fibrous. Daikon: Sow on 1-inch centers (in flat (seed needed per 100 square feet: 26 = .33 ounces). Transplant when seedlings have 3–4 good true leaves, about 2 weeks after sowing. To avoid bolting, transplant after June 21. Harvest after about 2½–3 months, before seed stalk begins to form.	D	4.1	91	122	:Raw, without tops. 10% refuse.
48 Rhubarb	Stalks: 70 / 140 / 280	D	D	Seeds: 3 yrs. Roots: 1 yr.	D	SP	Harvest stalks with hand-sized leaves every 5–10 days; be sure to keep 5–6 medium to medium-large shiny, newer leaves with some red on the stem on the plant.	".03"	2.3	95	374	:Raw, without leaves. 14% refuse. Green parts poisonous.
49 Rutabagas	200 / 400 / 800+	"68.0+"	5.4	13	4+	SP, FA	Transplant when seedlings are about 2–3 inches tall. Harvest when roots are mature (a "neck" will begin to form when the root has reached maximum size; quality will decline as neck elongates).	D	4.2	163	254	:Raw. 15% refuse. Very flavorful when grown using GROW BIOINTENSIVE methods.
50 Salsify	100 / 200 / 400+	D	27.7	17	4+	SP, FA	For transplanting, see Carrots. Harvest after 4–5 months in ground, before leaves become dull.	D	11.4	372	185	

Δ Approximately 12% of the protein, 8% of the calories, and 18% of the calcium eaten worldwide is in the form of potatoes grown on 2.4% of the cropland.

CROP	A Approx. No. Seeds per Ounce[4] (Range: larger–smaller seed)	B Minimum Legal Germination Rate[5]	C Ounces / Volume Seed per 100 Square Feet (adj. for germ. rate, offset spacing, and curv. surf.)[6,7,8]	D Short/Long/Extra-Long Germination Time	E Plant Initially in Flats/Beds; Space in First Flat (in order of preference)	F Approx. No. of Plants per Flat (adj. for germ. rate)[14]	G No. First Flat(s) per 100 Sq Ft	H Approx. No. Weeks in First Flat[16]	I Depth of Second Flat and Spacing (Inches)	J No. Plants in Second Flat[14]	K No. Second Flats per 100 Sq Ft	L Approx. No. Weeks in Second Flat[16]	M In-Bed Spacing (Inches)	N MAXIMUM No. Plants per 100 Square Feet[7]
51 Shallots	8[Y] (bulbs)	.75[Y]	14.0 / 7 qt (bulbs)	L	B	—	—	—	—	—	—	—	4	1,343
52 Spinach, New Zealand, Malabar	350	.40	1.14 / 6 T	L	F	24	6.6	3–4	—	—	—	—	12	159
53 Spinach, Regular	2,800	.60	.37 / 2 t	S	F	150	4.2	3–4	—	—	—	—	6	621
54 Squash, Crookneck	218–281	.75	.5–.4 / 2–1½ T	S	F 2	45	1.9	3–4[LG]	—	—	—	—	15	84
55 Squash, Patty Pan	300	.75	.37 / 1⅓ T	S	F 2	45	1.9	3–4[LG]	—	—	—	—	15	84
56 Squash, Winter	100–250+	.75	12" C: 2.12–.84 / 9½–3¾ T 15" C: 1.12–.45 / 5–2 T 18" C: .71–.28 / 3⅕–1¼ T	S	F 2	45	3.5 / 1.9 / 1.2	3–4[LG]	—	—	—	—	12 / 15** / 18	159 / 84 / 53
57 Squash, Zucchini	300	.75	.24 / 2²⁄₅ t	S	F 2	45	1.2	3–4[LG]	—	—	—	—	18	53
58 Tomatoes	10,000–12,000	.75	.006 / .004 / .003 / 1⁄16–1⁄32 t	S	F	187	0.3 / 0.2 / 0.14	4–6	6 / 2	60	0.9 / 0.6 / 0.4	3–4[LG]	18 / 21 / 24[TD]	53 / 35 / 26
59 Turnips	9,375–12,500	.80	.18–.13 / ²⁄₃	S	F	200	6.7	2–3	—	—	—	—	4	1,343
60 Watermelon	Small seed: 500–625 Large seed: 187–312	.80	**Small seed:** 12°C: .45–.36 / 3–2³⁄₈ t • 18°C: .15–.12 / 1¹⁄₈–³⁄₄ t • 21°C: .10–.08 / ⁵⁄₈–¹⁄₂ t • 24°C: .07–.06 / ⁷⁄₁₆–³⁄₈ t **Large seed:** 12°C: 1.2–.73 / 2³⁄₄ T • 18°C: .4–.24 / 2⁵⁄₈–1⁵⁄₈ t • 21°C: .27–.16 / 1³⁄₄–1¹³⁄₁₆ t • 24°C: .20–.12 / 1³⁄₈–³⁄₄ t	S	F	42	3.8 / 1.3 / 0.8 / 0.6	3–4[LG]	—	—	—	—	12 / 18 / 21 / 24w	159 / 53 / 35 / 26

CROP	O Possible GROW BIOINTENSIVE Yield in Pounds per 100-Square-Foot Planting[9]	P Average U.S. Yield in Pounds per 100 Square Feet[12,13]	Q Approx. Maximum Pounds Seed Yield per 100 Square Feet[19]	R Approx. No. of Weeks to Maturity in Ground[17]	S Approx. No. Weeks in Harvesting Period	T Time of Year to Plant (SP, SU, FA, WI)	U CROP PROCEDURES	V Pounds Consumed per Year by Average Person in U.S.[13,18]	W Protein Content per Pound in Grams (g) (454 g per pound)[25]	X Calorie Content per Pound[25,50]	Y Calcium Content per Pound in Milligrams (mg)[25]	Z NOTES
51 Shallots	60 / 120 / 240+	D	Bulbs: 240	17–26	—	SP, FA	Separate bulbs; use larger bulbs for transplanting. When leaves become abundant, 10–20% can be cut for flavoring without decreasing yield of bulbs. For curing, see Onions.	D	10.0	357	148	:Raw. 12% refuse.
52 Spinach, New Zealand, Malabar	180 / 225 / 270	D	17.2	10	42	SP, SU, FA	New Zealand: see Regular Spinach, except harvest when leaves are fully mature. Malabar: see Regular Spinach.	D	10.0	64	263	:Raw.
53 Spinach, Regular	50 / 100 / 225	Fresh: 34.6 Processing: 39.0	10.8	6–7	—	SP, FA	Transplant when seedlings have 3 true leaves. Timing is crucial (see Peas). Harvest large leaves just before they become dull; leave 5 good leaves per plant.	1.7	10.5	100	304[M]	:Raw. 28% refuse.
54 Squash, Crookneck	35 / 75 / 150	D	6.1	10	17+	SU	For transplanting, see Cucumbers. Harvest before fruit becomes dark yellow and hard.	D	5.3	86	124	:Raw. 2% refuse.
55 Squash, Patty Pan	75 / 150 / 307	D	6.1	7	17+	SU	For transplanting, see Cucumbers. White variety: harvest when bone-white with only a tinge of green left. Colored varieties: harvest before fruit becomes dark and hard.	D	4.0	82	124	:Raw. 2% refuse.
56 Squash, Winter	50 / 100 / 350	D	5.7	11–17**	4+	SU	For transplanting, see Cucumbers. Support squash on smooth rocks to keep them off the damp soil. Harvest when stem is dry and hard; cut off with 2 inches of stem.	D	5.2 4.4 4.2	152 171 117	107 102 57	:Acorn, raw. 24% refuse. :Butternut, raw. 30% refuse. :Hubbard, raw. 34% refuse.
57 Squash, Zucchini	160 / 319 / 478+	D	6.1	7–9	26	SU	For transplanting, see Cucumbers. Lightly tap open female flowers on new zucchini to push them off; if they do not come off easily, do not force them. Harvest preferably when approx. 8–10 inches long, 12–20 ounces; remove irregular and/or deformed fruit from plant.	D	5.2	64	121	:Raw. 5% refuse.
58 Tomatoes	100 / 194 / 418	Fresh: 67.0 Processing: 153.4	5.5	8–13	17+	SU	Transplant when seedlings are about 6 inches tall; set plants deeper than in flat. Harvest at full color and when fruit comes off easily.	Canned: 69.6 Fresh: 18.1	5.0	95	59	:Raw.
59 Turnips	Roots: 100 / 200 / 360 Greens: 100 / 200 / 360	D	14.7	5–10**	4+	SP, FA	See Rutabaga.	D	3.9 13.6	122 127	152 1,116	:Roots, raw. :Greens, raw.
60 Watermelon	50 / 100 / 320	58.7	2.6	10–13	13	SU	For transplanting, see Cucumbers. Harvest when the watermelon says "Plunk!" when you tap it with a knuckle; if it says "Plink!" or "Plank!" it is not yet mature enough.	13.8	1.0	145	15	:Raw. 54% refuse.

Master Charts

Calorie, Grain, Protein Source, and Vegetable Oil Crops

CROP	SEED			PLANTING		FLATS							BEDS	
	A: Approx. No. Seeds per Ounce[4] (Range: larger–smaller seed)	B: Minimum Legal Germination Rate[5]	C: Ounces / Volume Seed per 100 Square Feet (adj. for germ. rate, offset spacing, and curv. surf.)[6,7,8]	D: Short/Long/Extra-Long Germination Time	E: Plant Initially in Flats/Beds; Space in First Flat (in order of preference)	F: Approx. No. of Plants per Flat (adj. for germ. rate)[14]	G: No. First Flat(s) per 100 Sq Ft	H: Approx. No. Weeks in First Flat[16]	I: Depth of Second Flat and Spacing (Inches)	J: No. Plants in Second Flat[14]	K: No. Second Flats per 100 Sq Ft	L: Approx. No. Weeks in Second Flat[16]	M: In-Bed Spacing (Inches)	N: MAXIMUM No. Plants per 100 Square Feet[7]
1 Amaranth, Grain & Leaf	25,000–53,400	.70[A]	.035–.017 / 1/3–1/6 t .009–.004 / 1/40–1/80 t	S	F:BC	175	0.9 / 0.25	1	3 / 1.5	111	5.6 / 2.6	3	Greens: 6 Seed: 12	621 / 159
2 Barley	500 hulled	.70[A]	2.4 / 6 1/3 T	S	F:BC	175	4.7	1–2	—	—	—	—	5	833
3 Beans, Fava, Cold-Weather	15–70	.75	28.4–6.1 / 7 1/2–1 5/8 c	S	F1/BR	187	1.7	2	—	—	—	—	8	320
4 Beans, Fava, Hot-Weather	15–70	.75	55.2–11.8 / 14 1/2–3 c	S	F1/BR	187	3.3	2	—	—	—	—	6	621
5 Beans, Kidney	50	.70[A]	17.7 / 1 9/10 c	S	F1	175	3.5	1–2	—	—	—	—	6	621
6 Beans, Mung	500	.70[A]	3.8 / 7 5/8 T	S	F1	175	7.7	1–2	—	—	—	—	4	1,343
7 Beans, Pinto	70	.70[A]	12.7 / 2 c	S	F1	175	3.5	1–2	—	—	—	—	6	621
8 Beans, Red Mexican & Black	50–100	.70[A]	17.7–8.9 / 2 1/10–1 1/10 c	S	F1	175	3.5	1–2	—	—	—	—	6	621
9 Beans, White	90–180	.70[A]	9.9–4.9 / 1 3/4–5/6 c	S	F1	175	3.5	1–2	—	—	—	—	6	621
10 Cassava (Manioc/Yuca) (manihot esculenta)	—	—	D	—	B	—	—	—	—	—	—	—	36	18

For protein, also see: Beans, Lima; Buckwheat; Collards; Corn, Sweet; Garlic; Peas; Potatoes, Irish and Sweet

CROP	Possible GROW BIOINTENSIVE Yield in Pounds per 100-Square-Foot Planting[9] (O)	Average U.S. Yield in Pounds per 100 Square Feet[12,13] (P)	Approx. Maximum Pounds Seed Yield per 100 Square Feet[19] (Q)	Approx. No. of Weeks to Maturity in Ground[17] (R)	Approx. No. Weeks in Harvesting Period (S)	Time of Year to Plant (SP, SU, FA, WI) (T)	CROP PROCEDURES (U)	Pounds Consumed per Year by Average Person in U.S.[13,18] (V)	Protein Content per Pound in Grams (g) (454 g per pound)[25] (W)	Calorie Content per Pound[25,50] (X)	Calcium Content per Pound in Milligrams (mg)[25] (Y)	NOTES (Z)
1 Amaranth, Grain & Leaf	Edible greens-type: 68 / 136 / 272+ Seed: 4 / 8 / 16+ Biomass, air-dry (stalks): 12 / 24 / 48 Biomass, wet: 53 / 132 / 317	Seed: "4" Biomass, air-dry: "6"	16+	Greens: 6 Seed: 12	Greens: 4+ Seed: —	SU	Prick out when cotyledons have emerged and before first leaf emerges. Transplant when 2–3 inches tall and strong. For grain: harvest when seeds are mature and dry enough to rub out of head easily; be alert for birds. For leaves: harvest when they are large, green, and shiny and before they begin to lose their maximum green.	D	11.1 / 65.4	104 / 1,696	973 / 693	:Greens. Good calcium source. :Seed.
2 Barley	Seed: 5 / 10 / 24[K,U] Biomass, air-dry: 12 / 30 / 72	Seed: 6.5 Biomass, dry: est. 9.7	24	9–10 to 34[47]	—	SP, FA	Transplant when seedlings are about 1.5–2 inches tall, before roots become unmanageable. Harvest when entire plant is 85% golden; be alert for birds.	.7	37.2 / 43.5 / 3.2*	1,583 / 1,579 / 224	73 / 154 / 145	:Light. :Pearled or scotch. :Straw and chaff, dry. Hulling of regular varieties difficult. Use hull-less varieties.
3 Beans, Fava, Cold-Weather	Dry seed: 5 / 9 / 18 Biomass, air-dry: 18 / 36 / 72 Biomass, wet: 90 / 180 / 360	D	18	17–43	—	SP, FA	Transplant when seedlings are about 1 inch tall, before roots become unmanageable. For biomass, harvest when plants are at ~50% flower.	D	13.0 / 113.9	162 / 1,547	42 / 463	Excellent organic matter crop. Fixes up to .16+ lb nitrogen (for summer varieties) and .34 lb (for winter varieties) per 100 sq ft per year. Caution: Beans can be toxic to some people. :In pods. 66% refuse. :Dry beans.
4 Beans, Fava, Hot-Weather	Dry seed: 2 / 3 / 6 Biomass, air-dry: 6 / 12 / 24 Biomass, wet: 30 / 60 / 120	D	6	13–17	—	SP	For beans, harvest all pods when first pods begin to turn black, before they shatter.	D	13.0 / 113.9	162 / 1,547	42 / 463	:In pods. 66% refuse. :Dry beans.
5 Beans, Kidney	Seed: 4 / 10 / 24	"4.0"	24	12	8	SU	Transplant when seedlings have 2 true leaves but before seedlings reach 3–4 inches tall; bury up to half of stem up to cotyledons.	All edible dry beans: "13.5"	102.1	1,510	499	
6 Beans, Mung	Seed: 4 / 10 / 24	3.8	24	12	8	SU			109.8	1,574	535	
7 Beans, Pinto	Seed: 4 / 10 / 24	3.8	24	12	8	SU	Dry beans: pick when beans are bulging through pods so plants will set more beans. Beans may shatter (fall to the ground) if left on plant too long. Fixes up to .27 lb nitrogen per 100 sq ft per year.		103.9	1,542	612	:Dry seeds, raw.
8 Beans, Red Mexican & Black	Seed: 4 / 10 / 24	3.8	24	12	8	SU	Pinto beans: habit is often halfway between bush and pole. Ready to harvest when pods have delicate red pattern.		103.9 / 102.1	1,583 / 1,538	612 / 499	:Red Mexican. :Black.
9 Beans, White	Seed: 4 / 10 / 24	3.8	24	12	8	SU			101.2	1,538	653	
10 Cassava (Manioc/Yuca) (manihot esculenta)	Root: 30 / 60 / 120	D	D	26–52	D	—	Transplant stem cuttings 12–18 inches long and 1–1.5 inches in diameter at beginning of rains.	D	5.5	726	309	:Raw. Some varieties take 104 weeks to mature.

Master Charts

Letter codes on page 133, notes on pages 177–179

Calorie, Grain, Protein Source, and Vegetable Oil Crops

For protein, also see: Beans, Lima; Buckwheat; Collards; Corn, Sweet; Garlic; Peas; Potatoes, Irish and Sweet

CROP	A — Approx. No. Seeds per Ounce[4] (Range: larger–smaller seed)	B — Minimum Legal Germination Rate[5]	C — Ounces / Volume Seed per 100 Square Feet (adj. for germ. rate, offset spacing, and curv. surf.)[6,7,8]	D — Short/Long/Extra-Long Germination Time	E — Plant Initially in Flats/Beds; Space in First Flat (in order of preference)	F — Approx. No. of Plants per Flat (adj. for germ. rate)[14]	G — No. First Flat(s) per 100 Sq Ft	H — Approx. No. Weeks in First Flat[16]	I — Depth of Second Flat and Spacing (Inches)	J — No. Plants in Second Flat[14]	K — No. Second Flats per 100 Sq Ft	L — Approx. No. Weeks in Second Flat[16]	M — In-Bed Spacing (Inches)	N — MAXIMUM No. Plants per 100 Square Feet[7]
11 Chickpeas (Garbanzo)	50	.70[A]	38.4 / 6 c	S	F 1	175	7.7	1–2	–	–	–	–	4	1,343
12 Corn, Flour or Fodder, Dry	100–200	.70[A]	1.2–.6 / 3–2 T	S	F 1	175	0.5	3–5 days	–	–	–	–	7 / 12 / 15+++	84
13 Cowpeas	150	.75	1.5 / .25 / .17 3½ / 2–1¼ T	S	F 1	187	0.9 / 0.14	2	–	–	–	–	12 / 24	159 / 26
14 Lentils	600	.70[A]	3.2 / 6½ T	S	F 1	175	7.7	1–2	–	–	–	–	4	1,343
15 Millet, Japanese	10,000	.70[A]	.06 / ¾ t	S	F:BC	175	2.4	2–4	–	–	–	–	7	432
16 Millet, Pearl	2,200 unhulled	.70[A]	.3 / D	S	F:BC	175	2.4	2–3	–	–	–	–	7	432
17 Millet, Proso	5,000 unhulled	.70[A]	.12 / ⅖ T	S	F:BC	175	2.4	2–4	–	–	–	–	7	432
18 Oats	950 hulled	.70[A]	1.25 / 3 T	S	F 1	175	4.7	1–2	–	–	–	–	5	833

Column group headers: SEED (B, C, A) · PLANTING (D, E) · FLATS (F–L) · BEDS (M, N)

CROP	YIELD			TIMING			CROP PROCEDURES	PLANNING	NUTRITION			NOTES
	O — Possible GROW BIOINTENSIVE Yield in Pounds per 100-Square-Foot Planting[9]	P — Average U.S. Yield in Pounds per 100 Square Feet[12, 13]	Q — Approx. Maximum Pounds Seed Yield per 100 Square Feet[19]	R — Approx. No. of Weeks to Maturity in Ground[17]	S — Approx. No. Weeks in Harvesting Period	T — Time of Year to Plant (SP, SU, FA, WI)	U	V — Pounds Consumed per Year by Average Person in U.S.[13, 18]	W — Protein Content per Pound in Grams (g) (454 g per pound)[25]	X — Calorie Content per Pound[25, 50]	Y — Calcium Content per Pound in Milligrams (mg)[25]	Z
11 Chickpeas (Garbanzo)	Seed: 4 / 10 / 24	D	24	9	8	SU	See Beans.	D	93.0	1,651	680	:Dry seeds, raw.
12 Corn, Flour or Fodder, Dry	Seed: 11 / 17 / 23+ Biomass, air-dry: 24 / 48 / 96 Biomass, wet: 107 / 214 / 428	Seed: 18.2	23+	11–16[53] to 43	—	SP	Transplant when seedlings are 1 inch tall, before roots become too long. Harvest ears as husks dry out. To speed up drying, open up husks without removing. Remove husks for final drying. Remove grain from ear when thoroughly dry, or store ears with grain and shell as needed.	25.1 (food) 86.1 (sugar and starch)	40.4	1,656	100	:Dry seeds, raw. Also produces a lot of organic matter.
13 Cowpeas	Seed: 2.4 / 4.5 / 9 Biomass, wet: 91 / 183 / 366	D	9	9–12	8	SU	See Beans. Can harvest up to 1/3 of leaves from 21–30 days until flowering.	D	103.4	1,556	336	:Dry.
14 Lentils	Seed: 4 / 6 / 8+	"2.8"	8+	12	8	SP, SU	See Beans.	—	112.0	1,569	538	:Dry seeds, raw.
15 Millet, Japanese	Seed: 3 / 7 / 13+K Biomass, air-dry: 12 / 30 / 72	Seed: "3.4"	13+	6–8	—	SU	Use 45- to 60-day varieties. Transplant when ~1.5 inches tall. Harvest when plants are 85% golden. Difficult to thresh.	D	D	1,544	D	
16 Millet, Pearl	Seed: 3 / 6 / 12 Biomass, air-dry: 15 / 40 / 75 Biomass, wet: 70 / 185 / 350	D	12	17–21	—	SU	Transplant when ~1.5 inches tall. Harvest when plants are 85% golden; be alert for shattering and birds.	D	19.0*	1,522	D	:Dry. Seeds form in about 45 days when days become shorter. Yields can be 3 times higher in hot climate and good soil.
17 Millet, Proso	Seed: 3 / 6 / 12+K Biomass, air-dry: 6 / 15 / 36	Seed: 7.1	12+	10–13 to 38[47]	—	SU	Finger millet calories: 1,509 Foxtail millet calories: 1,550	D	44.9	1,715	91	:Dry. High in iron.
18 Oats	Seed: 3 / 7 / 13+K, U Biomass, air-dry: 12 / 30 / 72	Seed: 4.8 Biomass, dry: est. 7.2	13+	13–17 to 38[47]	—	SP, FA	See Barley.	4.5	64.4 / 3.2*	1,764 / 233	240 / 86	:Grain, dry. :Straw and chaff, dry. Hulling of regular varieties difficult. Use hull-less varieties.

Calorie, Grain, Protein Source, and Vegetable Oil Crops

		BEDS		FLATS							PLANTING		SEED		

CROP	A Approx. No. Seeds per Ounce[4] (Range: larger–smaller seed)	B Minimum Legal Germination Rate[5]	C Ounces / Volume Seed per 100 Square Feet (adj. for germ. rate, offset spacing, and curv. surf.)[6,7,8]	D Short/Long/Extra-Long Germination Time	E Plant Initially in Flats/Beds; Space in First Flat (in order of preference)	F Approx. No. of Plants per Flat (adj. for germ. rate)[14]	G No. First Flat(s) per 100 Sq Ft	H Approx. No. Weeks in First Flat[16]	I Depth of Second Flat and Spacing (Inches)	J No. Plants in Second Flat[14]	K No. Second Flats per 100 Sq Ft	L Approx. No. Weeks in Second Flat[16]	M In-Bed Spacing (Inches)	N MAXIMUM No. Plants per 100 Square Feet[7]
19 Peanuts	20–70 unshelled 30–90 shelled	.70[A]	11.8–3.9 / 4 3/8–1 1/2 c shelled	S	F1	42	5.9	2–4	—	—	—	—	9	248
20 Pigeon Peas	D	.70[A]	D	S	F1	175	0.02	2–3	—	—	—	—	60	4
21 Quinoa	10,000	.70[A]	.023 / 1/6 t	S	F:BC	175	0.9	1	3 / 1.5	111	1.4	3	12	159
22 Rapeseed (Canola)	8,000	.70[A]	.04 / 2 t	S	F:BC	175	0.7	1–2	—	—	—	—	9	248
23 Rice	1,100 unhulled	.70[A]	1.7 / 3 3/5 T	S	F:BC	175	3.8	2	—	—	—	—	4	1,343
24 Rye, Cereal	500 hulled	.70[A]	2.4 / 5 2/5 T	S	F:BC	175	2.4	1–2	—	—	—	—	5	833
25 Safflower	640 unhulled	.70[A]	1.8 / 2 3/5 c	S	F:BC	175	2.4	2–3	—	—	—	—	5	833
26 Sesame	11,000	.70[A]	.08 / 1/5 T	L	F:BC	175	3.5	3	—	—	—	—	6	621

For protein, also see: Beans, Lima; Buckwheat; Collards; Corn, Sweet; Garlic; Peas; Potatoes, Irish and Sweet

CROP	YIELD O: Possible GROW BIOINTENSIVE Yield in Pounds per 100-Square-Foot Planting[9]	YIELD P: Average U.S. Yield in Pounds per 100 Square Feet[12,13]	Q: Approx. Maximum Pounds Seed Yield per 100 Square Feet[19]	TIMING R: Approx. No. of Weeks to Maturity in Ground[17]	TIMING S: Approx. No. Weeks in Harvesting Period	TIMING T: Time of Year to Plant (SP, SU, FA, WI)	CROP PROCEDURES U	PLANNING V: Pounds Consumed per Year by Average Person in U.S.[13,18]	NUTRITION W: Protein Content per Pound in Grams (g) (454 g per pound)[25]	NUTRITION X: Calorie Content per Pound[25,50]	NUTRITION Y: Calcium Content per Pound in Milligrams (mg)[25]	NOTES Z
19 Peanuts	Seed: 4 / 10 / 24	7.2	24	17	—	SU	Transplant when ~1.5 inches tall. Harvest when leaves begin to lose their green color and become dull; check maturity by digging up a few peanuts.	".64"	117.9	2,572	313	:Shelled, raw. Shells 27% of unshelled weight. Can be carcinogenic if not stored properly.
20 Pigeon Peas	Seed: 2 / 4 / 16+	D	16+	22	26+	SU	—	D	92.5	1,556	485	:Dry. Hulls 61% of unhulled weight. Short-lived perennial in tropical climates.
21 Quinoa	Seed: 6 / 13 / 26 Biomass, air-dry: 18 / 39 / 78	D	26	16	—	SU	Prick out when cotyledons have emerged and before first leaf emerges. Transplant when 2–3 inches tall and strong. Harvest when seeds are mature and dry enough to rub out of head easily.	D	73.5	1,600	640	:Dry.
22 Rapeseed (Canola)	Seed: 5 / 12 / 20	D	20	D	D	SP, SU, FA	Transplant when seedlings are ~1.5–2 inches tall. Harvest for seed when plants are ~85% golden; be alert for birds and/or shattering. For biomass, see Fava Beans.	D	D	1,960	D	:Dry. Helps eradicate weeds.
23 Rice	Seed: 8 / 16 / 32K U Biomass, air-dry: 24 / 54 / 96	Seed: 15.3 Biomass, dry: est. 23.0	24	17	—	SU	Transplant when seedlings are about ~2 inches tall. Harvest when plants are ~85% golden; be alert for shattering and birds.	22.3	34.0 / 30.4 / 2.7*	1,642 / 1,656 / D	145 / 109 / 86	:Brown. :White. :Straw and chaff, dry.
24 Rye, Cereal	Seed: 4 / 10 / 24K U Biomass, air-dry: 12 / 30 / 72	Seed: 3.5 Biomass, dry: est. 5.2	24	17 to 38[47]	—	FA	See Barley.	.4	54.9 / D	1,520 / 90	172 / 118	:Dry, whole grain. :Straw and chaff, dry. 15% in wheat bread buffers phytates that otherwise tie up iron.
25 Safflower	Seed: 4 / 9 / 17+ Biomass, air-dry: 5 / 10 / 20	Seed: 3.0	17+	17	—	SU	Transplant when seedlings are ~1.5–2 inches tall. Harvest carefully after plant has begun to dry, when 98–100% of heads are dry, and before seeds begin to shatter.	Oil: "1.0"	86.6	2,345	D	:Dry, hulled. Source of organic matter and vegetable oil. Hulls 49% of unhulled weight.
26 Sesame	Seed: 1.5 / 3 / 6+	D	6+	13–17	8	SU	Transplant when seedlings are ~1.5 inches tall and strong. Harvest when pods are full and plants begin losing green color, and before seeds shatter.	D	84.4	2,599	5,262	:Dry. Very high in calcium. Seed = 40% oil.

Master Charts

CROP	SEED A Approx. No. Seeds per Ounce[4] (Range: larger–smaller seed)	SEED B Minimum Legal Germination Rate[5]	SEED C Ounces / Volume Seed per 100 Square Feet (adj. for germ. rate, offset spacing, and curv. surf.)[6,7,8]	PLANTING D Short/Long/Extra-Long Germination Time	PLANTING E Plant Initially in Flats/Beds; Space in First Flat (in order of preference)	FLATS F Approx. No. of Plants per Flat (adj. for germ. rate)[14]	FLATS G No. First Flat(s) per 100 Sq Ft	FLATS H Approx. No. Weeks in First Flat[16]	FLATS I Depth of Second Flat and Spacing (Inches)	FLATS J No. Plants in Second Flat[14]	FLATS K No. Second Flats per 100 Sq Ft	FLATS L Approx. No. Weeks in Second Flat[16]	BEDS M In-Bed Spacing (Inches)	BEDS N MAXIMUM No. Plants per 100 Square Feet[7]
For protein, also see: Beans, Lima; Buckwheat; Collards; Corn, Sweet; Garlic; Peas; Potatoes, Irish and Sweet														
27 Sorghum	1,000	.65[A]	Reg. type: .66 / 1 2/3 T Broom type: 1.9 / 6 4/5 T	S	F:BC	162	1.3 / 4.1	2–3	—	—	—	—	Reg. type: 7 Broom type: 4	432 / 1,343
28 Soybeans	100–250	.75	8.2–3.3 / 1 1/8–1/2 c	S	F 1	187	3.3	2	—	—	—	—	6	621
29 Sunflowers	650 in shell[Y]	.50+[Y]	0.08 / 0.16 / 0.5 / 0.76 / 3-1/3 T**, ++[55]	S	F 1	125+	0.2 / 0.4 / 1.3 / 2	2–3	—	—	—	—	24 / 18 / 12 / 9**,+++	26 / 53 / 149 / 248
30 Wheat, Durum	500 hulled	.70[A]	2.4 / D	S	F:BC	175	2.4	1–2	—	—	—	—	5	833
31 Wheat, Early Stone Age	800 unhulled	.70[A]	1.5 / D	L	F:BC	175	2.4	2–3	—	—	—	—	5	833
32 Wheat, Hard Red Spring	500 hulled	.70[A]	2.4 / 6 1/3 T	S	F:BC	175	2.4	1–2	—	—	—	—	5	833
33 Wheat, Red Winter	500 hulled	.70[A]	2.4 / 6 1/3 T	S	F:BC	175	2.4	1–2	—	—	—	—	5	833
34 Wheat, White	500 hulled	.70[A]	2.4 / 6 1/3 T	S	F:BC	175	2.4	1–2	—	—	—	—	5	833

CROP	YIELD			TIMING			CROP PROCEDURES	PLANNING	NUTRITION			NOTES
	O	P	Q	R	S	T	U	V	W	X	Y	Z
	Possible GROW BIOINTENSIVE Yield in Pounds per 100-Square-Foot Planting[9]	Average U.S. Yield in Pounds per 100 Square Feet[12,13]	Approx. Maximum Pounds Seed Yield per 100 Square Feet[19]	Approx. No. of Weeks to Maturity in Ground[17]	Approx. No. Weeks in Harvesting Period	Time of Year to Plant (SP, SU, FA, WI)		Pounds Consumed per Year by Average Person in U.S.[13,18]	Protein Content per Pound in Grams (g) (454 g per pound)[25]	Calorie Content per Pound[25,50]	Calcium Content per Pound in Milligrams (mg)[25]	
27 Sorghum	Seed: 8 / 16 / 24; Biomass, air-dry: 25 / 50 / 100+; Biomass, wet: 88 / 175 / 350+	Seed: 6.8; Biomass, wet: 52.3	24	13	—	SU	See Pearl Millet.	D	49.9 / 15.0*	1,538 / 351	127 / 154	:Grain, dry. :Fodder, dry. 1 gallon of sorghum syrup can be obtained from 100 sq ft from some varieties.
28 Soybeans	Dry seed: 4 / 8 / 14+	4.6	14	Green: 8–9; Dry: 16–17	2–4	SU	See Beans.	All purposes: 467.4"	49.9 / 154.7	608 / 1,887	304 / 1,025	:Green. :Hulled, dry.
29 Sunflowers	Seed, hulled: 24°C: 2.5 / 5 / 10; Stalks, air-dry: 9°C: 20 / 40 / 80	Seed, hulled: 3.5	10	12	—	SU	Transplant when seedlings have 2 true leaves, and a third one coming. If possible, set deep enough so cotyledons are at soil surface; for leggy seedlings, set so that true leaves are 1 inch above soil surface. Harvest for seeds when "fuzz" is dry and black. May need to be protected from birds.	D	108.9	2,585	544	:Dry seeds without hulls. Hulls 46% of unhulled weight. Seed = approx. 20% oil. ~33 lb seeds required to produce 1T of oil.
30 Wheat, Durum	Seed: 4 / 10 / 26^K, U; Biomass, air-dry: 12 / 30 / 72	Seed: 4.6; Biomass, dry: est. 6.9	26	16–18 to 38^47	—	FA	See Barley.	See Wheat, Hard Red Spring	57.6 / 1.3*	1,538 / 100	168 / 95	:Grain, dry. :Straw and chaff, dry.
31 Wheat, Early Stone Age	Seed: 4 / 10 / 17^K, U; Biomass, air-dry: 12 / 30 / 51	D	17+	16–20 to 42^47	—	FA	See Barley.	D	83.0 / D	D / D	D / D	:Grain, dry. Triticum monococcum var. Hornemanii. Variety up to 12,500 years old. More difficult to thresh than other wheat.
32 Wheat, Hard Red Spring	Seed: 4 / 10 / 26^K, U; Biomass, air-dry: 12 / 30 / 72	Seed: 5.4; Biomass, dry: est. 8.1	26	16–18 to 38^47	—	FA	See Barley.	All purposes: 140.7	63.5 / 1.3*	1,492 / 100	163 / 95	:Grain, dry. :Straw and chaff, dry.
33 Wheat, Red Winter	Seed: 4 / 10 / 26^K, U; Biomass, air-dry: 12 / 30 / 72	Seed: 6.4; Biomass, dry: est. 9.6	26	16–18 to 38^47	—	FA	See Barley.		55.8 / 46.3 / 1.3*	1,483 / 1,483 / 100	209 / 191 / 95	:Grain, dry, hard variety. :Grain, dry, soft variety. :Straw and chaff, dry.
34 Wheat, White	Seed: 4 / 10 / 24^K, U; Biomass, air-dry: 12 / 30 / 72	Seed: "3.7"; Biomass, dry: est. 5.6	26	16–18 to 38^47	—	FA	See Barley.		42.6 / 1.3*	1,551 / 100	163 / 95	:Grain, dry. :Straw and chaff, dry. For milder, wetter climate, like the Pacific Northwest. Not widely used.

Master Charts

Compost, Carbon, Organic Matter, Fodder, and Cover Crops

CROP	A — Approx. No. Seeds per Ounce[4] (Range: larger–smaller seed)	B — Minimum Legal Germination Rate[5]	C — Ounces / Volume Seed per 100 Square Feet (adj. for germ. rate, offset spacing, and curv. surf.)[6,7,8]	D — Short/Long/Extra-Long Germination Time	E — Plant Initially in Flats/Beds; Space in First Flat (in order of preference)	F — Approx. No. of Plants per Flat (adj. for germ. rate)[14]	G — No. First Flat(s) per 100 Sq Ft	H — Approx. No. Weeks in First Flat[16]	I — Depth of Second Flat and Spacing (Inches)	J — No. Plants in Second Flat[14]	K — No. Second Flats per 100 Sq Ft	L — Approx. No. Weeks in Second Flat[16]	M — In-Bed Spacing (Inches)	N — MAXIMUM No. Plants per 100 Square Feet[7]
1 Alfalfa	14,000	.70[A]	.085 / 1/4 T	S	F:BC	175	1.2	8	—	—	—	—	5	833
2 Buckwheat	1,000	.70[A]	2.6 / 1/2 c	S	B:BC	—	—	—	—	—	—	—	Broad-cast	D
3 Cardoon	688	.60	.04 / 1 1/2 t	S	F1	150	0.12	2–3	6 / 2	60	0.3	3–4	36	18
4 Clover, Alsike	44,875	.70[A]	.55+-.3 / 1/6 t	S	F:BC	175	1.2	8	—	—	—	—	5	833
5 Clover, Crimson	7,000	.70[A]	.6+ / 1 1/4 t	S	F:BC	175	1.2	8	—	—	—	—	5	833
6 Clover, Medium Red	14,500	.70[A]	.08 for hay / .72 for green manure / 2 T / 1 1/10 c	S	F:BC	175	1.2	8	—	—	—	—	5	833
7 Clover, Sweet, Hubam	11,400	.70[A]	1.1 / 2/3 t	S	F:BC	175	1.2	8	—	—	—	—	5	833
8 Clover, White	45,750	.70[A]	.03 / 1/4 t	S	F:BC	175	1.2	8	—	—	—	—	5	833

Organic matter, also see: Artichoke, Jerusalem; Beans, Fava; Garlic

Group headings: SEED (A, B, C, D) · PLANTING (E) · FLATS (F, G, H, I, J, K, L) · BEDS (M, N)

CROP	O — Possible GROW BIOINTENSIVE Yield in Pounds per 100-Square-Foot Planting[9]	P — Average U.S. Yield in Pounds per 100 Square Feet[12,13]	Q — Approx. Maximum Pounds Seed Yield per 100 Square Feet[19]	R — Approx. No. of Weeks to Maturity in Ground[17]	S — Approx. No. Weeks in Harvesting Period	T — Time of Year to Plant (SP, SU, FA, WI)	U — CROP PROCEDURES	V — Pounds Consumed per Year by Average Person in U.S.[13,18]	W — Protein Content per Pound in Grams (g) (454 g per pound)[25]	X — Calorie Content per Pound[25,50]	Y — Calcium Content per Pound in Milligrams (mg)[25]	Z — NOTES
1 Alfalfa	Biomass, air-dry: 37 / 69 / 103, Biomass, wet: 148 / 275 / 412, 5–6 cuttings	Biomass, air-dry: 14.9; Biomass, wet: 49.9	1.8+	12 to first cutting, 5–9 thereafter	3–50+ years	SP	Grown as a perennial. Transplant when seeding is 2–3 months old. Can last up to 25+ years. Harvest at 10–50% flower or when leaves are dull/gray, stems are falling over, or leaves have holes. Cut back to 2 inches above growing crown. AC	"611.9"	Air-dry: 53.1*	411	667	Air dry at 10% bloom point. Fixes .35–.57 lb nitrogen/100 sq ft/year.
2 Buckwheat	Biomass, air-dry: 2 / 4 / 6, Grain: 4 / 8 / 16+	D	16+	9–13 (13 for maximum seed yield with sequential harvesting as seeds mature)	—	SP, mid-SU	Japanese variety may produce more dry biomass.	D	53.1	1,520	517	Dry grain. Hulling difficult. Good honeybee plant. 1/2 lb honey/100 sq ft.
3 Cardoon	Biomass, air-dry: 20 / 40 / 80	D	D	Harvest when stalks mature	1 harvest	SP	Perennial. Harvest flowers for income just as the blue is beginning to appear or for biomass before seeds begin to disperse. Harvest stalks for biomass when they become woody and the upper leaves wither.	D	—	—	—	Flower market potential. Can become a noxious weed; do not allow seeds to disperse.
4 Clover, Alsike	Biomass, air-dry: 12 / 25 / 38 (6-mo. yield)	Biomass, air-dry: "4.3"		17–26	1 cutting	SP			36.7*	436	522	Dry. Fixes up to 27 lb nitrogen/100 sq ft/year.
5 Clover, Crimson	Biomass, air-dry: 15 / 30 / 45, Biomass, wet: 60 / 120 / 180 (6-mo. yield)	Biomass, air-dry: "4.3"		17–26	1 cutting	SP	Annual. For harvest, see Alfalfa.		44.5*	391	558	Dry. Fixes up to 21 lb nitrogen/100 sq ft/year.
6 Clover, Medium Red	Biomass, air-dry: 18 / 36 / 54, Biomass, wet: 90 / 180 / 270 (6-mo. yield)	Biomass, air-dry: "8.7"	2.2+	17 to first cutting, 5–9 thereafter	2–3 years	SP	See Voisin books in the bibliography (under "Compost Crops") for ways to increase grazing yields significantly. Try 3–5 times the seeding rate for hay if growing crop seed. Roots can equal biomass weight above ground. Short-lived perennial. For harvest, see Alfalfa. More productive than other clovers.	"547.5"	51.3*	450	767	Dry. Before bloom. Fixes up to .23–.3 lb nitrogen/100 sq ft/year.
7 Clover, Sweet, Hubam	Biomass, air-dry: 15 / 30 / 45, Biomass, wet: 68 / 136 / 204 (6-mo. yield)	Biomass, air-dry: "4.3"		17–26	1 cutting	SP			42.6	355	567	Dry.
8 Clover, White	Biomass, air-dry: 10 / 25 / 38, Biomass, wet: 50 / 100 / 150 (6-mo. yield)	Biomass, air-dry: "4.3"		17–26	3–5 years	SP	Short-lived perennial. For harvest, see Alfalfa.		42.6*	355	567	Dry. Fixes up to .23–.3 lb nitrogen/100 sq ft/year.

Compost, Carbon, Organic Matter, Fodder, and Cover Crops

CROP	SEED — A: Approx. No. Seeds per Ounce[4] (Range: larger–smaller seed)	B: Minimum Legal Germination Rate[5]	C: Ounces / Volume Seed per 100 Square Feet (adj. for germ. rate, offset spacing, and curv. surf.)[6,7,8]	PLANTING — D: Short/Long/Extra-Long Germination Time	E: Plant Initially in Flats/Beds; Space in First Flat (in order of preference)	FLATS — F: Approx. No. of Plants per Flat (adj. for germ. rate)[14]	G: No. First Flat(s) per 100 Sq Ft	H: Approx. No. Weeks in First Flat[16]	I: Depth of Second Flat and Spacing (Inches)	J: No. Plants in Second Flat[14]	K: No. Second Flats per 100 Sq Ft	L: Approx. No. Weeks in Second Flat[16]	BEDS — M: In-Bed Spacing (Inches)	N: MAXIMUM No. Plants per 100 Square Feet[7]
Organic matter, also see: Artichoke, Jerusalem; Beans, Fava; Garlic														
9 Comfrey, Russian	—	—	53 roots	S	B	—	—	—	—	—	—	—	12	159
10 Grass, Rye, Italian	16,875	.70[A]	3.6 / 1 1/3 c	S	B:BC	—	—	—	—	—	—	—	Broadcast	D
11 Kudzu	2,000	.70[A]	D / D	S	B:BC	Propagated by seeds, cuttings, and roots. More research needs to be performed. For some information see *The Book of Kudzu*, by Bill Shurtleff, in the bibliography.								
12 Roots, General						An important hidden compost crop beneath the ground. Root matter in the soil can range from 45–120% of aboveground biomass at the end of the growing season (Brady and Weil, *The Nature and Properties of Soils*, 12th ed., p. 423).								
13 Sainfoin	In pods: 1,560 Cleaned: 2,040	.50[A]	.82 hulled / D	S	F:BC	125	3.3	8	—	—	—	—	5	833
14 Sunn hemp, Giant	3,000	.70[A]	.2 / 1 1/2 t	S	F:BC	175	2.5	2–3	—	—	—	—	7	432
15 Teosinte	440	.70[A]	.11 / 2/3 T	S	F1	175	0.2	2–3	—	—	—	—	21	35
16 Timothy	82,500	.70[A]	.01 / 1/8 t	S	F:BC	175	1.2	8	—	—	—	—	5	833
17 Vetch, Purple, Hairy, or Woolly Pod[BB]	800	.70[BB]	5.5 (.63 if interplanted) / 3/4 c (1 1/2 T)	S	B:BC	—	—	—	—	—	—	—	Broadcast	D

CROP	O — Possible GROW BIOINTENSIVE Yield in Pounds per 100-Square-Foot Planting[9]	P — Average U.S. Yield in Pounds per 100 Square Feet[12,13]	Q — Approx. Maximum Pounds Seed Yield per 100 Square Feet[19]	R — Approx. No. of Weeks to Maturity in Ground[17]	S — Approx. No. Weeks in Harvesting Period	T — Time of Year to Plant (SP, SU, FA, WI)	U — Crop Procedures	V — Pounds Consumed per Year by Average Person in U.S.[13,18]	W — Protein Content per Pound in Grams (g) (454 g per pound)[25]	X — Calorie Content per Pound[25,50]	Y — Calcium Content per Pound in Milligrams (mg)[25]	Z — Notes
9 Comfrey, Russian	Biomass, air-dry: 10 / 20 / 30; Biomass, wet: 92 / 184 / 276 (6-mo. yield)	Biomass, air-dry: "62.6" world high (12-mo. season)	D	12–17 to first cutting	Years	SP	Perennial. Divide roots and plant. Harvest for biomass when plants begin to flower; cut back to 2 inches.	D	3.4	D	D	
10 Grass, Rye, Italian	D	D	6.9+	D	D	SP		D	15.4*	D	—	Not good for soil. Use cereal rye to build soil and for food.
11 Kudzu	Biomass, air-dry: 13 / 26 / 53; Biomass, wet: 53 / 105 / 211					D			13.3 / 11.3	D / D	D / D	:Dried root. :Cured hay. Plus cloth can be made from the root. Can be invasive.
12 Roots, General						—			—	—	—	
13 Sainfoin	Biomass, air-dry: 10 / 20 / 30 (6-mo. yield)	D	.46+	17 to first cutting, 9 thereafter	D	SP		D	34.0*	D	—	:Dry. Does best in slightly dry climate. Significantly less productive than alfalfa.
14 Sunn hemp, Giant	Biomass, air-dry: 18 / 44 / 108; Biomass, wet: 79 / 198 / 475	D	D	17+	D	SU	For harvest, see Alfalfa. Or allow to grow, and harvest seeds before they shatter.	D	D	D	D	Grain legume.
15 Teosinte	Grain: 2 / 4 / 6; Biomass, air-dry: 17 / 34 / 68; Biomass, wet: 88 / 166 / 232	D	D	D	D	SU	Harvest grain before it shatters.	D	22.2*	D	D	Less productive of biomass and significantly less productive of grain than corn, but produces an extensive root system.
16 Timothy	Biomass, air-dry: 18 / 35 / 51; Biomass, wet: 45 / 87 / 127 (6-mo. yield)	Biomass, air-dry: "4.3"	.46+	17	D	SP	Perennial. Harvest when earliest heads are straw-colored for highest biomass yield.	D	18.6*	D	186	:Dry, early bloom.
17 Vetch, Purple, Hairy, or Woolly Pod[BB]	Biomass, air-dry: 5 / 9 / 18; Biomass, wet: 24 / 45 / 90 planted alone	D	1.1+	D	D	SP, FA	For better germination, soak seeds overnight in warm water; mix with dry sand or soil to minimize clumping; chop seed in very lightly with rake. Harvest at 10%–50% flower. Can become weedy if seeds disperse.	D	69.0*	D	513	:Dry. Fixes up to .25 lb nitrogen/100 sq ft/year.

CROP	A — Approx. No. Seeds per Ounce[4] (Range: larger–smaller seed)	B — Minimum Legal Germination Rate[5]	C — Ounces / Volume Seed per 100 Square Feet (adj. for germ. rate, offset spacing, and curv. surf.)[6,7,8]	D — Short/Long/Extra-Long Germination Time	E — Plant Initially in Flats/Beds; Space in First Flat (in order of preference)	F — Approx. No. of Plants per Flat (adj. for germ. rate)[14]	G — No. First Flat(s) per 100 Sq Ft	H — Approx. No. Weeks in First Flat[16]	I — Depth of Second Flat and Spacing (Inches)	J — No. Plants in Second Flat[14]	K — No. Second Flats per 100 Sq Ft	L — Approx. No. Weeks in Second Flat[16]	M — In-Bed Spacing (Inches)	N — MAXIMUM No. Plants per 100 Square Feet[7]
1 Bamboo, Paper	Under research						—				—			
2 Bamboo, Regular	Under research						—				—			
3 Beets, Sugar	1,600	.65[A]	.4[AA] / 2 T	L	F 1	162	2.7	3–4	—	—	—	—	7	432
4 Cheese	Approx. 1 lb per gallon of milk. Heat milk to 180°F. Add 1/2 cup vinegar per gallon of milk. Stir. Let sit for 5 minutes. Pour through cheesecloth lining a colander. Let drain until excess moisture is gone. Result: soft cheese.													
5 Cotton, Regular	300	.70[A]	.76 / varies	L	F 1	175	0.9	3–4	—	—	—	—	12	159
6 Cotton, Tree	An African perennial variety. Under research.						—							
7 Eggs, Chicken	See Ecology Action's *Backyard Homestead, Mini-Farm and Garden Log Book*.						—							
8 Flax	6,000	.70[A]	Seed: .2 / 1/2 t Fiber: .6 / 1 2/3 t	S	F 1	175	4.8 / 14.3	2–3	—	—	—	—	Seed: 5 Fiber: 3	833 / 2,507

CROP	YIELD			TIMING			CROP PROCEDURES	PLANNING	NUTRITION			NOTES
	O — Possible GROW BIOINTENSIVE Yield in Pounds per 100-Square-Foot Planting[9]	P — Average U.S. Yield in Pounds per 100 Square Feet[12,13]	Q — Approx. Maximum Pounds Seed Yield per 100 Square Feet[19]	R — Approx. No. of Weeks to Maturity in Ground[17]	S — Approx. No. Weeks in Harvesting Period	T — Time of Year to Plant (SP, SU, FA, WI)	U	V — Pounds Consumed per Year by Average Person in U.S.[13,18]	W — Protein Content per Pound in Grams (g) (454 g per pound)[25]	X — Calorie Content per Pound[25,50]	Y — Calcium Content per Pound in Milligrams (mg)[25]	Z
1 Bamboo, Paper	Under research	General: "27.5"				—		All paper and paperboard: "699"	—	—	—	Probably any abundant local species, reasonably priced, may be used. Better grades of paper are made from young and still leafless culms; older, mature culms are too lignified for easy processing but can be used for coarse, dark-fibered paper. 40% paper yield. For wrapping paper, newsprint, and book-quality paper. Paper can also be made from many fibrous plants, including cabbage.
2 Bamboo, Regular	Under research					—	Use clumping bamboo to minimize spreading; roots may need to be restrained. For building, furniture, and pipeline, harvest after 3 years of growth.		—	—	—	Building materials, piping.
3 Beets, Sugar	91 / 182 / 364	104.7	"30.6"	12	—	SP, SU, FA		All sugars: "67.1 lbs" All syrups: "10+ gal"	D	1,746	D	~5.2 lb of sugar beets are required to produce 1 T of sugar.
4 Cheese						—			36.3	1,696	281	:Cream cheese. Add parsley, dill seeds, chives for flavor.
5 Cotton, Regular	1.2 / 2.4 / 4.8+	1.7	22.7	17–26		SU	Harvest when seeds are fully developed.	D	—			Minimum clothes replacement rate per year: 2.5 lbs. Thousands of years ago in India, people placed a mineral in the soil with the cotton plants, and colored fibers resulted!
6 Cotton, Tree	Under research					SU			—	—	—	
7 Eggs, Chicken					—	—		Eggs: "240 (30 lb)"	52.1	658	218	:11% refuse.
8 Flax	seed: 2 / 4 / 8 biomass, air-dry: 4 / 8 / 16+	"1.4"	D	12–14	—	SP	For seed, harvest before seeds shatter. For fiber, harvest when seeds are beginning to turn :color from green to brown and bottom of plant is beginning to turn yellow.	D	89	2,419	1,115	

Energy, Fiber, Paper, and Other Crops

CROP	SEED			PLANTING			FLATS						BEDS	
	A — Approx. No. Seeds per Ounce[4] (Range: larger–smaller seed)	B — Minimum Legal Germination Rate[5]	C — Ounces / Volume Seed per 100 Square Feet (adj. for germ. rate, offset spacing, and curv. surf.)[6,7,8]	D — Short/Long/Extra-Long Germination Time	E — Plant Initially in Flats/Beds; Space in First Flat (in order of preference)	F — Approx. No. of Plants per Flat (adj. for germ. rate)[14]	G — No. First Flat(s) per 100 Sq Ft	H — Approx. No. Weeks in First Flat[16]	I — Depth of Second Flat and Spacing (Inches)	J — No. Plants in Second Flat[14]	K — No. Second Flats per 100 Sq Ft	L — Approx. No. Weeks in Second Flat[16]	M — In-Bed Spacing (Inches)	N — MAXIMUM No. Plants per 100 Square Feet[7]
9 Gopher Plant	For automotive oil. Under research. Also, a toxic plant for gopher control. Not to be used around young children.						–							
10 Gourds	150	.70A	.5 / varies	S	F	42	1.25	3-4	–	–	–	–	18	53
11 Guayule	For rubber. Under research.						–							
12 Jojoba	50	D	For oil. Under research.				–							
13 Kenaf	For newsprint, toilet paper, fiber, twine, rope. Grows up to 18 ft high. 8–10 tons of fiber yield per acre possible annually (5 times the pulp per acre compared with wood).													
14 Milk, Cow	See Ecology Action's *Backyard Homestead, Mini-Farm and Garden Log Book*. A cow requires about twice the fodder as a goat and produces about twice the milk.						–							
15 Milk, Goat							–							
16 Sprouts, Alfalfa	To be developed. Nutritious, but a large area is required for the production of the seed.						–							
17 Sprouts, Wheat							–							

CROP	O — Possible GROW BIOINTENSIVE Yield in Pounds per 100-Square-Foot Planting[9]	P — Average U.S. Yield in Pounds per 100 Square Feet[12,13]	Q — Approx. Maximum Pounds Seed Yield per 100 Square Feet[19]	R — Approx. No. of Weeks to Maturity in Ground[17]	S — Approx. No. Weeks in Harvesting Period	T — Time of Year to Plant (SP, SU, FA, WI)	U — CROP PROCEDURES	V — Pounds Consumed per Year by Average Person in U.S.[13,18]	W — Protein Content per Pound in Grams (g) (454 g per pound)[25]	X — Calorie Content per Pound[25,50]	Y — Calcium Content per Pound in Milligrams (mg)[25]	Z — NOTES
9 Gopher Plant	For automotive oil. Under research. Also, a toxic plant for gopher control. Not to be used around young children.	D	D			SP		—	—	—	—	
10 Gourds	D	D	D	16	—	SU	For transplanting, see Cucumbers. Support gourds on smooth rocks to keep them off the damp soil. Harvest when stem is dry and hard; cut off with 2 inches of stem.	D	—	—	—	
11 Guayule	For rubber. Under research.											
12 Jojoba	For rubber. Under research.											
13 Kenaf												For more information on kenaf, write to the American Kenaf Society, PMB 440, 1001 South 10th Street, Ste G, McAllen, TX 78501.
14 Milk, Cow						—		Fluid milk and cream: 207.0 lbs (25.9 gal)	15.9	299	531	:3.7% fat.
15 Milk, Goat						—		D	14.5	304	585	Has only 1/3 the vitamin B12 that cow's milk has.
16 Sprouts, Alfalfa						All year			Nutritive amounts given for sprouts differ.			
17 Sprouts, Wheat						All year						

Column key:

- **BEDS**
  - N — Square Feet Required per Plant
  - M — In-Bed Spacing (feet)
- **FLATS**
  - L — Approx. No. Weeks in Second Flat[16]
  - K — No. Second Flats per 100 Sq Ft
  - J — No. Plants in Second Flat[14]
  - I — Depth of Second Flat and Spacing (Inches)
  - H — Approx. No. Weeks in First Flat[16]
  - G — No. First Flat(s) per 100 Sq Ft
- **PLANTING**
  - F — No. Plants in First Flat (adj. for germ. rate)[14]
  - E — Flat spacing for First Flat and Second Flat (inches)
  - D — Short/Long/Extra-Long Germination Time
- **SEED**
  - C — Aprpox. No. Plants per Acre
  - B — Minimum Legal Germination Rate[5]
  - A — Approx. No. Seeds per Ounce[4] (Range: larger–smaller seed)

CROP	A	B	C	D	E	F	G	H	I	J	K	L	M	N
1 Almond	12–15	D	160	L	4 / 1	D	Minimal	D	—	—	—	D	16.5	272
2 Apple, Dwarf	600–1,000	D	681	EL	2 / 1	D	Minimal	D	—	—	—	D	8	64
3 Apple, Regular	600–1,000	.65A	27	EL	2 / 1	39	Minimal	D	—	—	—	D	40	1,600
4 Apple, Semidwarf	600–1,000	D	194	EL	2 / 1	D	Minimal	D	—	—	—	D	15	225
5 Apricot, Dwarf	18–20	D	681	L	4 / 1	D	Minimal	D	—	—	—	D	8	64
6 Apricot, Regular	18–20	.90A	70	L	4 / 1	14	Minimal	D	—	—	—	D	25	625
7 Apricot, Semidwarf	18–20	D	303	L	4 / 1	D	Minimal	D	—	—	—	D	12	144
8 Avocado, Tall Dwarf	D	D	302–193 / 681	D	4 / 1	D	Minimal	D	—	—	—	D	12–15 / 8	144–225 / 64
9 Banana, Tall Dwarf	—	D	302–193 / 681	D	4 / 1	D	Minimal	D	—	—	—	D	12–15 / 8	144–225 / 64
10 Blackberries	10,000	—	2,723	D	6 / 1	D	4 / 1	D	6 / 4	1.5	6.7 / 1	D	1–4	1–16

CROP	Possible GROW BIOINTENSIVE Yield in Pounds per 100 Square Feet[10, 11] (O)	Average U.S. Yield in Pounds per 100 Square Feet[12, 13] (P)	Approx. Maximum Pounds Seed Yield per 100 Square Feet[19] (Q)	Approx. No. Years to Bearing / Max Bearing (R)	Approx. No. Weeks in Harvesting Period / Possible Bearing Years (S)	Time of Year to Plant (T)	CROP PROCEDURES (U)	Pounds Consumed per Year by Average Person in U.S.[13, 18] (V)	Protein Content per Pound in Grams (g) (454 g per pound)[25] (W)	Calorie Content per Pound[25, 50] (X)	Calcium Content per Pound in Milligrams (mg)[25] (Y)	NOTES (Z)
							For varietal and other information, see [HPW] *Western Fruit, Berries and Nuts: How to Select, Grow and Enjoy*, by Lance Walheim and Robert L. Stebbins (under Fruits, Berries, and Nuts in Bibliography), and/or [DW] Dave Wilson Nursery catalog (under Seed Catalogs in Bibliography), or [HPC] *Citrus: How to Select, Grow and Enjoy*, by Richard Ray and Lance Walheim (under Fruits, Berries, and Nuts in Bibliography).					
1 Almond	Shelled: 1.4 / 2.8 / 4.2+	7.2	In shell: 8.4	3–4	D / D	Early SP	HPW, DW.	".4"	84.4	2,713	1,061	:Shelled. Shells 49% of unshelled weight.
2 Apple, Dwarf	50 / 75 / 100	51.4	D	3 / D	D / D	Early SP	[1] Harvest according to varietal maturation time. Also, harvest before first frost, before significant drop occurs, and before or as bird damage begins to occur. Optimum harvest time will vary from year to year depending on climatic conditions. [2] Consider grafting several varieties on 1 tree for harvest during a significant part of the growing season, depending on climate. [3] Note that one full-sized tree at maturity can produce approximately 3 lb of apples per day, at intermediate yields. You do not need many fruit trees to have enough fruit. Consider doing a few trees well. It takes less time! 1.5 gallons of apple cider or apple cider vinegar can be obtained per 100 sq ft.		.8	242	29	:Raw. 8% refuse. Spur-type yields higher. Thin to 6 to 8 in.
3 Apple, Regular	50 / 75 / 100	51.4	D	5 / 10	35–50 / D	Early SP		"16.0"	.8	242	29	:Raw. 8% refuse. Thin to 6 to 8 in.
4 Apple, Semidwarf	50 / 75 / 100	51.4	D	4 / 10	D / D	Early SP			.8	242	29	:Raw. 8% refuse. Thin to 6 to 8 in.
5 Apricot, Dwarf	25 / 50 / 100	25.1	D	2 / D	D / D	Early SP	See [1] and [2] under Apples. HPW, DW.		4.3	217	72	:Raw. 6% refuse. A fall-yielding variety also exists.
6 Apricot, Regular	25 / 50 / 100	25.1	D	3 / D	D / D	Early SP		".17"	4.3	217	72	:Raw. 6% refuse. 30 ft high.
7 Apricot, Semidwarf	25 / 50 / 100	25.1	D	3 / D	D / D	Early SP			4.3	217	72	:Raw. 6% refuse.
8 Avocado, Tall Dwarf	9 / 18 / 36	16.0	D	D / D	D / D	Early SP	HPW	"1.3"	7.1	568	34	:25% refuse.
9 Banana, Tall Dwarf	27 / 60 / 92+	38.3	—	D / D	D / D	Early SP	HPW	D	3.4 / 3.7	262 / 278	25 / 31	:Yellow. :Red. 32% refuse
10 Blackberries	24 / 36 / 48+	15.0	—	2 / D	D / 6–25	Early SP	Propagated by cuttings. Beds 2–3 ft wide. Some people use 2-ft centers. See [1] under Apples. HPW.	D	5.3	264	145	:Raw.

Master Charts

CROP	A — Approx. No. Seeds per Ounce[4] (Range: larger–smaller seed)	B — Minimum Legal Germination Rate[5]	C — Approx. No. Plants per Acre	D — Short/Long/Extra-Long Germination Time	E — Flat spacing for First Flat and Second Flat (inches)	F — No. Plants in First Flat (adj. for germ. rate)[14]	G — No. First Flat(s) per 100 Sq Ft	H — Approx. No. Weeks in First Flat[16]	I — Depth of Second Flat and Spacing (Inches)	J — No. Plants in Second Flat[14]	K — No. Second Flats per 100 Sq Ft	L — Approx. No. Weeks in Second Flat[16]	M — In-Bed Spacing (feet)	N — Square Feet Required per Plant
11 Blueberries, Low Bush, High Bush	—	—	10,890 / 2,723	D	— / —	D	8.5 / 1	D	—	D	—	D	2 / 4	4 / 16
12 Boysenberries	—	—	681	D	— / F	D	4 / 1	D	—	—	—	D	1–8	64
13 Cherry, Sour, Bush	D	D	4,840	L	— / 3	D	1	D	—	—	—	D	3	9
14 Cherry, Sour, Dwarf	200–250	.80A	681	L	— / 3	22	0.3	D	—	—	—	D	8	64
15 Cherry, Sour, Regular	200–250	D	1,089	L	— / 3	D	Minimal	D	—	—	—	D	20	400
16 Cherry, Sweet, Bush	D	D	4,840	L	— / 3	D	1	D	—	—	—	D	3	9
17 Cherry, Sweet, Dwarf	150–160	D	681	L	— / 3	D	0.3	D	—	—	—	D	8	64
18 Cherry, Sweet, Regular	150–160	.75A	481	L	— / 3	20	Minimal	D	—	—	—	D	30	900
19 Chestnut	1	.72A	27	D	1 / 6	5	Minimal	D	—	—	—	D	40	1,600

For varietal and other information, see (HPW) *Western Fruit, Berries and Nuts: How to Select, Grow and Enjoy*, by Lance Walheim and Robert L. Stebbins (under Fruits, Berries, and Nuts in Bibliography), and/or (DW) Dave Wilson Nursery catalog (under Seed Catalogs in Bibliography), or (HPC) *Citrus: How to Select, Grow and Enjoy*, by Richard Ray and Lance Walheim (under Fruits, Berries, and Nuts in Bibliography).

CROP	O — Possible GROW BIOINTENSIVE Yield in Pounds per 100 Square Feet[10,11]	P — Average U.S. Yield in Pounds per 100 Square Feet[12,13]	Q — Approx. Maximum Pounds Seed Yield per 100 Square Feet[19]	R — Approx. No. Years to Bearing / to Max Bearing	S — Approx. No. Weeks in Harvesting Period / Possible Bearing Years	T — Time of Year to Plant	U — CROP PROCEDURES	V — Pounds Consumed per Year by Average Person in U.S.[13,18]	W — Protein Content per Pound in Grams (g) (454 g per pound)[25]	X — Calorie Content per Pound[25,50]	Y — Calcium Content per Pound in Milligrams (mg)[25]	Z — NOTES
11 Blueberries, Low Bush, High Bush	19 / 37 / 75	D	—	3–4 / D	6–7 / 10–15	Early SP	Propagated by cuttings in late SP. Remove blossoms for first 2 years. Use bird netting. See (1) under Apples. HPW, DW.	".12"	2.9	259	63	:Raw. 8% refuse.
12 Boysenberries	26 / 39 / 52+	"25.7"	—	2 / D	6–10 / D	Early SP	Propagated by cuttings. 2-ft-wide beds. 4–8 canes/center. See Blackberries.	D	3.2	163	86	:Canned. 8% refuse. Bearing season: Logan (midsummer); Young (midsummer); Olallie (late summer).
13 Cherry, Sour, Bush	8 / 17 / 34	D	D	3 / D	D / D	Early SP	See (1) under Apples. HPW, DW.	".62"	5.0	242	92	:Raw. 8% refuse.
14 Cherry, Sour, Dwarf	17 / 34 / 51	14.0	D	3 / D	D / D	Early SP			5.0	242	92	:Raw. 8% refuse.
15 Cherry, Sour, Regular	17 / 34 / 51	14.0	D	4 / 10–20	D / D	Early SP			5.0	242	92	:Raw. 8% refuse.
16 Cherry, Sweet, Bush	8 / 17 / 34	D	D	3 / D	D / D	Early SP			3.6	195	68	:Canned, without pits.
17 Cherry, Sweet, Dwarf	17 / 34 / 51	15.0	D	3 / D	D / D	Early SP			3.6	195	68	:Canned, without pits. One self-pollinating variety exists.
18 Cherry, Sweet, Regular	17 / 34 / 51	15.0	D	4 / 10–20	D / D	Early SP			3.6	195	68	:Canned, without pits.
19 Chestnut	In shell: 3.5 / 7 / 15	D	In shell: 15.0	D / D	D / D	Early SP	HPW, DW.	D	30.4	1,710	236	:Dried and shelled: 18% of unshelled weight. Problems with blight.

Master Charts

Crop	A. Approx. No. Seeds per Ounce[4] (Range: larger–smaller seed)	B. Minimum Legal Germination Rate[5]	C. Approx. No. Plants per Acre	D. Short/Long/Extra-Long Germination Time	E. Flat spacing for First Flat and Second Flat (inches)	F. No. Plants in First Flat (adj. for germ. rate)[14]	G. No. First Flat(s) per 100 Sq Ft	H. Approx. No. Weeks in First Flat[16]	I. Depth of Second Flat and Spacing (Inches)	J. No. Plants in Second Flat[14]	K. No. Second Flats per 100 Sq Ft	L. Approx. No. Weeks in Second Flat[16]	M. In-Bed Spacing (feet)	N. Square Feet Required per Plant
20 Coconut	—	D	48	D	4 / —	D	Minimal	D	—	—	—	D	30	900
21 Currants, Black	—	—	2,723	D	6 / —	D	4 / 1	D	—	—	—	D	1–4	16
22 Dates	40	—	48	D	9 / —	D	Minimal	D	—	—	—	D	30	900
23 Fig	—	—	194	D	9 / —	D	Minimal	D	—	—	—	D	15	225
24 Filbert	10–20	—	194	L	9 / —	D	Minimal	D	—	—	—	D	15 (18–25)	225
25 Grapefruit	150–200	D	76	D	3 / —	D	Minimal	D	—	—	—	D	24	576
26 Grapes, Raisin	—	—	681	D	6 / —	D	0.3	D	—	—	—	D	8	64
27 Grapes, Table	—	—	681	D	6 / —	D	0.3	D	—	—	—	D	8	64
28 Grapes, Wine	—	—	681	D	6 / —	D	0.3	D	—	—	—	D	8	64
29 Guava	D	D	303	D	2 / —	D	Minimal	D	—	—	—	D	12	144

Master Charts

CROP	YIELD — O: Possible GROW BIOINTENSIVE Yield in Pounds per 100 Square Feet[10,11]	YIELD — P: Average U.S. Yield in Pounds per 100 Square Feet[12,13]	YIELD — Q: Approx. Maximum Pounds Seed Yield per 100 Square Feet[19]	TIMING — R: Approx. No. Years to Bearing and Approx. No. Years to Max Bearing	TIMING — S: Approx. No. Weeks in Harvesting Period and Possible Bearing Years	TIMING — T: Time of Year to Plant (SP, SU, FA, WI)	CROP PROCEDURES — U	PLANNING — V: Pounds Consumed per Year by Average Person in U.S.[13,18]	NUTRITION — W: Protein Content per Pound in Grams (g) (454 g per pound)[25]	NUTRITION — X: Calorie Content per Pound[25,50]	NUTRITION — Y: Calcium Content per Pound in Milligrams (mg)[25]	NOTES — Z
(General)							For varietal and other information, see (HPW) *Western Fruit, Berries and Nuts: How to Select, Grow and Enjoy*, by Lance Walheim and Robert L. Stebbins (under Fruits, Berries, and Nuts in Bibliography), and/or (DW) Dave Wilson Nursery catalog (under Seed Catalogs in Bibliography), or (HPC) *Citrus: How to Select, Grow and Enjoy*, by Richard Ray and Lance Walheim (under Fruits, Berries, and Nuts in Bibliography).					
20 Coconut	3 / 6 / 13	D	D	D / D	D / D	Early SP	D	D	8.3 / 15.9	816 / 1,569	31 / 59	:Fresh. 48% refuse. :Meat
21 Currants, Black	D	D	—	3	D / D	Early SP	2-foot-wide beds. See (1) under Apples. HPW. Propagated by cuttings.	D	7.6	240	267	:Raw. 2% refuse.
22 Dates	23 / 46 / 70	14.2	D	5–6 / 10–15	D / D	Early SP	1 male to 100 female plants for pollination. Propagated by cuttings.	D	10.0	1,243	268	:Dry and pitted. Pits: 13% of dried weight.
23 Fig	Raw: 12 / 24 / 36++	17.1	D	D / D	17 / D	Early SP	See (1) under Apples. HPW, DW. Propagated by cuttings.	D	5.4 / 19.5	363 / 1,243	159 / 572	:Raw. Drying ratio 3:1. :Dried. 23% moisture.
24 Filbert	Shelled: 7 / 15 / 30	6.2	In shell: 55.0	D / D	D / D	Early SP	See (1) under Apples. HPW, DW. Propagated by cuttings.	".07"	57.2	2,876	948	:Shelled: 54% of unshelled weight. 46% refuse.
25 Grapefruit	63 / 95 / 126	73.7	D	3	D / D	Early SP	HPC	"6.7"	1.0	84	33	:Raw. 55% refuse.
26 Grapes, Raisin	Fresh, for drying: 45 / 67 / 90	"45.4"	D	3	D / D	Early SP	See (1) under Apples. HPW, DW. Propagated by cuttings.	Dry: "2.0"	11.3	1,311	281	:Dry. 18% moisture. Drying ratio 4.3:1.
27 Grapes, Table	45 / 67 / 90	31.2	D	3	D / D	Early SP	Propagated by cuttings.	"4.6"	2.4	270	48	:Raw. 11% refuse.
28 Grapes, Wine	32 / 48 / 64	"31.6"	D	3	D / D	Early SP	Propagated by cuttings.	"20.4"	3.7	197	46	:Raw. 37% refuse.
29 Guava	D	28.9	D	D / D	D / D	Early SP	HPW	D	3.5	273	101	:Raw. 35% refuse. 15 ft high.

Tree and Cane Crops

CROP	SEED — A: Approx. No. Seeds per Ounce[4] (Range: larger–smaller seed)	SEED — B: Minimum Legal Germination Rate[5]	SEED — C: Aprpox. No. Plants per Acre	PLANTING — D: Short/Long/Extra-Long Germination Time	PLANTING — E: Flat spacing for First Flat and Second Flat (inches)	FLATS — F: No. Plants in First Flat (adj. for germ. rate)[14]	FLATS — G: No. First Flat(s) per 100 Sq Ft	FLATS — H: Approx. No. Weeks in First Flat[16]	FLATS — I: Depth of Second Flat and Spacing (Inches)	FLATS — J: No. Plants in Second Flat[14]	FLATS — K: No. Second Flats per 100 Sq Ft	FLATS — L: Approx. No. Weeks in Second Flat[16]	BEDS — M: In-Bed Spacing (feet)	BEDS — N: Square Feet Required per Plant
30 Hickory	1–5 depends on variety	.55–.80 J depends on variety	27	D	4 / —	8–12	Minimal	D	—	—	—	D	40	1,600
31 Honey Locust	180	.50 J	27	D	4 / —	8	Minimal	D	—	—	—	D	40	1,600
32 Lemon	200–300	D	76	D	2 / —	D	Minimal	D	—	—	—	D	24	576
33 Lime	300–400	D	194	D	2 / —	D	Minimal	D	—	—	—	D	15	225
34 Mango	D	D	48	D	2 / —	D	Minimal	D	—	—	—	D	30	900
35 Mesquite	D	D	109	D	2 / —	D	Minimal	D	—	—	—	D	20	400
36 Nectarine, Dwarf	D	D	681	D	—	—	Minimal	—	—	—	—	D	8	64
37 Nectarine, Regular	D	D	194	D	4 / —	D	Minimal	D	—	—	—	D	15	225
38 Olive	D	D	27	D	2 / —	D	Minimal	D	—	—	—	D	40	1,600

Column descriptions:
- **O** — Possible GROW BIOINTENSIVE Yield in Pounds per 100 Square Feet[10,11]
- **P** — Average U.S. Yield in Pounds per 100 Square Feet[12,13]
- **Q** — Approx. Maximum Pounds Seed Yield per 100 Square Feet[19]
- **R** — Approx. No. Years to Bearing and Approx. No. Years to Max Bearing
- **S** — Approx. No. Weeks in Harvesting Period and Possible Bearing Years
- **T** — Time of Year to Plant (SP, SU, FA, WI)
- **U** — Crop Procedures. For varietal and other information, see (HPW) *Western Fruit, Berries and Nuts: How to Select, Grow and Enjoy*, by Lance Walheim and Robert L. Stebbins (under Fruits, Berries, and Nuts in Bibliography), and/or (DW) Dave Wilson Nursery catalog (under Seed Catalogs in Bibliography), or (HPC) *Citrus: How to Select, Grow and Enjoy*, by Richard Ray and Lance Walheim (under Fruits, Berries, and Nuts in Bibliography).
- **V** — Pounds Consumed per Year by Average Person in U.S.[13,18]
- **W** — Protein Content per Pound in Grams (g) (454 g per pound)[25]
- **X** — Calorie Content per Pound[25,50]
- **Y** — Calcium Content per Pound in Milligrams (mg)[25]
- **Z** — Notes

Crop	O	P	Q	R	S	T	U	V	W	X	Y	Z
30 Hickory	D	D	D	D / D	D / 25–350	Early SP	See [1] under Apples.	D	59.9	3,053	Trace	Shelled: 65% of unshelled weight.
31 Honey Locust	Pods and beans: 6 / 13 / 26+	D	In shell: 13.0	D / D	D / 10–100	Early SP	See *Forest Farming*, by J. Sholto Douglas and Rebecca Hart and/or *Tree Crops*, by J. Russell Smith (in Bibliography under Trees).	D	72	D / D	D	Can make a flour from the beans. Pods and beans a good fodder. A very important tree. *Gleditsia trianconti.*
32 Lemon	75 / 112 / 150	76.2	D	3 / D	D / 50+	Early SP	HPW, HPC.	3.8	3.3	82	79	33% refuse.
33 Lime	D	32.3	D	3 / D	D / D	Early SP	HPW, HPC.	.3	2.7	107	126	16% refuse.
34 Mango	D	68.8	D	D / D	D / D	D	HPW. Propagated by seed or grafting.	.02	2.3	294	45.7	33% refuse. 90 ft high at maturity.
35 Mesquite	Seeds: D / Pods: D	29.0	D	D / D	D / D	Early SP	See [1] under Apples. HPW, DW.	D	17.0 / 76.2	D / D	260 / D	Seed. / Pod.
36 Nectarine, Dwarf	40 / 60 / 80	29.0	D	3–4 / 8–12	D / D	Early SP			2.5	267	263	8% refuse. 8 ft high. Thin to 6 to 8 in (10 in for early varieties).
37 Nectarine, Regular	40 / 60 / 80	29.0	D	D / D	D / D	Early SP		1.8	2.5	267	263	8% refuse. 25 ft high. Thin to 6 to 8 in (10 in for early varieties).
38 Olive	8 / 17 / 35	15.0	D	D / D	D / D	Early SP		D	5.3 / 8.0	442 / 1,227	232 / —	Green. 16% refuse. Ripe. 20% refuse. Pasquale, up to 40% oil. All others, 16.5–21.8% oil.

CROP	A — Approx. No. Seeds per Ounce[4] (Range: larger–smaller seed)	B — Minimum Legal Germination Rate[5]	C — Aprpox. No. Plants per Acre	D — Short/Long/Extra-Long Germination Time	E — Flat spacing for First Flat and Second Flat (inches)	F — No. Plants in First Flat (adj. for germ. rate)[14]	G — No. First Flat(s) per 100 Sq Ft	H — Approx. No. Weeks in First Flat[16]	I — Depth of Second Flat and Spacing (Inches)	J — No. Plants in Second Flat[14]	K — No. Second Flats per 100 Sq Ft	L — Approx. No. Weeks in Second Flat[16]	M — In-Bed Spacing (feet)	N — Square Feet Required per Plant
39 Orange, Sweet	200–300	D	97 / 76	D	— / 2	D	Minimal	D	—	—	—	D	22 / 24	484 / 576
40 Peach, Dwarf	610	D	681	D	—	—	Minimal	—	—	—	—	D	8	64
41 Peach, Regular	610	D	194	D	— / 4	D	Minimal	D	—	—	—	D	15	225
42 Pear, Dwarf	750	D	681	D	—	D	Minimal	D	—	—	—	D	8	64
43 Pear, Regular	750	D	170	EL	— / 1	D	Minimal	D	—	—	—	D	16 (-20)	256
44 Pecan	6	.50[J]	27	L	— / 4	8	Minimal	D	—	—	—	D	40 (-70)	1,600
45 Persimmon	74	D	134	D	— / 1	D	Minimal	D	—	—	—	D	18	324
46 Pistachio	In shell: 28	D	109	D	— / 2	D	Minimal	D	—	—	—	D	20	400
47 Plum, Bush	D	D	4,840	D	—	—	2	—	—	—	—	D	3	9

Master Charts

Crop	O — Possible GROW BIOINTENSIVE Yield in Pounds per 100 Square Feet[10,11]	P — Average U.S. Yield in Pounds per 100 Square Feet[12,13]	Q — Approx. Maximum Pounds Seed Yield per 100 Square Feet[19]	R — Approx. No. Years to Bearing and Approx. No. Years to Max Bearing	S — Approx. No. Weeks in Harvesting Period and Possible Bearing Years	T — Time of Year to Plant (SP, SU, FA, WI)	U — Crop Procedures	V — Pounds Consumed per Year by Average Person in U.S.[13,18]	W — Protein Content per Pound in Grams (454 g per pound)[25]	X — Calorie Content per Pound[25,50]	Y — Calcium Content per Pound in Milligrams (mg)[25]	Z — Notes
39 Orange, Sweet	Navel: 32 / 48 / 64 Valencia: 42 / 63 / 84	67.0	D	3 / D	D / 50+	Early SP	HPW, HPC	"17.2"	4.0 / 4.1	157 / 174	123 / 136	Navels (winter-bearing). 32% refuse. Valencia (summer-bearing). 25% refuse.
40 Peach, Dwarf	Clingstone: 60 / 90 / 120	"60.3"	D	3 / D	D / D	Early SP	See (1) under Apples. HPW, DW.	"2.6"	2.4	150	36	13% refuse. 8 ft high. Thin to 6 to 10 in (10 in for early varieties).
41 Peach, Regular	Clingstone: 60 / 90 / 120 Freestone: 39 / 59 / 78	"53.4" 39.7	D	3–4 / 8–12	D / 8–12	Early SP	See (1) under Apples.		2.4	150	36	13% refuse. 25 ft high. Thin to 6 to 10 in (10 in for early varieties).
42 Pear, Dwarf	36 / 72 / 108	66.6	D	3 / D	D / D	Early SP	See (1) under Apples. HPW, DW.	"3.4"	2.9	252	33	9% refuse. 8 ft high.
43 Pear, Regular	36 / 72 / 108	66.6	D	4 / D	D / 50–75	Early SP		"3.4"	2.9	252	33	9% refuse. 30–40 ft high.
44 Pecan	In shell: 6 / 12 / 25+	D	In shell: 25.0+	D / D	D / 150	Early SP	See (1) under Apples. HPW, DW.	".4"	41.7	3,116	331	Shelled. 47% of unshelled weight.
45 Persimmon	8 / 16 / 32+	D	D	2–3 / D	D / 20–300	Early SP	See (1) under Apples. HPW, DW.	D	2.6	286	22	18% refuse. 30 ft high.
46 Pistachio	D	3.1	D	D / D	D / 30–50	Early SP	See (1) under Apples. HPW, DW.	D	87.5	2,694	594	Shelled. 50% of unshelled weight. 30 ft high.
47 Plum, Bush	9.5 / 19 / 38	D	D	3 / D	D / D	Early SP	See (1) under Apples. HPW, DW.	"2.0"	2.1	272	74	9% refuse. 3 ft high. Thin to 4 to 6 in.

Column U general note: For varietal and other information, see (HPW) Western Fruit, Berries and Nuts: How to Select, Grow and Enjoy, by Lance Walheim and Robert L. Stebbins (under Fruits, Berries, and Nuts in Bibliography), and/or (DW) Dave Wilson Nursery catalog (under Seed Catalogs in Bibliography), or (HPC) Citrus: How to Select, Grow and Enjoy, by Richard Ray and Lance Walheim (under Fruits, Berries, and Nuts in Bibliography).

	A	B	C	D	E	F	G	H	I	J	K	L	M	N
CROP	Approx. No. Seeds per Ounce[4] (Range: larger–smaller seed)	Minimum Legal Germination Rate[5]	Aprpox. No. Plants per Acre	Short/Long/Extra-Long Germination Time	Flat spacing for First Flat and Second Flat (inches)	No. Plants in First Flat (adj. for germ. rate)[14]	No. First Flat(s) per 100 Sq Ft	Approx. No. Weeks in First Flat[16]	Depth of Second Flat and Spacing (Inches)	No. Plants in Second Flat[14]	No. Second Flats per 100 Sq Ft	Approx. No. Weeks in Second Flat[16]	In-Bed Spacing (feet)	Square Feet Required per Plant
	SEED			PLANTING		FLATS							BEDS	
48 Plum, Regular	50–55	D	134	D	4 / —	D	Minimal	—	—	—	—	D	18 (-24)	324
49 Pomegranate	D	D	435	D	2 / —	D	Minimal	D	—	D	—	D	10	100
50 Raspberries	—	—	2,723	D	6 / —	D	4 1	D	—	—	—	D	1–4	16
51 Strawberries	40,000	D	43,560	D	1 / —	—	10	D	—	60	—	D	1	1
52 Tangelo	200–300	D	109	D	1 / —	D	Minimal	D	—	—	—	D	20	400
53 Tangerine	300–400	D	109	D	1 / —	D	Minimal	D	—	—	—	D	20	400
54 Walnut, Eastern, Black	3	.50ᴬ	27	EL	4 / —	6	Minimal	D	—	—	—	D	40	1,600
55 Walnut, English (Persian)	2	.80ᴬ	27	L	4 / —	12	Minimal	D	—	—	—	D	40	1,600
56 Walnut, No. Calif. Black	3	.40ᴬ	27	EL	4 / —	8	Minimal	D	—	—	—	D	40	1,600

General note (CROP PROCEDURES column): For varietal and other information, see (HPW) *Western Fruit, Berries and Nuts: How to Select, Grow and Enjoy*, by Lance Walheim and Robert L. Stebbins (under Fruits, Berries, and Nuts in Bibliography), and/or (DW) Dave Wilson Nursery catalog (under Seed Catalogs in Bibliography), or (HPC) *Citrus: How to Select, Grow and Enjoy*, by Richard Ray and Lance Walheim (under Fruits, Berries, and Nuts in Bibliography).

CROP	O — Possible GROW BIOINTENSIVE Yield in Pounds per 100 Square Feet[10,11]	P — Average U.S. Yield in Pounds per 100 Square Feet[12,13]	Q — Approx. Maximum Pounds Seed Yield per 100 Square Feet[19]	R — Approx. No. Years to Bearing / Years to Max Bearing	S — Approx. No. Weeks in Harvesting Period / Possible Bearing Years	T — Time of Year to Plant (SP, SU, FA, WI)	U — Crop Procedures	V — Pounds Consumed per Year by Average Person in U.S.[13,18]	W — Protein Content per Pound in Grams (g) (454 g per pound)[25]	X — Calorie Content per Pound[25,50]	Y — Calcium Content per Pound in Milligrams (mg)[25]	Z — Notes
48 Plum, Regular	Regular: 19 / 38 / 57; Dry prune: 18 / 36 / 72	26.7 / 36.8	D	4 / D	D / 20–25	Early SP		"2.0"	2.1 / 3.4	272 / 320	74 / 51	:Damson. 9% refuse. :Prune. 6% refuse. Thin to 4 to 6 in.
49 Pomegranate	50 / 75 / 100	D	D	D / D	D / D	Early SP	HPW, DW.	D	1.3	160	8	:44% refuse.
50 Raspberries	Berries: 12 / 18 / 24; Biomass, air-dry: 5 / 10 / 25	"12.3"	—	2 / D	D / 6–10	Early SP	Prune to 2–8 canes/ft of row. Beds 2–3 ft wide. Some people plant on 2-ft centers. See (1) under Apples. HPW. Propagated by cuttings.	D	6.6 / 5.3	321 / 251	132 / 97	:Black. :Red. Also yellow and purple varieties. 3% refuse.
51 Strawberries	40 / 80 / 160	102.4	D	2 / D	4 / D	Early SP	Use new plants on end of runners to renew bed by fifth year. Plant initially in fall for a better first-year crop. Usually propagated by runner rather than seed, except for Alpine variety. See (1) under Apples. HPW.	"3.3"	3.0	161	91	:4% refuse. Bear well second through fourth year.
52 Tangelo	D	53.3	D	3 / D	D / D	Early SP	HPW, HPC.	".34"	1.3	104	D	:44% refuse. 30 ft high.
53 Tangerine	D	47.9	D	3 / D	D / D	Early SP	HPW, HPC.	".7"	2.7	154	134	:26% refuse. 30 ft high.
54 Walnut, Eastern, Black	In shell: 5 / 7.5 / 10+	7.0	In shell: 10.0+	D / D	D / D	Early SP			67.1	2,953	Trace	:Shelled. 78% refuse. Up to 150 ft high. A good tree to plant for your great-great-grandchildren!
55 Walnut, English (Persian)	In shell: 5 / 7.5 / 10+	7.0	In shell: 10.0+	D / D	D / D	Early SP		"4.6"	93.0	2,849	449	:Shelled. 55% refuse. Up to 60 ft high.
56 Walnut, No. Calif. Black	In shell: 5 / 7.5 / 10+	7.0	In shell: 10.0+	D / D	D / D	Early SP	See (1) under Apples. HPW, DW.	D	D	D	D	30–60 ft high.

Flower Spacing Chart

Spacings vary for flowers depending on the variety and how the flowers are used. The following will help you start out with the most common flowers.

ANNUALS—REPLANT EACH YEAR IN SPRING FROM SEED			PERENNIALS—NEED A PERMANENT SPACE IN THE GARDEN		
	Height	Inches Apart*		Height	Inches Apart*
African daisy	4–6"	12	Alyssum (*Lobularia maritime*)**	4–6"	10–12
Aster	1–3'	10-12	Aubrieta	Trailing	12–15
Calendula***	1¹/₂–2'	12	Baby's breath	3–4'	14–16
California poppy***	9–12"	12	Bachelor's button	2'	12
Columbine	2–3'	12	Carnation	1'	12
Cosmos***	2–3'	12–18	Chrysanthemum	2–3'	18–24
Echinacea	1'	18–24	Coral bells (*Heuchera sanguinea*)**	2'	12
Flowering tobacco	2–3'	18–24	Coreopsis	2'	9–18
Hollyhock***	4–6'	12	Delphinium	1–5'	24
Marigold, African	2–4'	12-24	Foxglove	3'	12
Marigold, French	6–18"	8–12	Gaillardia	2–3'	12
Nasturtium, climbing***	Trailing	10	Gazania	6–12"	10
Nasturtium, dwarf***	1'	8	Iceland poppy	1'	12
Pansy	6–9"	8–10	Jacob's ladder (*Polemonium caeruleum*)**	6"–3'	12–15
Petunia	12–16"	12	Marguerite	2¹/₂–3"	18–24
Phlox (*Phlox drummondii*)**	6–18"	9	Oriental poppy	2¹/₂–3"	12–14
Portulaca	6"	6–9	Painted daisy	3'	12
Scarlet sage (*Salvia splendens*)**	1–1¹/₂'	12	Peony	2'	14–16
Schizanthus	1¹/₂–2'	12–18	Pinks (*Dianthus*)**	1'	12
Shirley poppy	1¹/₂–2'	12–18	Scabiosa	2'	12
Snapdragons	1¹/₂–3'	12	Sea pink (*Armeria*)**	4–6"	10–12
Stocks	1–2¹/₂'	12	Shasta daisy	2¹/₂–3'	12
Strawflower	2–3'	12–18	Sweet William	1–2'	12
Sweet peas	Climbing	12	Note: Most flowers have long-germinating seeds (8 to 21 days).		
Zinnia	1–3'	12–18	* Spacings for standard-sized plants. For smaller varieties, reduce the spacings in proportion to the reduced plant size. ** Botanical Latin names prevent possible confusion. *** Reseed themselves easily by dropping many seeds on the ground.		

Herb Spacing Chart

ANNUALS—PLANT SEED IN SPRING FOR LATE SUMMER HARVEST

	Height	Inches Apart*		Height	Inches Apart*
Anise	2'	8	Coriander	1–1½'	6
Basil, sweet	1–2'	6	Cumin	1'	18
Borage	1–1½'	15	Dill	2½'	8
Caraway	2½'	6	Fennel	3–5'	12
Chamomile (*Matricaria recutita*)	2½'	6–10	Parsley	2½'	5
Chervil	1–1½'	4	Savory, summer	1–1½'	6
Cilantro	1–1½'	5			

PERENNIALS††—NEED A PERMANENT SPACE IN THE GARDEN

		Height	Inches Apart*		Height	Inches Apart*
Angelica		4–6'	36	Marjoram	1'	12
Bee balm†		3'	30	Oregano†	2'	18–24
Burnet		15'	15	Peppermint	2½'	12#
Catnip		2–3'	15#	Pineapple sage†	4'	24–36
Chamomile, Roman (*Chamaemelum nobile*)†		3–12'	12	Rosemary	3–4'	18–24
Chives		10–24"	5	Rue	3'	18
Comfrey†		15–36"	12	Sage	2'	18
Costmary		2–6'	12	Santolina	2'	30
Feverfew		1–3'	10–15	Savory, winter	1'	12
Geraniums, scented†	Apple	10"	18	Southernwood	3–5'	30
	Coconut	8–12"	18	Spearmint†	2–3'	15#
	Lemon	2–3'	##	Stevia	1–1½'	12
	Lime	2'	18	Stinging nettle	4–6'	24#
	Peppermint	2'	48	St. Johns wort	2'	8
	Rose	3'	30	Tansy	4'	30
Good King Henry		1'	16	Tarragon	2'	12–18
Horehound		2'	9#	Thyme	1'	6
Hyssop		2'	12	Valerian	4'	18
Lavender		3'	18	Woodruff†	6–10"	8–12#
Lemon balm		3'	12#	Wormwood	3–5'	12–24
Lemon verbena		10'	24	Yarrow, common (*Achillea millefolium*)	3–5'	12–18
Lovage		6'	3	Yarrow, white-, red-, or pink-flowered†	2½–3'	12

Note: Many herbs have extra-long-germinating seeds (22 to 28 days). † Generally based on our experience. Others are from the Herb Chart by Evelyn Gregg, Biodynamic Farming and Gardening Association, Wyoming, Rhode Island. †† Normally started from cuttings or root divisions, they often take 1 to 4 years to reach full size from seed. # Spreads underground; keep it contained or plant where it can keep going. ## Unknown.

Planning Sheet

| | CROP | FOOD NEEDED | MATERIALS NEEDED | | | | | YIELDS | |
| | | AA | BB | CC | DD | EE | FF | GG |
		Pounds You Select	Approx. No. Plants You Need[20]	Approx. Square Feet You Need[21]	Approx. No. Flats You Need[22]	Approx. Ounces/ Volume Seeds You Need[23]	Your Actual Yield per 100 Square Feet	Your Actual Yield Compared with U.S. Average[24]
1								
2								
3								
4								
5								
6								
7								
8								
9								
10								

ENDNOTES

1 For more information on the potential yield figures in column E of the Master Charts and how they were and are determined, see Ecology Action's "Yields" information. Available for $1.00 plus a self-addressed long envelope with two first-class stamps to: Ecology Action, 5798 Ridgewood Rd., Willits, CA 95490.

2 V. T. Aaltonen, *Boden und Wald* (Berlin: Parey, 1948).

3 One good foot-treadle-powered mini-thresher is available from CeCeCo., P.O. Box 8, Ibaraki City, Osaka, Japan, or from Christy Hunt Agricultural, Ltd., Foxhills Industrial Estate, Scunthorpe, South Humberside, DN15 8QW, United Kingdom.

4 From Donald N. Maynard and George J. Hochmuth, *Knott's Handbook for Vegetable Growers* (New York: John Wiley & Sons, 1999), pp. 97–98; and other reference sources.

5 Ibid., p. 460; and other reference sources.

6 Column N ÷ Column A ÷ Column B.

7 The number of plants you will need may vary. The rise of a curved bed surface (approximate 10-inch rise) adds up to 10% to the planting surface, and a "flat-topped" raised bed adds up to 20% to the planting surface. Also, the hexagonal "offset" spacing uses up less space than spacing where plants are lined up opposite each other. Up to 159 plants fit in 120 square feet of curved surface on 12-inch (1-foot) centers, rather than fewer plants. You will probably have more plants ready than you need when using Column I to plan, so use the best plants first and save the rest for "spotting" areas that lose plants, or give the extras to friends. To calculate the distance between rows on offset spacing, multiply the spacing by 0.87. To calculate the number of plants on offset spacing in a flat bed, first calculate the number of plants on "square" spacing, then multiply by 1.13.

8 Less seed may be necessary if the seed of a given variety is particularly small and/or if there is not much rise to the bed.

9 Estimates based on our experience and research. Use lowest figure if you are a beginning gardener; middle if a good one; highest if an excellent gardener with exceptional soil and climate. (The testing and development process requires a long time and has involved many failures. Its direction, however, has been encouraging over the years, as the soil, our skills, and yields have improved, and as resource-consumption levels have decreased. There is still much left to be done.)

10 The approximate plant yield averages in some instances are much lower than one would expect. For example, a beginning gardener will get carrots much larger than the .04 lb noted, but all of their carrots will probably not germinate as well as a good or excellent gardener's will and they will probably not be as large. Therefore, it is estimated that the average weight of each carrot would be .04 lb, assuming the bed produces 2,507 carrots.

11 Column E 3 Column I 3 0.01.

12 From U.S. Department of Agriculture, Agricultural Statistics—2005, 2003 data (Washington, DC: U.S. Government Printing Office, 2000; see the index at the end of the volume); and other reference sources.

13 Numbers in quotes are approximations from other data, because official data are not available for this crop.

14 Assumes flat with internal dimensions of 13 inches by 21 inches (or 273 square inches) for both 3-inch- and 6-inch-deep flats, in which at least 250 plants fit on 1-inch centers and 60 plants on 2-inch centers; if half-sized flats are used, 125 plants fit on 1-inch centers and 30 plants on 2-inch centers.

15 When seeds are broadcast into a flat, it is possible to reduce the number of flats used. To calculate the number of flats needed for broadcast seed, determine the number of plants you need, divide by the number in Column L2, then divide by the number in Column L3. Broadcast the needed amount of seed evenly into the number of flats just calculated.

16 From Donald N. Maynard and George J. Hochmuth, *Knott's Handbook for Vegetable Growers* (New York: John Wiley & Sons, 1999), p. 51; and from our experience and research.

17 The Approximate Weeks to Maturity in Ground generally remains the same whether seeds are started in a flat or in a bed because the number of weeks to maturity indicated on the seed packet assumes optimal growing conditions that are rarely present.

18 From U.S. Department of Agriculture, Agricultural Statistics—2005, 2003 data (Washington, DC: U.S. Government Printing Office, 2000; see the index at the end of the volume); and other sources.

19 Based in part on standard field figures from James Edward Knott, *Handbook for Vegetable Growers* (New York: John Wiley & Sons, 1975), pp. 198–199, in combination with a multiplier factor based on our research and experience; and other reference sources. The result, however, is preliminary, for your guidance, and very experimental. If growing seed, remember to adjust for the germination rate when determining the amount to grow for your use.

20 Column BB ÷ Column F.

21 Column BB ÷ Column E 3 100. Use the lowest figure in Column E if you are a beginning gardener; middle if a good one working with good soil; highest if an excellent gardener working with excellent soil.

22 Column CC ÷ Column L2 or M3.

23 Column DD 3 Column D 3 .01.

24 Column GG ÷ Column G.

25 From U.S. Department of Agriculture, "Composition of Foods" (Washington, DC: U.S. Government Printing Office, 1963) and other reference sources, and from USDA food search website: www.nal.usda.gov/fnic/foodcomp/search/index.html.

26 In warm weather and/or with a good mini-greenhouse, 6 to 8 weeks; in cooler weather outdoors without a mini-greenhouse, 6 to 8 weeks; 9 to 12 weeks.

27 Johnny's Selected Seeds.

28 Smaller secondary and tertiary heads may also be used and may double the yield.

29 The Redwood City Seed Company carries an interesting tropical variety, Snow Peak, which heads only in the summer. A good variety with small heads for out-of-season growing.

30 Produces 4 times the general protein (not amino acids) and 8 times the calcium (free of oxalic acid) per unit of area compared to the milk produced by a cow or a goat fed on an equal area of alfalfa.

31 Be sure to obtain "seed" Irish potatoes; many potatoes in stores have been treated to retard sprouting. Sprout without soil in a 3-inch-deep flat or box with small air spaces between the tubers in a warm, dry, airy location in indirect light for up to 1 month, until sprouts are about 1/4 inch long. Caution: Avoid conditions of 90% humidity and 70°F, or more, for a period of 24 hours; they can encourage blight. Use pieces of potato weighing at least 1.5 to 2 ounces. Each potato piece should optimally have 2 or 3 sprouted eyes. For planting purposes, tubers are in dormancy for 5 to 20 weeks after harvest. For planting procedure, see note on p. 26.

32 Be sure to obtain "seed" sweet potatoes; many potatoes in stores have been treated to retard sprouting. Sprout in wide-mouth canning jars with water. Insert toothpicks into sweet potatoes around their outside to hold the upper half out of the water. Roots form on the portion in the water, and small plantlets grow from the eyes on the upper portion. Each 8-ounce sweet potato will make 3 to 4 of these "starts." When a shoot is about 1 to 1¹/₂ inches long, nick it off along with a very small piece of the sweet potato where it is attached, and plant it in a 3-inch-deep flat on 2-inch centers so only the last set of leaves is above the surface of the flat soil. Whole sweet potatoes may also be sprouted side by side in a flat; approximately 4 to 8 flats are needed for a 100-square-foot bed. When the seedlings are 7 to 9 inches tall, transplant them into the growing bed so at least 6 inches of the stem is beneath the soil.

33 Bountiful Gardens.

34 Use the French variety (Vilmorin's Cantalun—orange-fleshed) or the Israeli variety (Haogen—green-fleshed). Both have a smooth exterior without netting. This minimizes rotting.

35 Stokes Seeds.

36 Try the torpedo onion. Its long shape is particularly suited to intensive raised-bed gardening and farming, and it can produce twice the yield per unit of area.

37 Irish potatoes. Place your order for the entire year in January in order to ensure availability. Specify untreated seed and delivery date(s) desired (1 month before planting, so sprouts can develop properly).

38 Sweet potatoes: Jewel, Centennial, Garnett, and Jersey varieties. Order in September untreated, number 2 size, for the following summer in 40-pound boxes, to ensure availability. Joe Alvernaz, P.O. Box 474, Livingston, CA 95334, is a good source, although not organic. Ask for prices and include a stamped, self-addressed envelope.

39 Burpee's Triple Treat variety with hull-less seeds. No shelling of nutritious and tasty seeds!

40 Burpee's Sparkler variety: red top with white bottom half. Good-looking.

41 Burpee's New Hampshire Midget variety.

42 Native Seeds/SEARCH.

43 Vermont Bean Seed Co.

44 Fedco Seeds.

45 R. H. Shumway Seed.

46 J. L. Hudson, Seedsman.

47 If overwintering.

48 In some tropical regions.

49 Six inches deep in areas with cooler nights.

50 Some calorie values determined from USDA website.

51 Including for fodder.

52 Longer harvest period is for sequential harvesting of separate stalks on each plant as stalks become mature.

53 As high as 43 weeks in some other countries.

54 Polish Jenn and German Porcelin hardneck varieties: 15/30/60.

55 Spacing of 24" produces the largest and easiest to dehull seeds, but less calories and biomass; 9" produces the smallest and most difficult to dehull seeds, but the most calories and biomass; 12" spacing is the best chioce for most people: larger seeds and a good amount of biomass; 18" spacing is in between.

GOAL: To create a sustainable garden that produces food and compost for its sustainability

SAMPLE GARDEN PLANS

Now we come to the art of putting the theory into a garden design. No publication can make gardening foolproof! If growing plants did not involve real learning and experimentation it would not be nearly so satisfying. These plans were created based on what the average American consumes each year, experimentation with the 60/30/10 design concept (see pages 39–41) and considerations for soil fertility. Everyone has different preferences and your "average American diet" will change rapidly when you have abundant fresh vegetables, grains and other treats to eat from your garden! You will learn to incorporate your garden's abundance into your meals.

If you've never gardened before or are starting a garden in a new area, you should research local conditions and experiences. Talk to your neighbors who garden, check with the county agricultural agent, or ask at the local nursery.

You will want to know:

• When does the main planting season start?

• When are your first and last frosts?

- When are your first and last rainy season dates?

- How does precipitation play a role in your climate? Is there a rainy and dry season?

- Which crops and varieties grow well in your area? Which grow poorly?

- What are the special requirements of your specific soil?

- Are there any special climatic conditions to be aware of, such as heavy winds, hot dry spells, or excessive rains?

- How do people usually plan for these climatic conditions?

Do keep in mind the following questions related to Biointensive designs:

- What vegetables do I want to plant to eat? (10% vegetable crops)

- What crops do I want to plant for compost and calories? (60% carbon and calorie crops)

- How will the garden produce a lot of calories in a small space? (30% special root crops)

- Will I include any crops in my design solely for compost materials (for example, fava beans or grain crops cut when they are immature or alfalfa)? How will these areas affect the design?

Remember that a Biointensive focus means that one of your goals is to produce your own soil fertility and diet in a reduced space. The 60/30/10 concept is a guideline. In its simplest form, it refers to the division of your garden space into 60% carbon-and-calorie crops, 30% high-calorie root crops and 10% vegetable crops at a given time for the main growing season. In a more complex context, one can consider the garden over the course of a year.

For more in-depth planning tools, consider the GROW BIOINTEN-SIVE Diet Design and Planning Program (available at www.grow biointensive.org, or Booklet 31: *Designing a GROW BIOINTENSIVE Sustainable Mini-Farm—A Working Paper*. You will be able to measure your success with the amount of compost that you can create year after year and the yields and calories produced by your growing space.

Also consider that the basic 60/30/10 concept does not explicitly include using any materials exclusively for the immature part of your compost (for example, alfalfa, fava beans cut green, clover), however, they are a key part of sustainability. Remember: the measure to your success is the amount of food and compost materials created in your space combined with overall garden health.

Following are different sample plans. For those of you familiar with *The Sustainable Vegetable Garden* by John Jeavons and Carol Cox, you will recognize the first garden plan as an adaption of the garden presented in that work. The designs are varied and serve as examples for what is possible. Remember, these are simply a "jumping off" place for ideas and approach. Use the formats to develop your own plans.

When choosing a site for your garden, take into consideration the amount of available direct sunlight. Optimally, your garden area should have 11 hours of sunlight or more; 7 hours may allow plants to grow reasonably, and in some instances, 4 hours may work for cool season crops (see pages 98–99).

Assure that there is an easily accessible water source available as well as that the area is secure from "predators." Your garden will be considered very attractive by many: including unwanted guests. A fence will aid in keeping them at bay.

While planning, think about planting a wide range of flowers (composite flowers preferably) and herbs to attract thousands of pollinators and natural enemies of insects that can become pests if your system is not in balance. Five square feet of celery or parsley grown to seed will serve as dramatic pollen feeding stations for the predatory insects that eat or parasitize harmful insects. In addition these crops produce organic matter for the compost pile and tasty seed for cooking in the kitchen. (See chapter 7, "An Interrelated Food-Raising System," for more information.)

The correct tools will make your gardening experience more pleasurable and productive. Review each chapter to see which tools are recommended.

We also encourage you to start thinking about learning how to save seeds, as buying seeds for a backyard garden easily accumulates a large annual expense. In addition, as you learn to save seeds, you are saving the seeds best adapted to your own microclimate. Seed-saving can be very satisfying, but the space needs to be added into the design of your garden. On the average, it takes just 3% more area to grow all the seed for next year in this year's garden!

THE TEMPERATE CLIMATE GARDEN YEAR

Winter

- Plan the garden.

- Order open-pollinated, untreated seeds (remember to allow time for seeds to arrive!) and/or clean any saved seeds that are left over from the previous season for this purpose.

- Make flats, trellises, mini-greenhouses, and shade-netting units.[1]

Spring

- Plant flats so seedlings can mature while the soil is being prepared.

- Start new compost piles with weeds, grass clippings, and mature compost crop residues saved over winter.

- Harvest immature compost crops planted in the previous season.

- Dig garden beds and incorporate organic fertilizer and cured compost into the soil of your prepared growing area.

- Plant cool-winter crops in early spring and warm- and hot-weather crops in late spring and early summer. Generally, 7 to 11 hours of direct sunlight are needed to grow healthy crops.

Summer

- Plant summer crops.

- Keep the garden watered and weeded.

- Harvest and enjoy the fruits of your work.

- In mild-winter areas, plant fall gardens of cool-weather crops at the end of the summer.

Fall

- Start additional compost piles with plentiful leaves and garden waste.

- Harvest summer crops.

- Plant fall/winter compost crops.

Garden Plans

Cm = 60% crop grown to maturity   Ci = 60% crop harvested immature

R = 30% crop   V = 10% crop

Bed 1—Vegetables
MAIN GROWING SEASON—MAY 20 TO SEPTEMBER 30

Map of Bed (not in scale)

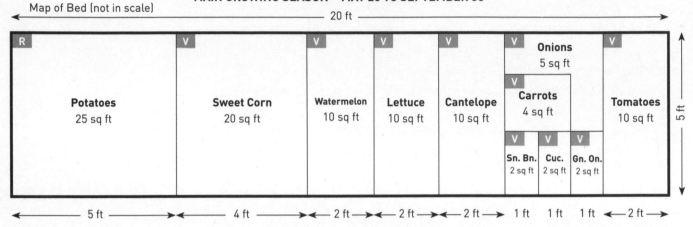

Bed 1—Compost Crops
COOL WEATHER GROWING SEASON—OCTOBER 1 TO MAY 20

Map of Bed (not in scale)

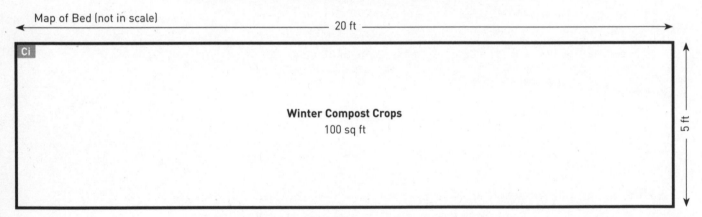

After each section finishes up its main season crop, consider the following possibilities:

Sow buckwheat for a summer catch cover crop, if needed (mostly to bring in beneficial insects and provide some compost materials) after the main crop.

And/or plant amaranth or sorghum after the main crop to cut as immature compost material before frost.

Note: The expected planting date IS NOT the same date for all the crops. Review Satisfactory (and Optimal) Plant-Growing Temperature ranges (pages 98–99) to determine the best times. Also check your area's recommended planting dates for your area. One good source for information can be found in part two in *The Backyard Homestead, Mini-Farm and Garden Log Book.*

Plant winter compost crops. One good mix (recipe per 100 square feet) should be planted about 6 weeks before first hard frost date. It is made up of:

- 2 ounces (about 1⅓ cups) hard red spring wheat—transplant or broadcast.

- .4 ounce (about 1 tablespoon) cereal rye—transplant or broadcast.

- .62 ounce (about 5¼ teaspoons) vetch broadcast after soaking seed overnight. (Mix seed with a small amount of dry soil before broadcasting so seeds do not stick together.)

- 1 ounce (about 1¼ cup) Banner fava beans sown on 21-inch centers—transplant or direct sow.

Bed 2—Grains and Beans (Winter 60% Crops)
COOL WEATHER GROWING SEASON—OCTOBER 1 TO MAY 20

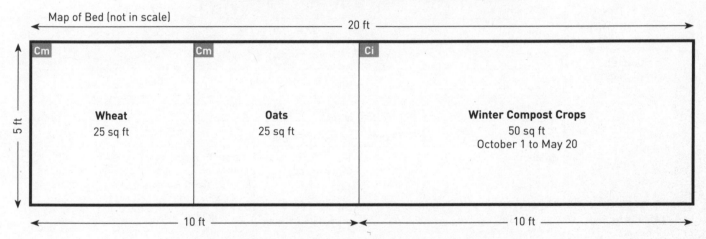

Map of Bed (not in scale)

20 ft

5 ft

Cm — Wheat — 25 sq ft

Cm — Oats — 25 sq ft

Ci — Winter Compost Crops — 50 sq ft — October 1 to May 20

10 ft — 10 ft

Bed 2—Corn and Beans (Summer Compost Crops)
MAIN GROWING SEASON—MAY 21 TO SEPTEMBER 30

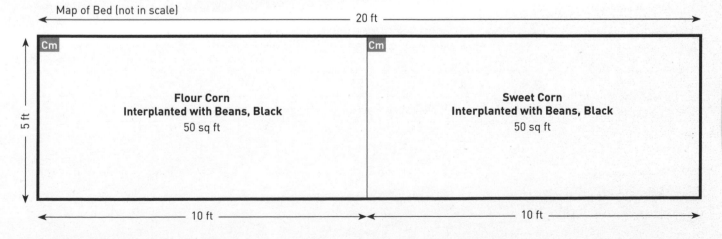

Map of Bed (not in scale)

20 ft

5 ft

Cm — Flour Corn — Interplanted with Beans, Black — 50 sq ft

Cm — Sweet Corn — Interplanted with Beans, Black — 50 sq ft

10 ft — 10 ft

Garden Plans

Beds 1 and 2—Planting
MAIN GROWING SEASON

6+ weeks before expected planting date	START IN FLATS			
	Crop	Square Feet	Bed Spacing	
	Tomatoes	10	21"	6 seeds to ensure 4 plants
	Regular onions	5	4"	100 seeds to ensure 70 plants
	Green onions	2	3"	75 seeds to ensure 50 plants
	Carrots	4	3"	200 seeds to ensure 100 plants
5 weeks before expected planting date	START IN FLATS			
	Crop	Square Feet	Bed Spacing	
	Lettuce	10	9"	35 seeds to ensure 25 plants (stagger planting to have longer harvest)
4 weeks before expected planting date	START IN FLATS			
	Crop	Square Feet	Bed Spacing	
	Watermelon	10	18"	7 seeds to ensure 5 plants
	Cucumbers	2	12"	3 seeds to ensure 2 plants
	Cantaloupe	10	15"	12 seeds to ensure 9 plants
	PRICK OUT			
	Crop	Lettuce		Tomatoes
	PREPARE			
	Crop	Square Feet	Bed Spacing	
	Potatoes	25	9" +9" deep	Sprout in warm area. Cut potatoes into pieces, cover cut surface with ash, and dry for 2–3 days. 7.5 pounds for area. Transplant when ready.
2 weeks before expected planting date	START IN FLATS			
	Snap beans	2	6"	16 seeds to ensure 13 plants
1 week before expected planting date	START IN FLATS			
	Corn, Sweet	70	12"	40 seeds to ensure 31 plants
	Corn, Flour	100	12"	212 seeds to ensure 159 plants
	Dry beans, black	100	6"	887 seeds (1.6 cups) to ensure 621 plants
On planting date	Broadcast carrots (alternatively)			
	Consult Master Charts for information on timing and tips for size for transplant.			

Beds 1 and 2—Planting			
COOL WEATHER GROWING SEASON			
	START IN FLATS		
2 weeks before expected planting date	Crop	Square Feet	Bed Spacing	
	Wheat	25	5"	300 seeds (about 2 tablespoons) to ensure 200 plants (Bed 2)
	Oats	25	5"	300 seeds (about 2 tablespoons) to ensure 200 plants (Bed 2)
	START IN FLATS		
6 weeks before first hard frost	**Sow Winter Compost Mix (recipe per 150 square feet) about 6 weeks before first hard frost date**		
	Hard red spring wheat	150	broadcast	3 ounces (about 7.8 tablespoons)
	Cereal rye	150	broadcast	0.6 ounce (about 1½ tablespoons)
	Vetch	150	broadcast	0.93 ounce (1¼ tablespoons)
	Fava Beans	throughout bed	21" centers	2.4 ounces (¾ cup) sown
On planting date	Transplant crops in indicated area on map. Choose healthiest plants. Consult Master Charts for information on timing and tips for best size to transplant. Record information about planting dates for future reference.		

LOOK CLOSER

- The mature materials for compost include: corn stalks and winter compost crops.

- Immature materials for compost are diverse: carrot tops, tomato plants after harvest, cucumber vines, etc. They also include any material like amaranth or buckwheat not grown to maturity after the main season. If you use sweet corn, let it continue to grow for 30 days after harvesting the ears. This will enable the corn plant to produce a lot more carbon in quantity and/or quality in a relatively short period of time.

- For more calories and mature compost material in a smaller space, use flour corn instead of sweet corn in the plan.

- If you only have a "main season" garden, you are missing out on many opportunities to have more compost materials and calories. In addition, by not having rooted plants in the ground, the soil microbiology is affected negatively.

- Review the Master Charts for all sorts of information about the crops you will be growing. You can find out how far to space the plants apart, when to expect to harvest, special tips, and much, much more.

Sustainable Diet Design[3]

5-Bed Unit (Seasons Vary According to Area)

COOL WEATHER GROWING SEASON—OCTOBER 1 TO MAY 20

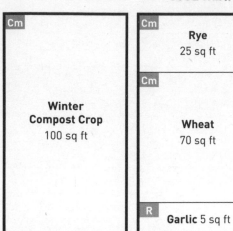

Cm **Winter Compost Crop** 100 sq ft	**Cm** Rye 25 sq ft **Cm** Wheat 70 sq ft **R** Garlic 5 sq ft	**Cm** **Winter Compost Crop** 100 sq ft	**Cm** **Fava Beans** 100 sq ft	**Cm** **Winter Compost Crop** 100 sq ft

MAIN GROWING SEASON—MAY 20 TO SEPTEMBER 30

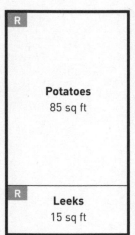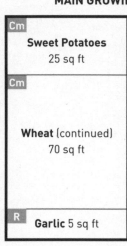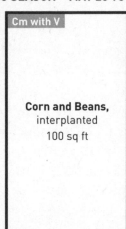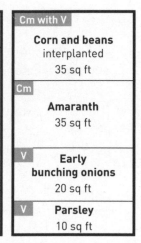

R **Potatoes** 85 sq ft **R** Leeks 15 sq ft	**Cm** Sweet Potatoes 25 sq ft **Cm** Wheat (continued) 70 sq ft **R** Garlic 5 sq ft	**Cm with V** **Corn and Beans,** interplanted 100 sq ft	**V** Cayenne 5 sq ft **V** **Pinto beans, dry** 75 sq ft **V** Tomatoes 25 sq ft	**Cm with V** Corn and beans interplanted 35 sq ft **Cm** Amaranth 35 sq ft **V** Early bunching onions 20 sq ft **V** Parsley 10 sq ft

LATE SEASON CATCH CROP

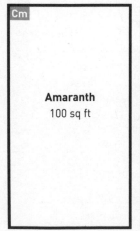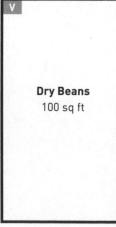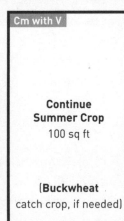

Cm **Amaranth** 100 sq ft	**V** **Dry Beans** 100 sq ft	**Cm with V** **Continue Summer Crop** 100 sq ft (Buckwheat catch crop, if needed)	**Cm with V** **Continue Summer Crop** 100 sq ft (Buckwheat catch crop, if needed)	**Cm with V** **Continue Summer Crop** 100 sq ft (Buckwheat catch crop, if needed)

Sustainable Diet Designs Planting
ALL SEASONS

6+ weeks before expected planting date	**START IN FLATS**			
	Crop	Square Feet	Bed Spacing	
	Leeks	15	6"	155 seeds to ensure 95 plants
	Peppers, cayenne	5	12"	16 seeds to ensure 8 plants
	Tomatoes	25	21"	11 seeds to ensure 9 plants
	Parsley	10	5"	135 seeds to ensure 85 plants
	Early bunching onions	20	3"	700 seeds (3/4 tablespoon) to ensure 500 plants
	Start sweet potato slips	25	9"	7.5 pounds to ensure 65 starts
5 weeks before expected planting date	**START IN FLATS**			
	Crop	Square Feet	Bed Spacing	
	Amaranth	100 + 35	12"	310 seeds (1/3 tablespoon) to ensure 230 plants
	PRICK OUT			
	Crop	Amaranth	Peppers	Parsley	Tomatoes
4 weeks before expected planting date	**PREPARE**			
	Crop	Square Feet	Bed Spacing	
	Potatoes	100	9"	(Put to sprout in warm, lighted area. When sprouts are at least 1/4 inch long, cut potatoes into pieces, cover cut surface with ash, and dry for 2 to 3 days.) 30 pounds
2 weeks before expected planting date	**START IN FLATS**			
	Fava, cold weather, small seeded	100	8"	426 seeds (1 5/8 cups) to ensure 320 plants
	Wheat	70	5"	430 seeds (4.4 tablespoons) to ensure 300 plants
	Cereal rye	25	5"	250 seeds (1.4 tablespoons) to ensure 175 plants
1 week before expected planting date	**START IN FLATS**			
	Beans, black	100	6"	887 seeds (1.1 cups) to ensure 621 plants
	Beans, pinto	75	6"	660 seeds (0.5 cup) to ensure 460 plants
	Beans, kidney (for interplanting)	135	6"	897 seeds (2.6 cups) to ensure 628 plants
	Corn, flour	135	12"	300 seeds (4 tablespoons) to ensure 210 plants
On planting date	**PLANT**			
	Crop	Square Feet	Bed Spacing	
	Garlic	5	4"	1 pound to ensure 70 plants

Garden Plans

LOOK CLOSER

- A simple "snapshot" analysis of the first season design shows that it does not achieve 60% in terms of carbon and calorie crops in the main season, but comes close with 50%. Summer and winter compost crops will move it closer to producing sufficient compost materials over the whole annual period. In the late winter/early spring of the first year, plant an additional 50 square feet of wheat and the design moves much closer to being sustainable while producing additional calories in a small space. The 50-square-feet sections of wheat, corn and summer vegetables can be rotated every year.

- Vary your vegetables over time to get to know new crops.

- Garlic can be added in the design to add more calories in the 30% category. Remember that the hardneck varieties: Polish Jenn and German Porcelain can produce a lot of mature organic matter—30 pounds, plus a lot of edible bulbs.

- The garden plan becomes more sustainable by adding more compost crops. Consider adding a perennial area for alfalfa and/or medium red clover. Take advantage of the area around the fruit tree and plant these crops underneath.

ENDNOTES

1 See Ecology Action's *The Backyard Homestead, Mini-Farm and Garden Log Book* for miniature mini-greenhouse and shade-netting house plans.

2 This garden is an adaption of the garden found in *The Sustainable Vegetable Garden* by John Jeavons and Carol Cox.

3 This is an adaptation of a design originally created by Margo Royer-Miller and then implemented by Margo and Dan Royer-Miller at the Ecology Action Research Garden in 2008. It grew out of a sustainable diet and compost design using Booklet 31: *Designing a GROW BIOINTENSIVE® Sustainable Mini-Farm–A Working Paper*.

Tools

One of Ecology Action's goals has been to develop Biointensive techniques that use as few procedures as possible, and as few tools as possible, preferably manual ones. Our philosophy has been to encourage the use of what we describe as sophisticated low-technology tools—tools that are inexpensive, simple, easy to build, yet highly functional. We wanted to avoid high initial capital investment and the high cost of running, maintaining, and repairing complex mechanical equipment.

Cars have important purposes, but consider the true cost of running one, not to mention the pollution it creates. Ivan Illich, author of *Tools for Conviviality* and advocate of a simpler life, one remarked that if everyone added up all the time spent earning the money to purchase, maintain, fuel, and drive an automobile, they would see that each person is really only traveling at four miles per hour in a car—the speed of the common bicycle! Recently, a study was made of the time the average stay-at-home mom in the United States spends working in, around, and for the home and family. It was discovered that, even with labor-saving tools, she spends the same amount of time that her counterpart spent one hundred years ago! Why not look for ways to maximize simplicity, sophistication, and quality, and yet get jobs done more quickly? This has been our goal in developing tools for mini-farming.

Early on in our research programs, we identified the need for four tools in particular that were available, but not quite in the form we needed. They were: 1) the **U-bar,** a large spading fork or kind of manual plow; 2) a versatile multi-use **mini-greenhouse** for temperature and pest control; 3) a **watering tool** that could water three times as rapidly and three times more gently (to avoid harming plants or compacting the soil) than any tool presently available; and 4) a low-cost **manual wheat thresher.** The U-bar and the mini-greenhouses are now a reality, and plans and specifications for these two tools are included in this chapter. In addition, there are plans and specs for a soil and compost sifter, seedling flat, and row marker.

We invite you to build these tools as presented here, and to make your own modifications. Any modifications to the U-bar should be performed with special care, however, as it is the result of a special, lengthy research, development and testing process. Any modifications which make it less strong could be dangerous for the user. Currently we are trying to find a good durable design for a U-bar with detachable handles so it can be more easily transported. We also believe that the mini-greenhouse can be improved upon to make interchangeable panels fit into a single structure, rather than two. Your suggestions can help us with this ongoing design process.

U-BAR OR MANUAL PLOW

Design: William Burnett and Robert Clark
Drawing Development: Dan Torjusen
Text: Marion Cartwright
Illustrations: Pedro J. Gonzalez

Deep soil preparation is of great importance in the biodynamic/French intensive method. Traditionally, the soil is loosened to a depth of 2 feet with a spade and spading fork in a process called the double-dig. The first time a plot of ground is worked, the double-dig can take anywhere from 2 to 6 hours per 100-square-foot raised bed, depending on the soil's condition and the skill of the practitioner. After the ground has been double-dug and cropped once, it generally takes about 2 hours thereafter to double-dig and shape a raised bed using a spade and fork.

There is a less time-consuming and less tiring way to prepare a raised bed while deeply aerating the soil. Once we have initially double-dug our beds, we often use a U-bar for subsequent cultivation in our test beds. Since the U-bar tines do not dig quite as deeply and do not aerate the soil as much as a double-dig with spade and fork, we still double-dig the soil periodically when significantly increased soil compaction is noticed. Another disadvantage of U-barring is that the gardener loses personal contact with the different strata of the soil and may not be aware of changes in soil quality due to different soil-preparation techniques, crops grown, or soil amendments used. Yet the time savings the U-bar offers is significant. Each person will need to decide which factors are most important.

The U-bar is essentially a very large spading fork with two handles mounted on opposite ends of a rack of 18-inch-long tines. The U-bar has cut our soil cultivation time from 2 hours per 100-square-foot bed to 10 to 30 minutes per bed. It is simple to use, and reduces the bending and lifting motions of digging. It loosens and aerates the soil with a minimum of soil strata mixing. Its only constraint is that it can only be used in well-loosened soil (usually soil that has been double-dug for at least one season).

Two undergraduate engineering students at Stanford University designed and built two types of U-bars for Ecology Action using two different designs as their starting point.[1] The design presented here is the one preferred by Ecology Action—both for ease of construction and for effectiveness in preparing the soil. The updated drawings should allow a competent welder to construct one with little difficulty. It is not intended to be a "do it yourself" for someone without welding experience.

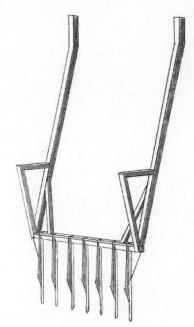

The U-bar

U-Bar Dimensions

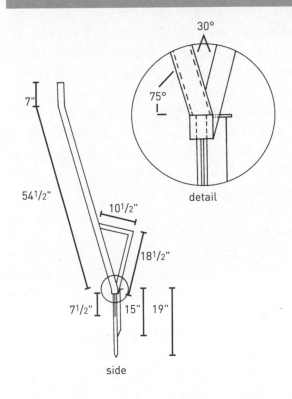

side

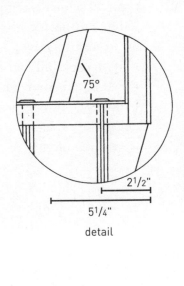

detail

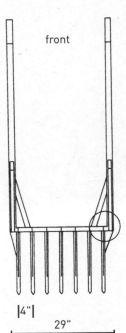

detail

front

The designers of the U-bar found that a 2-foot-wide tool with 18-inch-long tines is as large as the U-bar can be made. Otherwise it becomes too difficult for a person of average size and strength to operate.

The frame of the U-bar is $1^{1}/_{4}$-inch-square tubing with a wall thickness of 0.095 inches. The elbow and brace pieces are 1-inch-square tubing of the same thickness. The frame material is hot-rolled, low-carbon steel, also known as "mild" steel or 1010/1020 steel.

The tines of the U-bar are half-round bar, plow steel stock. If plow steel is unavailable, use cold-rolled steel. The gussets on the back of the tine are $^{1}/_{8}$ inch thick and 1 inch deep. The stand-up bar is made from the same $^{1}/_{8}$-inch-thick material and is welded to the tops of the gussets the whole width of the U-bar and is flush with the top of the square tubing.

Material costs are dependent upon the quantity ordered. If bought new from a dealer, steel is usually sold in 20-foot sections.

The U-bar makes a highly efficient form of personal food production possible. The design was kept simple so that the tool could be available to anyone. Often in this industrialized world, simple, efficient answers to problems are overlooked because they are thought of as *too* simple or not innovative enough. Yet, for us, the U-bar has been a breakthrough that makes Biointensive gardening more cost effective.

We especially wish to thank William Burnett and Robert Clark for designing and constructing the prototype U-bar; the Stanford University Mechanical Engineering Department; ARLO (Stanford University's Action Research Liaison Office); and Bill LeLand, who was instrumental in bringing us all together.

One easy carrying position. Be careful with tines, especially near your feet. The U-bar is balanced so its weight will be evenly dispersed.

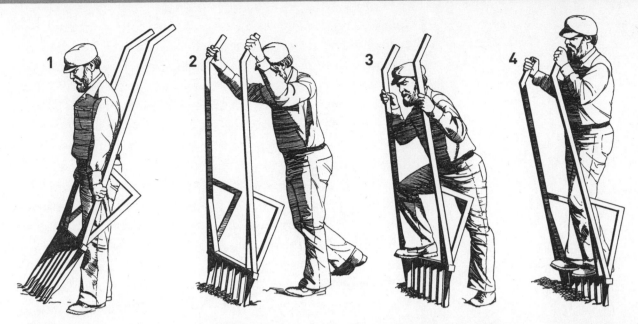

1. Place the points of the U-bar tines into soil at one corner of bed. You will be working your way backward the length of the bed. (U-bar is 2 feet wide, but loosens a 2¹/₂-foot-wide strip of soil; two passes with U-bar are required to dig a 5-foot-wide bed.)
2. Push the U-bar into soil. Your hands should be placed close to tines at first, then shifted to the handles as you continue to fix the tool firmly into the soil. Wiggle the tool right and left, if necessary.
3. Step onto the U-bar, first with your full weight on one foot.
4. Step onto the U-bar with your second foot, shifting your weight to make the tool parallel with the soil. (Caution: the U-bar should not be used on sloping areas.)

5. Shift your weight backward to gain maximum leverage. The tines will rotate through the soil.
6. Just before you start to fall onto the ground, step off the U-bar. Continue to rotate the tines through the soil by alternately pulling the handles toward you, then pushing them down,
7. After you have rotated the tines completely through the soil, clods of soil may remain on the tines. Push the U-bar handles up and down rapidly until the clods break up and fall through the tines. Drag the U-bar back about 8 inches (do not lift the tool—it weighs about 40 pounds and lifting can wear you out or strain your back). Using the handles, tilt the U-bar back into position as shown in step 2. Continue the U-barring process.

MODULAR, MULTI-USE MINI-GREENHOUSE
(For warmth, shade, and pest protection)

Design: Dan Torjusen and Robert Clark
Drawing Development: Patrick Long
Text: Gaye Carlson
Illustrations: Pedro J. Gonzalez

For many years, Ecology Action has searched for a mini-greenhouse, shadenetting house, and birdnetting house to extend the growing season and to protect crops. The following design, created by Dan Torjusen, comes closest to what we have been looking for. While it is not intended for winter use in areas with great amounts of snowfall, the mini-greenhouse can be assembled early in the spring and placed over a 50-square-foot growing bed. This will increase the temperature of the soil and the air surrounding the plants and allow the gardener to get an early start on the growing season. The double-walled construction of the design can keep the inside temperature above the freezing point when the outside temperature falls as low as 20°F. This makes the unit a good season extender for crops.

The lumber for the mini-greenhouse can last for up to 12 years or more. We recommend the 6-millimeter multi-year, clear plastic sheeting, for example, Klerks K50 Clear and Dura-film Super 4, although less expensive plastic sheeting may also be used.

Tools

1. Hand saw or circular saw

2. Hammer

3. Staple gun

4. Drill and $3/16$", $3/8$", and $5/8$" wood bits

5. Chisel

6. Measuring tape

7. Straight edge or carpenter's square

8. Protractor

9. Table saw (optional)

10. Bar clamps (optional)

The tools required to build the mini-greenhouse are basic, with the exception of a table saw. The table saw is not really necessary, but it is useful since it allows one to purchase 2 x 4s and rip them

Final Assembly of Mini-Greenhouse—Exploded View

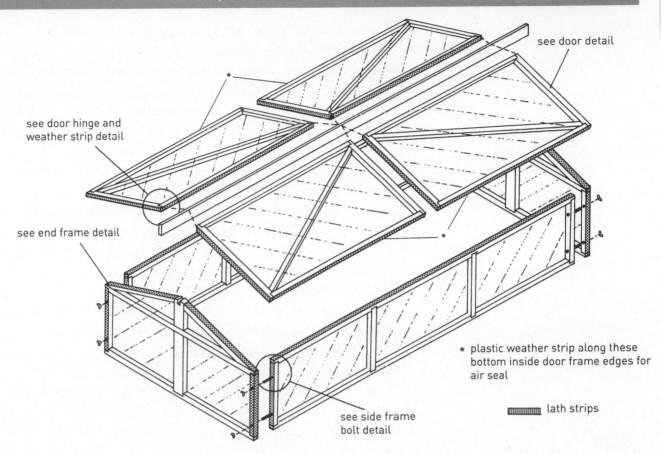

see door detail

see door hinge and
weather strip detail

see end frame detail

*

*

* plastic weather strip along these
bottom inside door frame edges for
air seal

see side frame
bolt detail

▨▨▨▨ lath strips

Mini-Greenhouse Frame Dimensions (Lath Omitted)

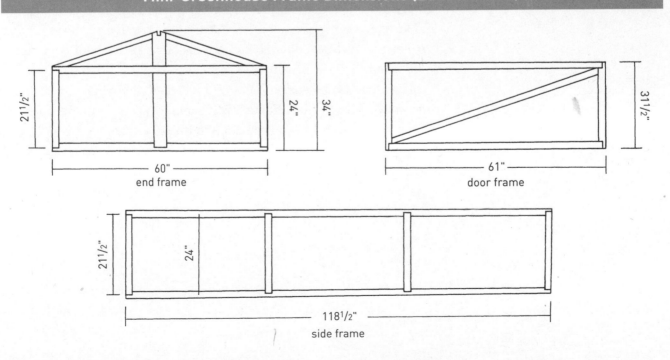

21¹/₂"   24"   34"

60"
end frame

31¹/₂"

61"
door frame

21¹/₂"   24"

118¹/₂"
side frame

in half. (Redwood 2 x 4s are less expensive than 2 x 2s, since 2 x 2s are generally sold as clear heartwood only.) With a table saw, it is also easier to make the necessary bevel cuts on the top rails of the doors. Bar clamps are handy when cutting the joints as several pieces can be clamped together and cut at one time.

The shadehouse/birdnetting unit costs about $2.50 per square foot for materials. The shadenetting is rated to last up to 15 years with good care and comes in different thread densities which screen out 3% to 98% of the sun's light. The 3% mesh can keep insects out while letting in most of the light; 30%, 45%, and 55% mesh fabric is used to grow cool-loving spring and fall crops in the summer. Experimentation will show which is best for your area at different times of the year and for different crops. Try a 30% mesh to begin with. Two or three meshes may be needed for one crop during the season as the weather gets hotter or cooler. Be careful not to overwater when using meshes 30% and over. The 90%+ meshes are reportedly used to let enough light in to keep the crops alive, but not enough to let them grow, for a 3- to 5-day period before marketing when more grown might involve their going to seed, bolting, or a general loss of crop quality.

If the entire 50-square-foot unit lasts for at least 10 years, the per year cost would also be about $12.50 per year. This would be much less than the value of the produce grown or protected underneath.

There is also another advantage of this design—interchangeable panels. It is possible to mix or match the functions: a greenhouse panel on a side and an end to block out growth-inhibiting prevailing winds, shadenetting top doors to filter out excessive sunlight, and birdnetting (or 3% shadenetting) panels on the other side and end to keep out birds or insect pests.

It would also be possible to build a large greenhouse out of these panels by adding pegs and stacking panels on top of one another. Think of it as an adult-appropriate technology tinker-toy set!

We hope you enjoy building and using this mini-greenhouse/ shadenetting house/birdnetting house and look forward to learning about your results in using it, or any modifications you have made.

Materials

(Use redwood or other weather-resistant wood, well seasoned to minimize warping.)

	QUANTITY	MATERIAL
Wood	6	2" x 2" x 10'
	15	2" x 2" x 8' (or 32" x 4" x 10')
	8	2" x 4" x 8' (if ripped to make 2 x 2s)
	1	2" x 4" x 8'
	1	1" x 4" x 12"
	28	$1/4$" x 8' lath strips
	4	$3/8$" x 3" dowels
Fasteners	8	$3/16$" x $2^1/2$" machine screws (No. 10 size), with 8 nuts and 16 washers
	4	$3/16$" x $1^1/4$" pan head wood screws (No. 10 size), with 4 washers
	8	$3/8$" x $5^1/2$" completely threaded carriage bolts, with 8 nuts, 8 wing nuts, and 16 washers
	1 lb.	8d galvanized box nails
	1 lb.	3d galvanized box nails
	8'	$3/4$"-wide nylon webbing
	1 box	$1/2$" staples
Plastic	36" x 312' roll	8 mm, 6-year, double-polished clear vinyl plastic film or other plastic sheeting. 100 5' x 36" pieces are needed for one double-glazed mini-greenhouse.
Shadenetting		Use 3% shadenetting.

Procedure

1. If you purchased 2 x 4s for 2 x 2s, rip all except one 8-foot 2 x 4 in half.

2. Cut pieces as specified below. (Notches and bevels will be cut later.)

   Side frames: (4) 1 x 2 x $118^1/2$" (will be notched)

   (8) 2 x 2 x $22^1/2$"

   Door frames: (4) 2 x 2 x $59^1/2$" (will be beveled)

   (4) 2 x 2 x $59^1/2$"

   (8) 2 x 2 x $31^1/2$" (will be notched)

   End frames: (4) 2 x 2 $22^1/2$"

   (4) 2 x 2 x 60"

   (2) 2 x 4 x 36"

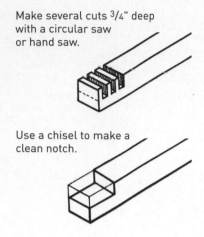

Make several cuts 3/4" deep with a circular saw or hand saw.

Use a chisel to make a clean notch.

3. Cut notches. The joins of the 2 x 2 frame can be made by cutting a notch 3/4-inch-deep to fit the end of a 2 x 2. This can be done quickly by setting the circular saw to cut 3/4-inch-deep and making several cuts about 1/8 inch to 1/4 inch apart across the notch area. The remaining material in the notch can be removed with a hammer and chisel. Several 2 x 2s can be cut at the same time this way by clamping them together with bar clamps.

   The joint between the 2 x 4 and the 2 x 2 in the end panel is a half-lapped joint where both pieces are continuous and notched to fit each other.

4. Assemble side frames with 8d nails. Install bolt assembly, locking carriage bolt in place with recessed nut.

5. Assemble door frames with 8d box nails. After nailing, but before cutting diagonals, be sure to check the doors for squareness by measuring across their diagonals. (When opposite diagonals are equal, then all corners will be 90°.) Once door is square, lay diagonal across frame in its position, mark and cut to length.

6. Assemble 2 x 2 end frame rectangle with 8d box nails. (Diagonals and center 2 x 4 are cut and installed in the next step.)

7. Make bevel cuts and roof of structure. Set 2 x 4 in its notched position on end frame, allowing it to extend longer than necessary. Two 18.5° angles now need to be cut in the 2 x 4s to form the roof peak. This angle can be determined with a protractor, and then lay the 2 x 2 diagonal in place and mark where you will be cutting the 2 x 2 across the 2 x 4. The bevel angle for the other end of the 2 x 2 may be marked and cut in a similar manner. The top edge of the doors where they will be hinged to the center ridge beam must also be bevel cut at an 18.5° angle for it to sit properly.

   Finally, before nailing, cut a 3/4-inch x 1 1/2-inch notch in the 2 x 4 for the 1 x 4 roof ridge beam.

8. Wrap with plastic. The plastic is stretched tightly over the frame and stapled frequently (2 to 3 inches apart) on the outside edges only. Each frame is double glazed with plastic wrapped on both the inside and outside. Excess plastic is trimmed after stapling.

9. Apply plastic weather strips on the top edge of the doors and where the doors meet in the middle. This is a simple 4-inch-wide

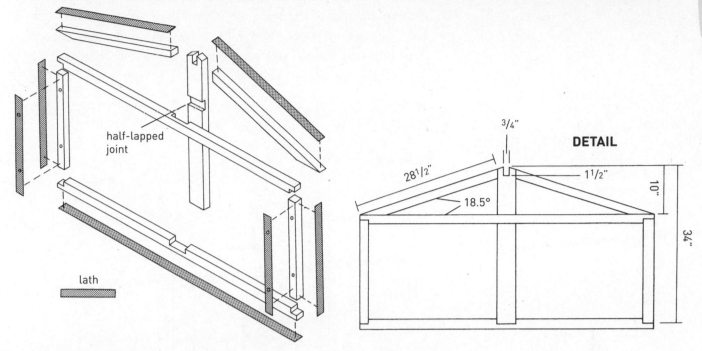

half-lapped joint

lath

DETAIL

3/4"

28¹/₂"

18.5°

1¹/₂"

10"

34"

piece of plastic, folded and secured by a piece of lath. (See door frame detail.) Also apply plastic weatherstrips along bottom inside door frame edges for air seal.

10. Cut and nail lath strips over all stapled edges using 3d galvanized box nails.

11. Attach side to end frames with wing nuts. Set 1 x 4 x 12 center ridge beam in slots in 2 x 4s but do not nail. This allows the mini-greenhouse to be quickly and easily disassembled for storage or changing of panels.

12. Assemble and install door hinges.

13. Corner dowels. On each corner of the greenhouse there is a 3/8-inch dowel which sets into a hole in the door (not shown in the diagrams). This is necessary for structural rigidity of the greenhouse and prevents the 1 x 4 center ridge beam from sagging under the weight of the doors. It can be installed simply by drilling a 3/8-inch hole in the corners of the end panel and tapping it halfway in with a hammer. Then the door is pressed onto the dowel, marking the position to be drilled on the door.

14. Spacers. It will be helpful during everyday operation of the greenhouse to attach a small piece of lath on top of the four bottom corners of each door to prevent the plastic from sticking together when the doors are open and laying upon the door opposite the open door.

Side Frame Bolt Detail

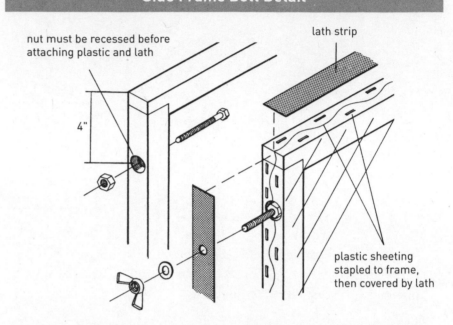

nut must be recessed before attaching plastic and lath

lath strip

4"

plastic sheeting stapled to frame, then covered by lath

Door Hinge and Weatherstrip Detail

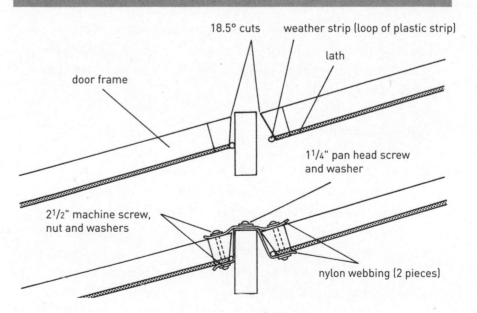

18.5° cuts

weather strip (loop of plastic strip)

lath

door frame

1 1/4" pan head screw and washer

2 1/2" machine screw, nut and washers

nylon webbing (2 pieces)

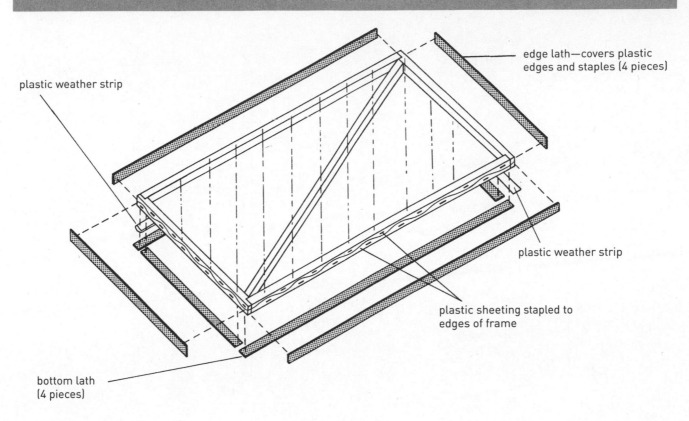

plastic weather strip

edge lath—covers plastic
edges and staples (4 pieces)

plastic weather strip

plastic sheeting stapled to
edges of frame

bottom lath
(4 pieces)

Other Possibilities

We have made a second mini-greenhouse, but instead of enclosing it
with plastic, we have used birdnetting as the covering of the panels.
Shadenetting, which screens out much more light than birdnetting
or pestnetting, can then be placed on top of the birdnetting in order
to control the amount of sunlight that the bed receives. (Shadenetting could be cut large enough to allow a 1- to 1^1/2-inch hem to be
sewn around the edges to prevent it from unraveling. It can then
simply be attached with machine screws and washers.)

Extra panels can be made so that plastic and netting panels can
be combined in the same greenhouse to meet specific weather or
horticultural requirements.

Another possibility would be the routing out of the 2 x 2 frames
and making removable panels instead of needing two separate
structures.

Let us know your experiences building and growing with this
mini-greenhouse/shadenetting house/birdnetting house/pestnetting
house. Suggestions for improvements are welcome.

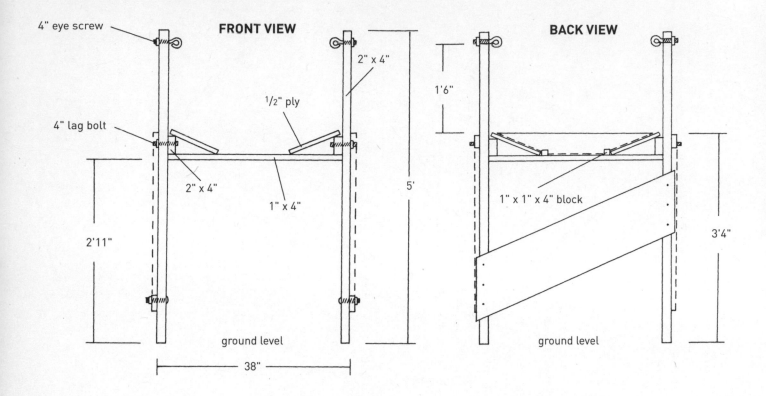

FRONT VIEW

4" eye screw

2" x 4"

½" ply

4" lag bolt

2" x 4"

1" x 4"

5'

2'11"

ground level

38"

BACK VIEW

1'6"

1" x 1" x 4" block

3'4"

ground level

WHEELBARROW SOIL AND COMPOST SIFTER

Design: Steve Shuck
Drawing Development: Pedro Klauder
Illustrations: Pedro J. Gonzalez

When we first started working the Common Ground Garden, Steve Shuck, a longtime Ecology Action member and supporter, saw we had a periodic need for large amounts of sifted soil and compost for seeding flats and sometimes for covering small seeds in the growing beds. As a result, he created a soil sifter for use with two 4-cubic-foot wheelbarrows. One wheelbarrow holds the soil to be sifted, while the second stands underneath the sifter to catch the refined soil.

The unsifted soil is placed on a screened "pan" that swings back and forth to speed the process. Pans with different mesh galvanized-wire "cloth" can be used depending on the size of the sifted particles needed. At the back of the pan is a hinged side which allows the clods which will not pass through the mesh to fall to the ground behind the sifter. The clods are later shoveled into the empty wheelbarrow and used as soil in the compost layering process. This tool made things a lot easier for us.

Wheelbarrow Soil and Compost Sifter

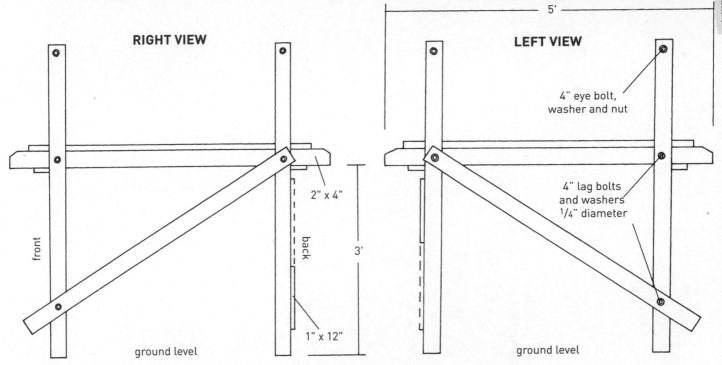

RIGHT VIEW

front

2" x 4"

back

3'

1" x 12"

ground level

LEFT VIEW

5'

4" eye bolt, washer and nut

4" lag bolts and washers 1/4" diameter

ground level

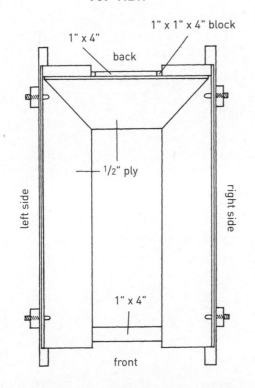

TOP VIEW

1" x 4"

1" x 1" x 4" block

back

1/2" ply

left side

right side

1" x 4"

front

	QUANTITY	MATERIAL
Wood	6	2" x 4" x 8'
	3	1" x 4" x 8'
	1	1" x 6" x 3'
	1	1" x 12" x 4'
	1	1/2" x 2' x 4' CDX plywood
	2	1/4" x 4' lath strips
Hardware	3' x 3'	1/2" galvanized wire mesh*
	2	3" x 3" x 1/2" L-bends
	2	small hook and eye sets
	4	4" eye screws
	4	4" eye bolts
	6	4" lag bolts with a 1/4"-diameter hole
	20	washers for 4" bolts
	4	1" pieces of chain
	2	2" hinge joints
	1 pkg.	3/8" staples
	1/2 lb.	3d galvanized nails

*other mesh sizes optional

TOP VIEW

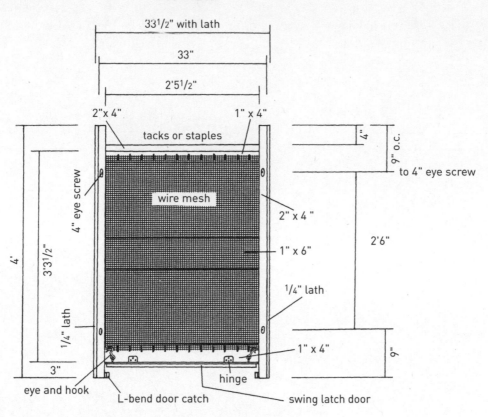

33¹/₂" with lath
33"
2'5¹/₂"
2" x 4"
1" x 4"
tacks or staples
4" eye screw
wire mesh
2" x 4"
1" x 6"
¹/₄" lath
¹/₄" lath
1" x 4"
4'
3'3¹/₂"
¹/₄" lath
3"
4"
9" o.c.
to 4" eye screw
2'6"
9"
eye and hook
L-bend door catch
hinge
swing latch door

BACK VIEW

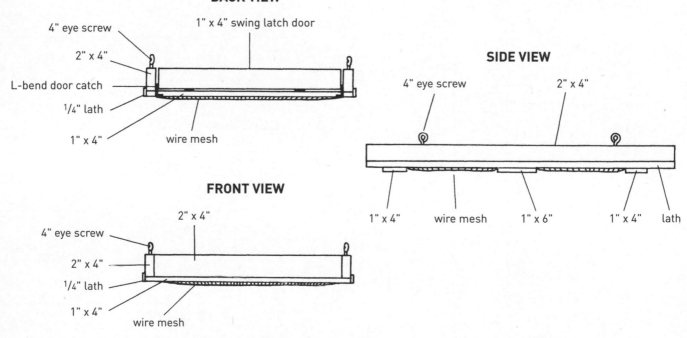

4" eye screw
2" x 4"
L-bend door catch
¹/₄" lath
1" x 4"
1" x 4" swing latch door
wire mesh

SIDE VIEW

4" eye screw
2" x 4"
1" x 4"
wire mesh
1" x 6"
1" x 4"
lath

FRONT VIEW

4" eye screw
2" x 4"
2" x 4"
¹/₄" lath
1" x 4"
wire mesh

SEEDLING FLATS

We like to use wooden flats when raising seedlings. They offer seedlings a home that can breathe and drain easily, and are made of natural materials. The design given below is for a standard flat, 14 inches wide by 23 inches long by 3¼ inches deep (all outer dimensions). A flat this size will contain about 250 1-inch planting centers, or about 60 2-inch planting centers. You can make a flat any size that you like, but remember that the larger the flat, the heavier it will be (because of the soil contained within it) and some shapes are awkward to carry.

Seedling Flat

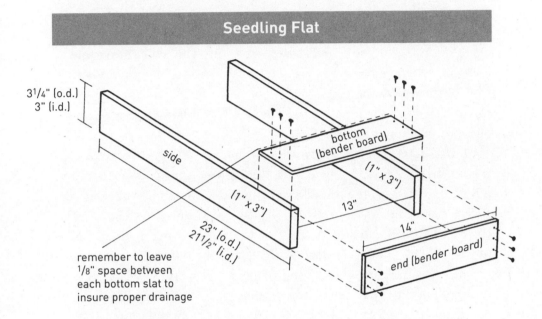

3¼" (o.d.)
3" (i.d.)

side

(1" x 3")

23" (o.d.)
21½" (i.d.)

remember to leave ⅛" space between each bottom slat to insure proper drainage

bottom (bender board)

(1" x 3")

13"

14"

end (bender board)

SEEDING BOARD OR FLAT ROW MAKER

A seedling flat row maker is a flat board with wooden ridges on it used to make rows in seed-starting flats

Seeding multiple vegetables or cultivars in trays can be time-consuming especially for market gardeners. This very simple tool performs a number of functions to aid in quantity and quality of seedlings available to be placed in bigger flats. The following are some of those functions:

- Provides uniform depth and texture to the soil in the flat.

- Ensures even planting depth for uniform germination.

- Keeps the various cultivars separate, avoiding intermingling.

- Allows for the maximum number of seedlings per flat—this saves space in heated germination areas, labor and supplies.

- The rows of seedlings can be removed easily, and with minimum disruption moved up/pricked out, or dibbled to the finishing flat.

- This may not seem like a lot, but it can really make a large difference as the gardener approaches production-scale gardening.

FLAT DIBBLE BOARD

Moving from flats with closely spaced seedlings to flats with more spacious spacing is called by various names such as pricking out, bumping up, or dibbling out. No matter what the name, it is time-consuming when you are dealing with thousands, and most likely tens of thousands, of transplants. The seeding board is the first tool in streamlining the process; the dibble board follows to create an efficient system.

Often the experienced grower can make pretty good time pricking out free-form with a widger (a mini trowel that is used to make a hole in the flat soil with a forward motion and covers the seeding with a backward motion). Even with the proficiency of such a skill, the dibble board is faster. Also, often the mini-farm may be utilizing newly skilled labor, apprentices, etc. This dibble board really helps to improve efficiency and get the spacing correct (to have consistent numbers in flats, maximize growth, and have uniform transplants).

The key to effectively using this tool is to have the proper flat soil, soil moisture, and correctly sized seedlings. The seedlings should have only two leaves and have no more than a few simple branched roots off the main root when they are placed in this soil. If they are too big they simply will not fit in. If they are too small they slide down the dibble hole, making it difficult to maintain the proper depth of the seedling. Flat soil can be used. Moisture should be sufficient to allow good penetration of the dibbles into the soil, but not enough moisture to stick to the dibbles or too little, which causes the walls of the dibble hole to cave in when the dibble is removed. If you get the moisture just right, it is a dream to use. When the process is working perfectly, the small plants can be set against the side of the dibble hole at the right depth (static attraction of the soil, water, and root keep the plant in place). When all the seedlings are in place, a bump to the side of the flat will settle the flat soil around the seedlings. A good watering afterward will provide the needed root-to-soil contact. You can really make time when it all works together!

The dibble board can be made of plywood (the size of your flats), and simple 1/2- to 9/16-inch by 31/2-inch wooden dowels can be used for the dibbles. The plywood is drilled to the diameter of the dowels for the seed tray, found on page 80, dipped in wood glue, and the dowels driven in until they are flush. Note: a drill press is very handy to keep all the holes perpendicular to the plywood.

Alternatively, a plastic assembly can be substituted for the wooden dowels. It is important to drill the holes for the drywall screw perpendicular to the plywood. It is important to cut the pvc pipe squarely on the ends so it remains perpendicular to the plywood.

For either type of dibble boards, a handle(s) or a simple board(s) can be attached to the back of the plywood to make it easier to use.

Flat Dibble Board

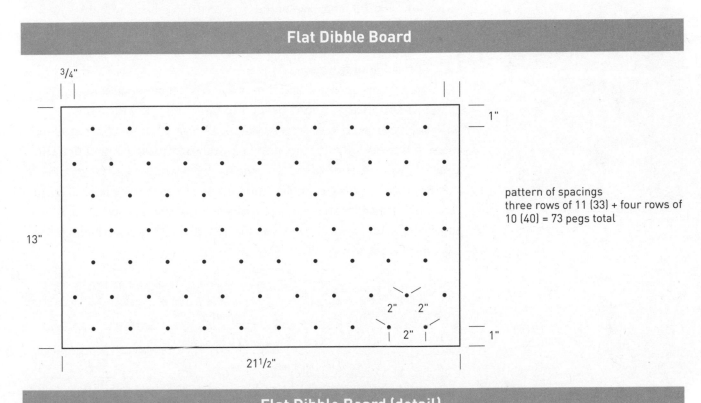

3/4"

1"

13"

pattern of spacings
three rows of 11 (33) + four rows of 10 (40) = 73 pegs total

2"   2"

2"

1"

211/2"

Flat Dibble Board (detail)

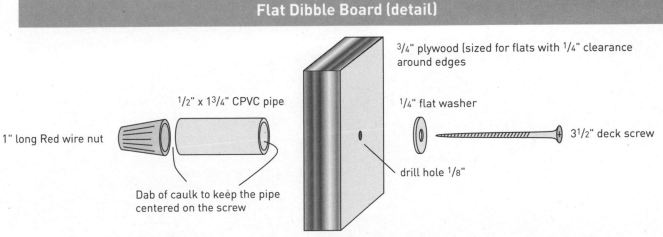

3/4" plywood (sized for flats with 1/4" clearance around edges

1/2" x 13/4" CPVC pipe

1/4" flat washer

31/2" deck screw

1" long Red wire nut

drill hole 1/8"

Dab of caulk to keep the pipe centered on the screw

ROLLING DIBBLE MARKER

For a biologically intensive production farmer, thousands, or tens of thousands, of transplants can be very time-consuming to plant. Using a rolling dibble marker, transplanting time can be dramatically reduced. In the case of onions, garlic, and leeks, a rolling marker can make holes on 6-inch offset centers deep enough to plant the seedlings. The marker shown here is for a 5-foot-wide bed and covers slightly more than half the growing bed. When one reaches the end of a bed, the marker is simply turned around and lined up with the holes and pulled down the other side of the bed. This allows the increased flexibility that is needed to bridge over the rounded beds and still make good deep holes. Once the holes are made, seedlings (or cloves in the case of garlic) are dropped in the holes and then settled within the earth and watered in. Using this technique, two skilled people can plant 621 transplants, a 100-square-foot bed, in less than 15 minutes.

The wheels on the dibble not only offer an easy mode of transport but supply the weight needed to force the individual dibbles into the ground. The wheels shown in the photo were old iron wheelbarrow wheels found at a junk yard—most any wheels will do. The dibble handle is flipped, so the wheels are down for transport and the handle flipped over when lined up on the bed for actual marking. A well-tilled soil with good soil structure and correct soil moisture are important to get proper penetration of the dibble while keeping the holes from caving in.

Partial Parts List	
QTY.	**MATERIAL**
33	1" x 2.5" dowels (old tool handles can be used)
6	1.5" x 2.5" x 36" (dowel support bars)
2	3/4" x 39 3/4" EMT (Electric conduit pipe for top handle and dibble axle)
2	1.5" x 1.5" x 60" Spruce framing lumber (Handle arms)
4	3/16" x 2" bolt/nut washer (These tie the axle and handle to the handle supports.)
1	diagonal 3/4" x 2.5" pine board cut to length, to be used as a diagonal brace to strengthen handle support arms
2	16" diameter transportation wheels; can be adapted to what is available
2	plywood supports for transport wheels
1	axle sized to wheel hubs
1	spacer pipe to keep transport wheels in place
2	cotter pins or bolts to keep the transport axle in place

Rolling Dibble Marker (front view)

41"

bolt through handle pipe

60"

57"

6" | 6" | 6" | 6" | 6" | 6"

bolt through roller axle pipe

1/4" wooden spacer/washer

3" | 6" | 6" | 6" | 6" | 6" | 3"

36"
37.5"

Wheel Axle (detail)

washers

doubled up nuts

all thread

wheel

Rolling Dibble Marker (side view)

plywood wheel support

16" diameter steel
wheelbarrow wheel
mounted on
all-thread axle

Rolling Drum (cross section)

1" dowel x 3.5"

2"

1.5"

2.5"

10.5" dia. 3/4"
plywood wheel

60°

Corners aligned
at 9.5" dia.

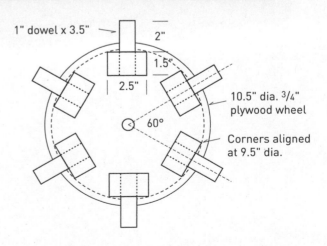

BED MARKER

Seldom does the production market gardener want to waste time keeping things pretty. So, keeping 900 beds in alignment can be viewed as a waste of time. It is, however, a good investment. It is easy for rows to drift over time and for us to sidestep a crop of broccoli, corn, or other crops that has oozed into the path and forced us to infringe on the adjoining bed. The multipurpose garden marker is a very simple tool to keep the paths and beds (and crops) in place, improving spacing efficiency and maximizing soil quality and improvement (no more walking where you should not). This tool combines measuring and string holding, winding and storage. It winds up the string quickly and keeps the string taught and nicely above the bed to be both accurate and convenient when working in the bed. (It is always a time waster and hassle to frequently go to the end of the bed to tighten the string.)

The tool height is equal to your bed width; the other leg of the device is the path width. Notches on the longest leg (bed width) provide a ready measure for plant spacings. This coupled with a piece of readily handy plant stem or tree twig can be measured against it and used as a quick planting stick. The bed maker is made of 3/8-inch concrete reinforcement rod. The reinforcement rod has some tensile strength which stiffens the steel. This tool requires some welding but lends itself to a great shop project for high school students. As an alternative, to avoid the need to weld, a less durable bed marker can be made out of pvc pipe and fitted with metal ground pin inserts (glued, auto body filler, or caulked) into the ground end of the pvc pipe.

ENDNOTES

1 Case Study B9: Design of a simple agricultural implement-France/Canada: *A Handbook of Appropriate Technology*, The Canadian Hunger Foundations, Ottawa, Canada and the Brace Research Institute, Quebec, Canada, co-publishers, April 1976. Maurice Franz, "Digging Without Pains and Aches," *Organic Gardening and Farming*, April 1976, pp. 76–77.

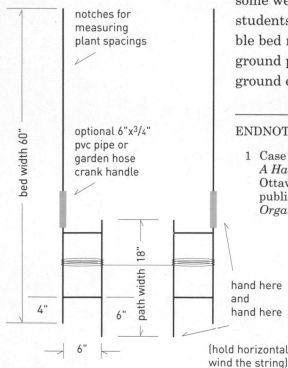

notches for measuring plant spacings

optional 6"x3/4" pvc pipe or garden hose crank handle

bed width 60"

path width 18"

4"

6"

6"

hand here and hand here

(hold horizontal to wind the string)

The Efficacy of the GROW BIOINTENSIVE Method in Increasing Sustainable Yields and Building Soils

As the charts below show, at some point during the years 2014 to 2021, there probably will not be enough land to produce all the nutrition needed for most of the world's population using current standard agricultural practices. These practices currently require about 7,000 to 63,000 square feet of farmable land per person, and most people will have access to only 9,000 square feet of arable soil as early as 2014. Further, most of the current practices are growing only *food* in the areas indicated, yielding insignificant net amounts of organic matter to produce the soil-nurturing humus needed to ensure the development of healthy soil. With many of these practices, an additional equal area will be needed to produce the amount of organic matter necessary to sustain soil fertility for both the food-growing farm area and the organic matter–growing farm area.

Approximate Area Required to Grow One Person's Diet Using Conventional Mechanized Chemical or Organic Techniques

High animal product diet (fossil fuels available) currently	31,000–63,000 sq ft
Average U.S. diets[1] (fossil fuels available) currently	15,000–30,000 sq ft
Average U.S. vegan (fossil fuels available) currently	7,000 sq ft
Average U.S. vegan diet (no animal products) (post-fossil fuel era)	21,000–28,000 sq ft
Average of actual areas needed for diets eaten in developing nations, using actual agricultural practices (fossil fuels available)	1977: 30,000 sq ft 1988: 22,000 sq ft 2000: 16,000 sq ft

Estimated Arable Land Available to Grow One Person's Diet with Different Levels of Water Availability

Year 2000, developing nations (where 80% of the world's population was living) with water available	16,000 sq ft
Year 2014–2021, developing nations (where 90% of the world's population will be living) with water available	9,000 sq ft
Year 2000, in water-scarce areas around the world	4,000 sq ft

Area Required to Grow One Person's Diet with the GROW BIOINTENSIVE Method, Including Crops That Produce a High Level of Calories per Unit of AREA (see pages 40–41)

GROW BIOINTENSIVE intermediate yields with soil fertility sustained	4,000 sq ft

By the years 2014–2021, with an average of 9,000 square feet available (see above), sufficient land and resources may be available in many developing-nation areas with GROW BIOINTENSIVE, leaving up to 5,000 square feet of surplus land for the preservation of plant and animal genetic diversity in situations with adequate water.

Will There Be Enough Land to Grow a Complete Diet for One Person Using Conventional Mechanized Chemical or Organic Techniques, or Using the GROW BIOINTENSIVE Method?

	DIET	High Animal Product	Avg. U.S.	Vegan	Vegan	Vegan with Special Root Crops
	AGRICULTURAL TECHNIQUE	Conventional or Organic	Conventional or Organic	Conventional or Organic	Conventional or Organic (post-fossil fuel)	GROW BIOINTENSIVE (intermediate yields/sustainable)
Land Available with Different Levels of Water — 16,000 sq ft (year 2000, water available)		Insufficient	Insufficient	Sufficient land and 9,000 sq ft surplus*	Insufficient	Sufficient land and 12,000 sq ft* surplus
9,000 sq ft (year 2014–2021, water available)		Insufficient	Insufficient	Sufficient land and 2,000 sq ft surplus*	Insufficient	Sufficient land and 5,000 sq ft* surplus
4,000 sq ft (year 2000, water scarce)		Insufficient	Insufficient	Insufficient	Insufficient	Sufficient land and no surplus

*Number of square feet represents the area that is in surplus (not needed for food production), that could be left in a natural state to preserve plant and animal genetic diversity and ecosytems.

GROW BIOINTENSIVE Applications

The GROW BIOINTENSIVE method, is eminently practical for serious small-scale food production. Some possible applications are:

- One mini-farmer may be able to net $20,000 to $40,000+ a year on a 1/8-acre mini-farm. He or she might work a 40-hour week and take a 4-month vacation each year. (For more details, see Ecology Action's *The Backyard Homestead, Mini-Farm and Garden Log Book* and *Cucumber Bonanza,* Self-Teaching Mini-Series Booklet.)

- A backyard gardener in the United States could grow a year's supply of vegetables and soft fruits (322 pounds) on 200 square feet in a 6-month growing season, assuming GROW BIOINTENSIVE intermediate yields. This food would be worth more than $600 and could eventually be grown in about 30 minutes (for 2 beds) a day, making the gardener's time worth $20 to $40+ per hour.

Perhaps it is unfair to compare the yields we obtained in our hard clay subsoil in Palo Alto with commercial agricultural yields. The stunted broccoli plant on the left was grown using normal backyard techniques, loosening the soil and adding chemical fertilizer. The broccoli shown in the middle was obtained by loosening the soil 12 inches deep and incorporating a 3-inch layer of aged manure with some compost. The broccoli on the right demonstrates the superiority of the GROW BIOINTENSIVE method, with soil loosened 24 inches deep and compost incorporated.

- An entire balanced diet could be grown at intermediate yields on as little as 1,000 square feet per person in an 8-month growing season with another 1,000 square feet needed to make it sustainable (for a total of 2,000 square feet). (See David Duhon and Cindy Gebhard's *One Circle,* published by Ecology Action, and Ecology Action's *Designing a GROW BIOINTENSIVE® Sustainable Mini-Farm* for more information. More usually it will take about 4,000 square feet to sustainably grow a complete diet for one person.) Using commercial agricultural techniques, it takes approximately 22,000 square feet per person in India, 7,000 square feet in the United States, and 3,400 square feet in Japan to grow similar diets unsustainably.

- Eventually we hope to produce as much food per hour by hand as commercial agriculture produces with machines.

- Key points such as the low start-up cost, low water usage, and diversity of crops make the GROW BIOINTENSIVE approach especially viable for small farmers in the developing world.

- This decentralized, self-sufficient approach is consistent with the current emphasis on enabling countries and communities to provide their own food.

Potential of Small-Scale GROW BIOINTENSIVE Food-Raising as indicated by ecology action's research to date

Potential production ranges as compared to local averages, per unit area

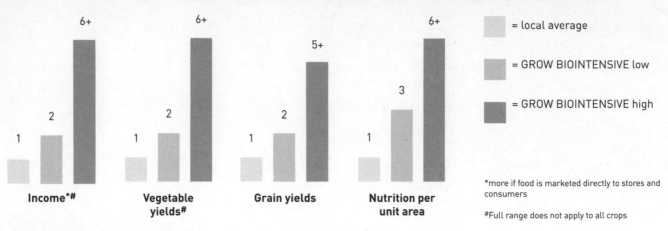

= local average

= GROW BIOINTENSIVE low

= GROW BIOINTENSIVE high

Income*#

Vegetable yields#

Grain yields

Nutrition per unit area

*more if food is marketed directly to stores and consumers

#Full range does not apply to all crops

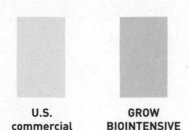

U.S. commercial agricultural average

GROW BIOINTENSIVE potential

Pounds of food produced per hour

Potentially can reach the same yield per hour as with machines, as soil and practitioner's skills improve and yields increase, and through the the use of simple, labor-saving hand devices—when all labor inputs for both approaches are evaluated.

Potential resource use ranges as compared with local averages, per pound of food produced

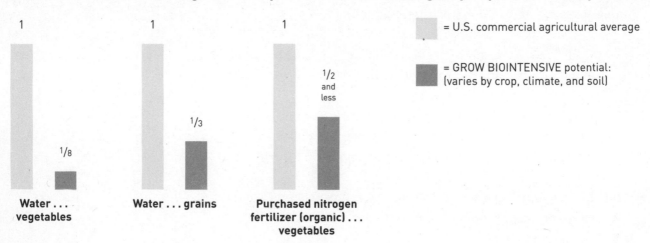

= U.S. commercial agricultural average

= GROW BIOINTENSIVE potential: (varies by crop, climate, and soil)

Water . . . vegetables

Water . . . grains

Purchased nitrogen fertilizer (organic) . . . vegetables

Soil Build-Up Rate with GROW BIOINTENSIVE Practices at Palo Alto Site Compared with Normal Build-Up Rate

A. Observed increase (buildup) in carbon soil (which was subsoil to begin with) at the Ecology Action Research Site (tentative figures). The program began in June 1972.
B. Normal buildup of soil by natural processes.
C. Natural development?

*% C Times,1.7 ≅ % Organic Matter

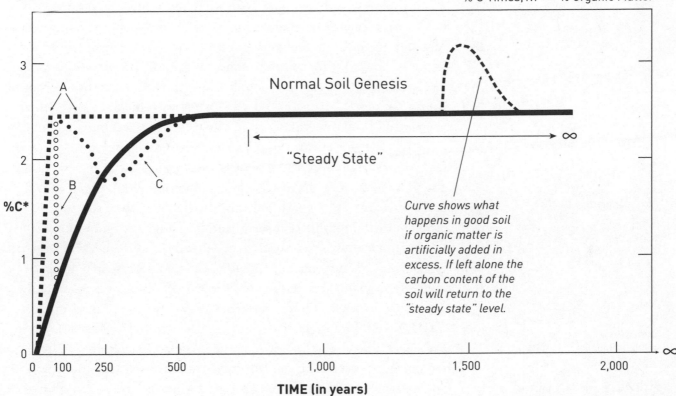

Normal Soil Genesis

"Steady State"

Curve shows what happens in good soil if organic matter is artificially added in excess. If left alone the carbon content of the soil will return to the "steady state" level.

%C*

TIME (in years)

Question: What would the fate of the carbon curve (or nitrogen curve) be if the bed were now left fallow after the normal "intense" organic matter input?

A. ■ ■ ■ ■ ■ ■ ■ ■ ■ ■ ■ ■ ■

Remains at "natural" steady-state level?

—Unlikely.

B. ○ ○ ○ ○ ○ ○ ○ ○ ○ ○ ○ ○

Drastic drop back down to zero?

—Unlikely.

C. ● ● ● ● ● ● ● ● ● ● ● ●

Substantial drop, but leveling off, then rising again under "natural development"?

—Most likely. Accelerated gain of hundreds of years of soil development (in as little as 6 months or as much as 8 years time with Ecology Action-type cultivation).

Sustainability

Biointensive techniques are being used to improve people's diets in over 142 countries around the world.

The most important element in assessing agricultural systems is whether or not the yields are sustainable in an environmentally balanced way. For thousands of years the Chinese practiced a manual, organic form of intensive farming using only fertilizers grown or produced on the farmstead. They were able to feed 1.5 to 2 times more people per acre than the United States presently does with mechanized chemical or mechanized organic techniques (assuming similar nonmeat diets). In addition, chemical techniques deplete the soil's capacity to produce. Wilson Clark, in the January 1975 issue of *Smithsonian,* noted: "Even though more corn was produced per acre in 1968 than in the 1940s, the efficiency with which crops used available [nitrogen] fertilizer actually declined fivefold."

Chemical agriculture requires ever-increasing amounts of fertilizer at an increasing cost as petroleum supplies dwindle. The use of chemical fertilizers depletes beneficial microbial life, breaks down soil structure, and adds to soil salinity. Impoverished soil makes crops more vulnerable to disease and insect attack and requires increasing amounts of pesticides to sustain production. "A modern agriculture, racing one step ahead of the apocalypse, is not ecologically sane, no matter how productive, efficient, or economically sound it may seem" (John Todd, in *The New Alchemy Institute Bulletin,* No. 2). Biointensive agriculture can sustain yields because it puts back into the soil those elements needed to sustain fertility. A small-scale personal agriculture recycles the nutrients and humus so important to the microbial life-forms that fix atmospheric nitrogen and produce disease-preventing antibiotics.

Preliminary studies by soil scientists at the University of California, Berkeley, indicate that in as little as a 6-month period (and in as many as 8 years), the soil involved in our tests (which was only a "C-horizon" subsoil material at the beginning) was built up to a humified carbon level equal to hundreds of years of natural soil development! If maintained, this improvement may make possible not only the maintenance of sustainable soil fertility, but also the reclamation of deteriorated and marginal lands (see the preceding graph). The GROW BIOINTENSIVE method also nurtures the soil life and structure, utilizes renewable resources, can be productive economically on a small manual scale, and provides higher yields.

For more information about Ecology Action's history, current programs, workshops, and classes, or to become a member and support our work, go to www.growbiointensive.org or write to:

Ecology Action
5798 Ridgewood Road
Willits, CA 95490-9730.

To order Ecology Action's other publications, see page 227.

ENDNOTES

1 Assuming average amounts of vegetables, fruits, grains, beans, eggs, milk, cheese, and meat are eaten.

Ecology Action Publications

Beeby, John. *Future Fertility: Transforming Human Waste into Human Wealth.* Willits, CA: Ecology Action, 1995. 168 pp.

Duhon, David, and Cindy Gebhard. *One Circle: How to Grow a Complete Diet in Less Than 1,000 Square Feet.* Willits, CA: Ecology Action, 1984. 200 pp. This book helps you to explore your nutritional needs and to design and produce a smallest-scale complete diet.

Gridley, Karen, ed. *Man of the Trees: Selected Writings of Richard St. Barbe Baker.* Willits, CA: Ecology Action, 1989. This collection of excerpts from Richard St. Barbe Baker's most important writings provides a fascinating glimpse of one of this century's most farsighted individuals. Beyond mere human interest, however, the book carries an urgent message about the vital role of trees in planetary survival. (Also available in Spanish.)

Jeavons, John. *How to Grow More Vegetables, Fruits, Nuts, Berries, and Other Crops Than You Ever Thought Possible on Less Land Than You Can Imagine.* 8th Edition. Berkeley, CA: Ten Speed Press, 2012. 288 pp. Ecology Action's popular primer gives the most complete instructions and information for the GROW BIOINTENSIVE method.

———. *Cultivo Biointensivo de Alimentos: Más Alimentos en Menos Espacio.* Willits, CA: Ecology Action, 2002. Spanish translation of the 6th edition of *How to Grow More Vegetables.*

———. *Comment Faire Pousser.* Berkeley, CA: Ten Speed Press, 1982. 192 pp. French translation of the 2nd edition of *How to Grow More Vegetables.*

———. *Mehr Gemuse im Eigenen Garten.* Willits, CA: Ecology Action, 1981. 82 pp. German translation of the 1st edition of *How to Grow More Vegetables.*

———. *Kak Vyraschivat' Bol'she Ovoschei.* Moscow: BVL Publishers, 1997. 220 pp. Russian translation of the 5th edition of *How to Grow More Vegetables.*

———. Arabic translation of the 5th edition of *How to Grow More Vegetables.* Willits, CA: Ecology Action, 1997. 300 pp.

———. Braille version of the 3rd edition of *How to Grow More Vegetables*. Willits, CA: Ecology Action, 1981. For details on how to obtain a copy, write Monterey County Braille Transcribers, P.O. Box DF, Pacific Grove, CA 93950.

———. Hindi translation of the 1st edition of *How to Grow More Vegetables*. Willits, CA: Ecology Action, 1987. 70 pp.

———. *1972 Preliminary Research Report*. Palo Alto, CA: Ecology Action of the Midpeninsula, 1973. 22 pp. Ecology Action's first data report on the Biointensive method and implications for small farmers.

———. *1972–1975 Research Report Summary*. Palo Alto, CA: Ecology Action, 1976. 19 pp. Summary of data and projections of Ecology Action's first four years of research with Biointensive techniques.

———. "Quantitative Research on the Biodynamic/French Intensive Method." In *Small Scale Intensive Food Production—Improving the Nutrition of the Most Economically Disadvantaged Families,* pp. 32–38. Washington, DC: League for International Food Education, 1977. Workshop proceedings prepared on behalf of the Office of Nutrition, Bureau for Technical Assistance, U.S. Agency of International Development.

Jeavons, John, and Carol Cox. *The Sustainable Vegetable Garden*. Berkeley, CA: Ten Speed Press, 1999. 118 pp. The basic GROW BIOINTENSIVE book for those just starting. Also gives specific recommendations on the best crops to grow and how much to grow for an entire family.

Jeavons, John, J. Mogador Griffin, and Robin Leler. *The Backyard Homestead, Mini-Farm and Garden Log Book*. Willits, CA: Ecology Action, 1983. 224 pp. A handbook for everyday use in developing greater self-sufficiency in a backyard homestead or in actually earning an income from a small farm. There is material covering tools and crop testing, as well as calendars, graphs, charts, and plenty of space for record keeping. It also includes information on creating your own self-fertilizing herbal lawns.

Roberts, Hugh, ed. *Intensive Food Production on a Human Scale: Proceedings of the Third International Conference on Small Scale and Intensive Food Production*. Willits, CA: Ecology Action, 1982. 224 pp. The result of a gathering of 100 people representing projects in 16 countries.

———. *Proceedings of the Soil, Food, and People Conference*. Willits, CA: Ecology Action, 2001, 180 pp. The result of a gathering of 276 people from 26 countries focusing on the role of Biointensive food raising in the new century.

Shepard, Michael, and John Jeavons. *Appropriate Agriculture*. Menlo Park, CA: Intermediate Technology, 1977. 14 pp. Paper given by Peter N. Gillingham at the "Small Is Beautiful" conference, featuring Dr. E. F. Schumacher, at the University of California at Davis.

SELF-TEACHING MINI-SERIES AND OTHER BOOKLETS

Annual Report. 1993. 30 pp.

Another Way to Wealth. Booklet 1. 1991. 16 pp.

Backyard Garden Research. Booklet 17. 1988. 32 pp. Improving your garden's performance through observation. (Also available in Spanish.)

Biointensive Mini-Farming: A Rational Use of Natural Resources. Booklet 0. 1985. 15 pp. Explains what Ecology Action is doing and why. (Also availabe in Spanish, French, German, Russian, Portuguese, and Chinese.)

Biointensive Micro-Farming: A Seventeen-Year Perspective. Booklet 19. 1989. 20 pp. (Also available in Spanish.)

A Complete 21-Bed Biointensive-Bed GROW BIOINTENSIVE Mini-Farm: Fertility, Nutrition, and Income. Booklet 14. 1986. 28 pp. Explores sustainably growing all your own food and composting crops and making an income, in as little as 2,100 square feet at high-level yields.

A Complete 33-Bed Biointensive Bed GROW BIOUNTENSIVE Mini-Farm: Fertility, Nutrition, and Income. Booklet 36. 2011. 32 pp. Explores sustainably growing all your own food, composting crops, and making an income in as little as 3,300 square hundred square feet at intermediate-level yields.

Cucumber Bonanza. Booklet 1. 1979. 24 pp. Takes cucumbers as an example of a crop history and goes through 7 years of work, bringing the 1973 yield of 140 pounds of marketable cucumbers per 100 square feet to over 400 pounds in 1979. An excellent introduction to mini-farming and the variables that can be examined in obtaining improved yields. (Also available in Spanish.)

Cultivating Our Garden. A detailed article on GROW BIOINTENSIVE methods. 4 pp. (Also available in Spanish, Russian, Arabic, and Japanese.)

Designing a GROW BIOINTENSIVE® Sustainable Mini-Farm—A Working Paper. Booklet 31. 2003. 45 pp.

Dried, Cut, and Edible Flowers for Pleasure, Food, and Income. Booklet 18. 1990. 61 pp. (Also available in Spanish.)

An Ecology Action Reading Guide. Booklet 20. 1989. 36 pp. Design your own curriculum.

Ecology Action's Comprehensive Definition of Sustainability. Booklet 24. 2005. 4 pp. (Also available in Spanish.)

Examining the Tropics: A Small-Scale Approach to Sustainable Agriculture. Booklet 11. 1982. 31 pp. (Also available in Spanish.)

Foliar Feeding. Booklet 16. 1987. 9 pp. (Also available in Spanish.)

Food for the Future, Now: A Survival Garden Plan. 2010. 48 pp. Also explores a key 1,600 calorie diet.

GROW BIOINTENSIVE® Apprentice Possibilities. 2005. 28 pp.

GROW BIOINTENSIVE® Composting and Growing Compost Materials. Booklet 32. 2004. 35 pp.

GROW BIOINTENSIVE® Sustainable Mini-Farming Teacher Training and Certification Program—Revised. Booklet 30. 2005. 43 pp.

Grow Your Manure for Free. Booklet 22. 1989. 32 pp. Summary of compost crops to grow for improving your soil's fertility. (Also available in Spanish.)

Growing and Gathering Your Own Fertilizers. Booklet 12. 1984. 125 pp. (Also available in Russian.)

Growing More Food with Less Water. Booklet 35. 2011. 28pp.

Growing Medicinal Herbs in as Little as Fifty Square Feet—Uses and Recipes. Booklet 27. 1995. 40 pp.

Growing to Seed. Revised. Booklet 13. 1999. 45 pp. How to grow your own seed in the smallest possible area while preserving genetic diversity. (Also available in Spanish.)

Learning to Grow All Your Own Food: One-Bed Model for Compost, Diet, and Income Crops. Booklet 26. 25 pp. A companion to Booklet 14.

Learning to Grow All Your Own Food: One-Bed Model for Compost, Diet, and Income Crops. Booklet 36. 2012. 225 pp. A companion to Booklet 35. 2012.

Micro-Farmers as a Key to the Revitalization of the World's Agriculture and Environment. Booklet 21. 1989. 13 pp.

One Basic Kenyan Diet: With Diet, Income, and Compost Designs in a Three-Growing-Bed Learning Model. Booklet 25. 1991. 28 pp.

One Basic Mexican Diet. Booklet 15. 1987. 32 pp. Explores complete nutritional self-sufficiency in a small area with 1 Mexican diet as a focal point. (Also available in Spanish.)

One Crop Test Booklet: Soybeans. Booklet 2. 1980. 24 pp. Contains step-by-step instructions for conducting comparative tests for spacing and yield (with optional water monitoring) for soybeans—an important protein crop throughout the world. This booklet lets you participate in Ecology Action's research or simply grow better soybeans for yourself.

A Perspective. Booklet 9. 1981. 17 pp. Speech given by John Jeavons at the Second International Conference on Small-Scale Intensive Food Production, October 1981.

The Smallest Possible Area to Grow Food and Feed. Booklet 28. 1997. 45 pp.

Solar Water Heater. 2000. 12 pp.

Test Your Soil with Plants. Booklet 29. 1997. 86 pp.

INFORMATION PACKETS

Topical treatments on the latest information from our garden research, and our work around the world. Topics range from "Data for Common Compost Crops" (in the Sustainable Soil Fertility packet) to "Double-Digging vs. the U-Bar" (in the Gardening Techniques packet) to "About Amaranth and Quinoa" (in the Crops packet). The information is presented as short complete articles on a given subject area, and the information tends to be interrelated.

Children's Gardening Resources. 3 pp.

Cooking with Sunshine. 2 pp.

Crops. 9 topics, 15 pp. Information on specific crops and things to look for in certain useful crops.

Data Report for One Crop. 2 pp., free. The form to use to send data from your garden to Ecology Action.

Gardening Techniques. 12 topics, 31 pp. Some greening-edge techniques and observations on the art of gardening.

GROW BIOINTENSIVE Projects. 5 topics, 14 pp. Profiles of some of the major Biointensive projects around the world.

Insect and Animal Life. 5 topics, 10 pp. Useful hints and tips for dealing with our wilder neighbors.

Inspiration. 6 topics, 13 pp. The bigger picture. Articles that are Ecology Action's key position papers and put our work in perspective.

Limited Water Growing. 4 topics, 6 pp. Water-saving techniques.

Small Cabin / Land Trust Information. 2 pp.

Sustainable Soil Fertility. 16 topics, 41 pp. The heart of our work—finding out how to have a really sustainable garden or mini-farm.

Yields. 4pp. Outlines the factors master yield figures are based upon.

REPRINTS

Composting for the Tropics. 28 pp.

Living Quarters for Plant Roots. 6 pp.

Plant Species Index for the Pacific Northwest and General Reference. 20 pp.

RELATED PUBLICATIONS BY OTHER ORGANIZATIONS

Intensive Small Farms and the Urban Fringe. Sausalito, CA: Landal Institute for Small Farm Research, 1976. 93 pp. Based in part on Ecology Action's research.

Jeavons, John. "Biointensive Sustainable Mini-Farming: I. The Challenge; II. Perspective, Principles, Techniques, and History; III. System Performance—Initial Trials; IV. System Performance—Continuing Trials in a More Difficult Environment and Soil; V. Future Potential, Some Representative World Applications, Future Challenges, and Research Opportunities." *Journal of Sustainable Agriculture,* pp. 49–105. Birmingham, NY: Haworth Press, 2001.

Martinez, Juan Manuel. *Huertos Familiares.* ECOPOL: (c.o. Edif. H10-1-2. Col. Lomas de Plateros, Mexico, D.F. CP 01480, Mexico), 1992. Booklet used by the nationwide program in Mexico to teach Biointensive mini-farming at the introductory level.

———. *Rotofolio Huertos Familiares.* Rotofolio Huertos Familiares. ECOPOL: (c.o. Edif. H10-1-2. Col. Lomas de Plateros, Mexico, D.F. CP 01480, Mexico), 1992. Flipchart used for teaching Biointensive mini-farming in villages in Mexico.

A Preliminary Assessment of the Applicability of French Intensive/Biodynamic Gardening Techniques in Tropical Settings. Santa Barbara, CA: Direct International Development/Direct Relief Foundation, 1978. 47 pp. Report from on-site visits to 4 intensive demonstration gardens in Central America.

Seshadri, C. V., et al. *Biodynamic Gardening.* Vol. 4. Tharamani, Tamil Nadu: Shri AMM Murugappa Chettiar Research Centre (Tharamani, Tamil Nadu, 600 113, India), 1980. 38 pp.

———. *Biodynamic Horticulture—Improvements & Extension.* Vol. 15. Tharamani, Tamil Nadu: Shri AMM Murugappa Chettiar Research Centre (Tharamani, Tamil Nadu, 600 113, India), 1983. 43 pp.

Yang, Y. K. "Home Gardens as a Nutrition Intervention," in *Small Scale Intensive Food Production: Improving the Nutrition of the Most Economically Disadvantaged Families,* pp. 60–80. Washington, D.C.: League for International Food Education, 1977.

Ecology Action / GROW BIOINTENSIVE

Ecology Action teaches people worldwide to better feed themselves while feeding the soil and conserving resources. Ecology Action is a 501(c) (3) nonprofit organization with its headquarters and Common Ground Mini-Farm located at 5798 Ridgewood Road, Willits, CA 95490. Also visit www.growbiointensive.org; for a synopsis of initiatives in and results from this work since 1972, see "The Story So Far . . ." on this website. Become a member to support this growing-edge work. Be sure to see Self-Teaching Section: www.growbiointensive.org/self_teaching.html

ECOPOL, Latin America

Ecology Action's international partner for the Spanish speaking world is ECOPOL. Contact: Juan Manuel Martinez Valdez, Director, ECOPOL, Apartado Postal Numero 2, Aculco, Estado de Mexico, Mexico; ecopolac@aol.com and onaledar@yahoos.com; tel 011-52 (55) 565-111-43 or 011-52 (55) 130-860-40.

Grow Biointensive Agriculture Center of Kenya

Ecology Action's international partner in Kenya is Grow Biointensive Center of Kenya, G-BIACK, which works with small-scale farm holders in Central, Eastern, and Nairobi Provinces in Kenya. Contact: Samual Nderitu, PO Box 4171, Madaraka, Thika, Kenya; growbiointensivecenterkenya@gmail.com or gbiacenterkenya@yahoo.com; tel +254-720-323-134.

Kilili Self Help Project

You can help support a Kenyan villager's training at a basic Biointensive Skills Workshop. To make this happen, send a tax-deductible donation to the Kilili Self Help Project, 260 Marion Avenue, Mill Valley, California 94141: $50 will train 10 farmers and $100 will train 20. Help the world grow!

Manor House Agricultural Centre, Africa

Ecology Action's international partner for Africa is Manor House Agricultural Centre. Contact: Emmanuel Omondi, Director, Manor House Agriculture Centre, Private Bag, Kitale, Kenya.

Memberships and Ordering

I would like to be part of Ecology Action's work. Enclosed is my membership donation for one year, which includes Ecology Action's newsletter.

❑ $20 Newsletter   ❑ $40 Supporting   ❑ $60 Family
❑ $100 Sustaining   ❑ $250 Outreach Supporter
❑ $400 Research Supporter   ❑ $1,000 Lifetime Membership
❑ Gift membership at $_____   ❑ Other _____

Please also send:
❑ *How to Grow More Vegetables*. 2012 edition, by John Jeavons, $19.95 (U.S. funds). California residents add 7.25% sales tax. For shipping and handling please add $4.95 for U.S., $12.00 for Canada, and $14.00 for all other countries.

❑ *The Sustainable Vegetable Garden*. 1999 edition, by John Jeavons and Carol Cox, $12.95 (U.S. funds). California residents add 7.25% sales tax.

❑ For shipping and handling please add $4.00 in U.S., $4.95 for Canada, and $10.00 for all other countries.

❑ *Proceedings of the Soil, Food, and People Conference: A Biointensive Model for the New Century*. $30 (U.S. funds). California residents add 7.25% sales tax. For shipping and handling please add $6.65 for U.S., $10.00 for Canada, and $19.00 for all other countries.

❑ Sample Newsletter, $2.50 postpaid.

Name _____

Address _____

Send to: ECOLOGY ACTION, 5798 Ridgewood Road, Willits, CA 95490-9730

PLEASE JOIN US.

Membership donations provide a reliable financial base that secures continued education and research programs for sustainable GROW BIOINTENSIVE food-raising worldwide. Our thanks to all of our friends who are investing in the future by making this work possible.

Order online from
Bountiful Gardens at
www.bountifulgardens.com
— or —
By mail from **Ecology Action**
(see left)

INDEX

A

Acidic plants in compost, 57
Aeration and compost, 58
Africa
    biointensive work in, 226
    North Africa, overfarming in, 6
Agricultural recycling, 105
    companion planting as, 108
Agroforestry, 4
Air space in soil, 31
Alfalfa
    green manures with, 56
    guide for adding alfalfa meal, 74
    nitrogen (N), alfalfa meal for, 68
    nutrients from, 35
Allergies to fava beans, 108
Amaranth
    as carbon-and-calorie crop, 11
    rotation planting with, 108
Anaerobic decomposition, 54
Animals. *See also* specific animals
    companion planting and, 114
Ants, 120
    companion planting to control, 114
    plant controls for, 127
Aphids
    companion planting to control, 114
    plant controls for, 127
Arable land for one person's diet, 214
ARLO (Stanford University's Action
    Research Liaison Office), 194
Ash for potassium (K), 68–69
Asian blue-green algal wet rice
    farming, 4
Asparagus
    companion planting with, 116
    soil temperature conditions for, 99

B

*The Backyard Homestead, Mini-Farm
    and Garden Log Book* (Ecology
    Action), 26, 129, 130–131, 215
    sifters for compost, 55
    starter garden plan information,
    184
Bacteria, composting and, 48–49
Baltimore orioles, 122
Barley as carbon-and-calorie crop, 11
Barriers for insect control, 124, 126
Basil, companion planting with, 117
Bay laurel in compost, 57
Beans
    companion planting with, 116
    compost efficiency and, 40
    green manures with, 56
    soil temperature conditions for, 99
    in starter garden plan, 185
Bed markers, 212
Beds
    40-bed design, 41–42
    laying out, 18–19
    poor soil, preparation for, 23–24
    prepared beds, 29–32
    raised beds, 16
    rows *vs.,* 16
    starter garden plan with 2 beds,
    184–187
    widths for, 29–31
Bee balm, companion planting with, 117
Beeby, John, 66
Bees, companion planting and, 114
Beets
    companion planting with, 116
    root system of, 19
    rotation planting with, 108
    soil temperature conditions for, 99

Beginning gardeners, 10–11
Bent beds for rainfall capture, 95
Bermuda grass in compost, 57
Bibb lettuce, spinach panted with, 101
Biodynamic composting method, 55
Biointensive for Russia, 225
Biopshere2, 42–43
Birds
    companion planting and, 114
    insect/pest control with, 122
Black flea beetles, plant controls
    for, 127
Black flies, plant controls for, 127
Black wood ash, 68
Borage
    companion planting with, 117
    for tomato worm control, 114
Bountiful Gardens, 225
    membership information for, 227
Bow rakes, 17, 18
Breakfast-lunch-dinner concept, 83
Broadcasting fertilizers, 72
Broadcasting seeds, 77–78
Broccoli, companion planting with, 116
Brown, Lester, 6
Buckwheat family, rotation planting
    with, 108
The Bug Book (Philbrick), 128
Building compost piles, 53–54
Burdock, compost efficiency and, 40
Burnett, William, 194
Bush beans, companion planting
    with, 116
Butterflies, 123–124
    plant controls for, 127

C

Cabbages
    companion planting with, 116
    soil temperature conditions for, 99
    watering, 90
Cabbage worms, 120
    plant controls for, 127
Calcite, 69
Calcium
    in Oyster Shell Flour, 67
    recommended sources for, 69
Calcium sulfate, 69
Calendula, companion planting
    with, 118
California bay laurel in compost, 57
Calorie-efficient crops, 2–3
    Master Chart for, 146–157
Cane crops, Master Chart for, 162–173
Caraway, companion planting with,
    117
Carbonaceous materials, 35
Carbon-and-calorie crops, 2, 11
    design ratios for, 41
Carbonic acid, 35
Carbon/nitrogen ratio of compost pile,
    60–61
Carrots
    companion planting with, 116
    root system of, 19
    soil temperature conditions for, 99
Cassava, compost efficiency and, 40
Castor beans
    in compost, 57
    for gopher control, 114
Caterpillars, 120
Cat manure in compost, 58
Catnip, companion planting with, 117
Cauliflower
    companion planting with, 116
    root system of, 19
    soil temperature conditions for, 99
Celery
    companion planting with, 116
    soil temperature conditions for, 99
Cereal rye
    as carbon-and-calorie crop, 11
    nitrogen (N) from, 104
    roots of, 44, 45
Chadwick, Alan, 8–9, 10–11, 43, 46,
    48, 64, 77–78
    breakfast-lunch-dinner concept, 83
    moon, planting by phases of,
    86–89
    seedling plant soil mixture, 82

Chamomile, companion planting
    with, 103–104, 117
Chervil, companion planting with, 117
Chickens, 120
    for insect control, 114–115
China
    biologically miniaturized
    agriculture, 37
    urbanization in, 5
Chives, companion planting with,
    116, 117
Circle of the Sun Farm and
    Education Center, 225
Clark, Robert, 194
Clark, Wilson, 218
Classes in BIOINTENSIVE
    mini-farming, 224
Clay soils, compost for, 28
Closed-system living project, 42–43
Clove, green manures with, 56
Cold compost piles, 60, 61
Cold frames for seedlings, 81
Cole family, rotation planting with,
    108
Colorado potato beetles, plant
    controls for, 127
Comfrey, nutrients from, 35
Common Ground Garden, 9
    Supply and Education Center,
    225
Companion planting, 101–118
    beneficial companions, 103–104
    crystallization method, 102–103
    fast/slow maturing requirements,
    112
    herbs, list of, 117–118
    insect/pest control and, 113–114,
    126–127
    physical complementarity, 112
    planning for, 110–111
    rotations, 104–108
    shallow/deep rooting
    requirements, 112
    soil nutrients and, 108–112
    spacing for, 103, 109–112
    sun/shade needs, 112
    2-crop companion planting, 110
    3-crop companion planting, 111
    vegetables, list of, 116
    vertical location of plant's edible
    portion, 112, 113
    weed control and, 113
*Companion Plants and How to Use
    Them* (Philbrick), 128

Complete texturizing double dig,
    24–25, 27
Compost and composting, 2. *See also*
    Manures
    adding compost, techniques for, 72
    application rates, 54–55
    avoidable materials for, 57–58
    benefits of, 58–60
    biodynamic composting method,
    55
    building piles, 53–54
    carbon-and-calorie crops and, 11
    carbon/nitrogen ratio of compost
    pile, 60–61
    cold composting, 60, 61
    containers for piles, 50–51
    curing rates, 54–55
    different crops in pile, 49
    double-digging, adding to, 23
    Ecology Action's goals, 37–38
    efficient composting, 60–61
    functions of compost, 46
    goals for, 40
    hot compost piles, 61
    locating piles, 49–51
    maximum maintenance dressing
    of, 55
    methods, comparison of, 55–57
    in nature, 44–45
    non-soil compost, 29
    nutrients from, 35, 46, 59
    from outside garden sources, 28
    and pH of soil, 67
    process of, 46–48
    Rodale composting method,
    55–56
    sheet composting, 56
    sifting compost, 55
    size of pile, 51–52
    smell of compost pile, 53–54
    soil in pile, 48–49, 54
    soil modifier, compost as, 70–71
    source of compost, 18
    starter garden plan, composting
    crops in, 184, 185
    step-by-step guide to building
    piles, 59–60
    timing for building, 51–52
    turning compost pile, 54–55
    types of piles, 50
    watering piles, 54
    weeds in compost pile, 97
    wheelbarrow soil and compost
    sifter, 204–206

Containers for compost piles, 50–51
Cool-season crops, 98
Corn
    as carbon-and-calorie crop, 11
    companion planting with, 116
    in compost pile, 53
    cucumbers grown with, 112
    root system of, 19
    soil temperature conditions for, 99
Cornell University, 128
Cotyledons, 83–84
Cox, Carol, 182
Crop rotation. *See* Rotations in planting
Crushed granite, 69
    guide for adding, 74
Crystallization method, 102–103
Cucumber Bonanza (Self-Teaching Mini-Series Booklet), 215
Cucumbers
    companion planting with, 116
    corn, planting with, 112
    soil temperature conditions for, 99
    stems, turning, 85
    sun/shade needs, 112
Curing compost pile, 54–55
Cutworms, plant controls for, 127
Cypress in compost, 57

D

Daffodils for gopher control, 114, 124
Daily watering, 90
Dandelion, companion planting with, 103, 104
Dead nettle, companion planting with, 117
Deep soil, 2, 15–32
    types of preparation, 19, 24–28
Depth of beds, 29
Designing a GROW BIOINTENSIVE Sustainable Mini-Farm— A Working Paper, 181
Destruction of soil, 1–2
D-handled flat spades, 16, 17
D-handled spading forks, 16, 17
Diamond-shaped growing areas, 95, 96
Dibbers, 17
Dibble boards
    flat dibble boards, 208–209
    rolling dibble markers, 210–211

Diet Design and Planning Program, 181
Digging boards, 18, 31
    as planting boards, 78
Dill, companion planting with, 117
Diseased plants in compost, 57, 58
Diversity
    of microbes, 49
    preservation of, 38
Dog manure in compost, 58
Dolomitic lime, 69
Double-digging, 16–32
    complete texturizing double dig, 24–25, 27
    goal of, 19
    initial double dig, 25
    ongoing double dig, 25
    for poor soils, 23–28
    procedure for, 20–23
    step-by-step process, 20–23
    time for, 18
    U-bar dig, 25–26, 28
Drooping plants, watering, 93
DVDs, list of, 224

E

Earwigs, 120
Ecology Action, 9, 226. *See also* GROW BIOINTENSIVE Sustainable Mini-Farming
    information on, 219
    joining and assisting, 12–13
    membership information for, 227
    publications, list of, 219–224
    sustainability goals, 37–38
ECOPOL, 226
Eelworms, controlling, 114
Eggplants
    companion planting with, 116
    soil temperature conditions for, 99
Eggshells, dried crushed, 69
Einkorn hornemanni, 42
Elderberry for gopher control, 114
Energy
    GROW BIOINTENSIVE Sustainable Mini-Farming and, 3
    Master Chart for energy crops, 158–161
English Haws watering can, 90
Environmental Research Laboratory, University of Arizona, 42–43
Eucalyptus in compost, 57

F

Fall crops, rotation for, 105
Fava beans
    allergies, 108
    green manures with, 56
    nitrogen (N) from, 104
Fennel, companion planting with, 117
Fertility
    fertilization and, 46
    in perspective, 65
Fertilization, 63–75
    compost and, 58
    fertility and, 46
    sustainable fertilization, 72–74
Fertilizers
    adding, techniques for, 72
    analysis of NPK minerals, 66
    GROW BIOINTENSIVE Sustainable Mini-Farming and, 3
    history of, 7–8
    organic fertilizers, 34
Fiber crops, Master Chart for, 158–161
Flat dibble boards, 208–209
Flats for seedlings. *See* Seedling flats
Flat spades, 16, 17
Flax, companion planting with, 117
Flies, 120
    black flies, plant controls for, 127
    plant controls for, 127
    syrphid flies, insect/pest control with, 123
    Tachinid flies, 120, 123
    white flies, companion planting to control, 113
Flowering tobacco for white fly control, 113
Flowers
    in garden planning, 182
    Master Chart for spacing, 174
40-bed design, 41–42
French marigold for nematode control, 114
Fukuoka food raising, 4
Fully experienced gardeners, 11

G

Gandhi, M., 12
Gardening Without Poisons (Hunter), 128

Olsen, Mary, 224

One Circle, the Sustainable Vegetable Garden, 42

One Crop Test Booklet: Soybeans (Ecology Action), 131

One person's diet, area required to grow, 214

Ongoing double dig, 25

Onions
  companion planting with, 116
  compost efficiency and, 40
  rotation planting with, 108
  soil temperature conditions for, 99
  transplanting seedlings, 85

Open compost pile, 50

Open-pollinated seeds, 3
  information on growing, 131
  planting, 77

Oregano, companion planting with, 103

Organic fertilizers, 34

Organic matter, 46
  analysis in fertilizers, 67
  key functions of, 52
  watering and, 95

Organic Method Primer (Rateaver & Rateaver), 73

Organizations, list of, 225–226

Overplanting and watering, 96–97

Oyster Shell Flower, 67

P

Pallet-type compost pile, 50

Paper crops, Master Chart for, 158–161

Parsley
  companion planting with, 116
  rotation planting with, 108
  soil temperature conditions for, 99

Parsnips
  compost efficiency and, 40
  soil temperature conditions for, 99

Peanuts and compost efficiency, 40

Peas
  companion planting with, 116
  green manures with, 56
  rotation planting with, 108
  soil temperature conditions for, 99
  watering, 90

Pennyroyal for ant control, 114

Peppermint, companion planting with, 117

Peppers
  companion planting with, 116
  soil temperature conditions for, 99

Pernicious weeds in compost, 57, 58

Pesticides, 8
  disadvantages of, 128
  soil structure and, 15–16

Pests. *See* Insect/pest control

Petunia, companion planting with, 118

Pfeiffer, Ehrenfreid, 73, 102–103

pH
  analysis of, 67
  of compost, 57, 58
  of soil, 35, 67

Philbrick, Helen, 128

Philosophy of GROW BIOINTENSIVE Sustainable Mini-Farming, 7–10

Phosphate
  guide for adding, 74
  recommended source of, 68

Phosphate rock, 68
  guide for adding, 74

Phosphorus (P)
  analysis in fertilizers, 66–67
  guide for adding, 74
  insect/pest control and, 121
  recommended source for, 68–71

Pigweed, companion planting with, 118

Pine needles
  in compost, 57
  and pH of soil, 67

Planting. *See also* Companion planting; Transplanting
  by moon phases, 86–89
  season, planting in, 98–99
  seeds, 77–79
  starter garden plan for, 186–187

Plant lice, plant controls for, 127

Plant spacing. *See* Spacing

Poisonous plants in compost, 57

Pole beans, companion planting with, 116

Poor soils, preparing, 23–28

Potash
  insect/pest control and, 121

Potassium (K)
  analysis in fertilizers, 66–67
  guide for adding, 74
  recommended sources for, 68–69

Potato bugs, plant controls for, 127

Potatoes
  companion planting with, 116
  compost efficiency and, 40
  double-digging for, 26
  nutrients in, 132

Pot marigold, companion planting with, 118

Praying mantids, insect/pest control with, 123

Pricking out seedlings, 83–84

Professional soil tests, 64

Protein source crops, Master Chart for, 146–157

Pumpkins
  companion planting with, 116
  soil temperature conditions for, 99
  stems, turning, 85

Purslane, companion planting with, 118

R

Radishes
  companion planting with, 116
  soil temperature conditions for, 99

Rainfall conditions, 94–97
  natural rainfall "arid" farming, 4

Rakes, 17, 18

Rateaver, Bargyla, 73

Rateaver, Gylver, 73

Recycling
  agricultural recycling, 105, 108
  compost and, 59
  human waste recycling, 73

Re-digging beds, 32

Redwood compost and germination, 82

Refuse factor for crops, 132

Reprints, list of, 223

Rodale composting method, 55–56

Rogers, Will, 1

Rolling dibble markers, 210–211

Root-bound seedlings, 84–85

Root-eating pests, controlling, 114

Roots
  compost and composting and, 45
  humus and, 47
  of seedlings, 79, 80
  shallow/deep rooting requirements, 112

Rosemary, companion planting with, 118

Ross watering fans, 90

Rotation in space, 104, 105

Rotation over time, 105

Rotations in planting, 104–108
  plant families for, 108
  2-year rotation plans, 107
  3-year rotation plan, 106

Index

Succulents in compost, 57
Sulphur and pH of soil, 67
Summer savory, companion planting with, 118
Sunflowers
    companion planting with, 116
    rotation planting with, 108
    sun needs of, 112
Sun/shade needs, 112
Surface cultivation, 29, 49
Sustainability, 33–43
    designing for fertility, 39–43
    Ecology Action's goals, 37–38
    garden plan for sustainable diet design, 188–190
    goals for achieving, 63–64
    GROW BIOINTENSIVE Sustainable Mini-Farming and, 218
    loss of nutrients and humus, 34–35
    99% sustainability, need for, 36–37
    100% sustainability, 36
The Sustainable Vegetable Garden (Jeavons & Cox), 182
Sweet potatoes and compost efficiency, 40
Swiss chard, soil temperature conditions for, 99
Synergistic planting, 2
Syntex Corporation, 9
Syrphid flies, insect/pest control with, 123

T

Tachinid flies, 120
    insect/pest control with, 123
Tack trap, blocking ants with, 124
Tanglefoot Pest Barrier, 124, 126
Tansy
    for ant control, 114
    companion planting with, 118
Tarragon, companion planting with, 118
Temperate climate, garden plan for, 183–187
Temperature
    key air temperatures, 130
    soil temperature conditions, 99
Test Your Soil with Plants (Beeby), 66
3-year rotation plan, 106
Threshing wheat, 131
Thyme, companion planting with, 118

Timberleaf soil testing service, 64–65
    sampling soil for, 65–66
Toads, 120
    insect/pest control with, 122
Tobacco family
    flowering tobacco for white fly control, 113
    rotation planting with, 108
Todd, John, 218
Tomatoes
    companion planting with, 116
    root system of, 19
    soil temperature conditions for, 99
    stinging nettle planted with, 103
    watering, 90, 91
Tomato worms, controlling, 114
Tools, 16–18, 191–212
Tools for Conviviality (Illich), 191
Toxins in fertilizers, 67
Transpiration, 93, 95
Transplanting, 79
    benefits of, 79
    methods for, 84–85
    starter garden plan information, 185
    surplus seedlings, saving, 85
    time for, 85
    triangulation process for, 77
Transplanting trowels, 17
Traps for insects, 124, 125
Tree crops, 130
    Master Chart for, 162–173
Trees, compost piles under, 50
Triangular spacing template for placing seeds, 77–78
Tricogramma wasps, insect/pest control with, 123
Triple-digging method, 96
Turning compost pile, 54–55
Turnips
    companion planting with, 116
    compost efficiency and, 40
    soil temperature conditions for, 99
Twist dig sifting in of fertilizers, 73
2-year rotation plans, 107

U

U-bar, 191–192
    dig, 25–26, 28
    dimensions of, 193
    working with, 192–195
UN-FAO, 5

University of Arizona, Environmental Research Laboratory, 42–43
University of California, Berkeley, 218
University of California, Santa Cruz, 8–9
Urbanization, 5–6

V

Valerian, companion planting with, 103, 118
Vaseline, blocking ants with, 124
Vegetable oil crops, Master Chart for, 146–157
Vegetables
    Master Charts for, 135–145
    in starter garden plan, 184
Vetch
    green manures with, 56
    nitrogen (N) from, 104
Volume, compost by, 53

W

Walnut plants in compost, 57
Warm-season crops, 98
Wasps, 120
    tricogramma wasps, insect/pest control with, 123
Water and watering. *See also* Soil moisture
    availability of, 5
    beds *vs.* rows and, 16
    compost pile, watering, 54
    GROW BIOINTENSIVE Sustainable Mini-Farming and, 3
    key water factors, 94–97
    one person's diet, availability for, 214
    rainfall conditions, 94–97
    seeds and seedlings, 79, 90–93
    time for, 91
Watering can, English Haws, 90
Watering tools, 192
Watering wands, 91–92
Watermelons, soil temperature conditions for, 99
Weather and watering, 90–92
Weed killers and germination, 82
Weeds and weeding, 97–98
    companion planting and, 113
    compost, weeds in, 57
    methods for weeding, 31
    in plant community, 101–102

ABOUT THE AUTHOR

JOHN JEAVONS is the leading method developer, teacher, and consultant for the small-scale sustainable agricultural method known as GROW BIOINTENSIVE Sustainable Mini-farming. He has authored, co-authored, or edited more than forty publications on this high-yielding, resource-conserving approach. His food-raising methods are being practiced in 142 countries and recommended by such organizations as UNICEF, Save the Children, and the Peace Corps.

A political science graduate of Yale University, Jeavons worked for the United States Agency for International Development (USAID) and Stanford University before devoting the past 40 years to the development of Biointensive techniques. He is the recipient of the 1988 Boise Peace Quilt Award, the 1989 Giraffe Award for public service, the 1989 Santa Fe Living Treasure Award, and the Steward of Sustainable Agriculture Award in 2000.

In 2006, Jeavons catalyzed the Pan-Latin America GROW BIOINTENSIVE Sustainable Mini-Farming Workshop in Costa Rica with participants from 21 countries. In 2007, he facilitated the Pan-Africa GROW BIOINTENSIVE Workshop and Symposium in Kitale, Kenya. In 2008, Jeavons co-taught a Pan-Africa GROW BIONTENSIVE Workshop in South Africa with participants from 7 countries. And in 2010, he taught at a Pan-Latin America Conference and Workshop in Mexico with participants from 21 countries. Today, Jeavons travels constantly, advising students, teachers, local producers, and representatives of private, nonprofit, and governmental organizations.

The comprehensive and sustainable cropping system developed by Jeavons enables people in all regions of the world to grow a balanced diet on a small plot of land. Former U.S. Secretary of Agriculture Bob Bergland said of his work, "There are probably a billion people in the world who are malnourished. The Jeavons approach could enable that segment of the population to feed itself adequately for the first time ever. That would be a remarkable development in this world, and would do more to solve the problems of poverty, misery and hunger than anything else we've done."

More on John Jeavons and GROW BIOINTENSIVE can be found at the links below:

- www.johnjeavons.info

- Google+ page, which has tons on information about GROW BIOINTENSIVE: https://plus.google.com/106507624180546136919/posts

- Google Talk: www.youtube.com/watch?v=afHd9EhsJ1U